JUDGING LAW AND POLICY

To what extent do courts make social and public policy and influence policy change? This innovative text analyzes this question generally and in seven distinct policy areas that play out in both federal and state courts—tax policy, environmental policy, reproductive rights, sex equality, affirmative action, school finance and same-sex marriage. The authors address these issues through the twin lenses of how state and federal courts must and do interact with the other branches of government and whether judicial policymaking is a form of activist judging.

Each chapter uncovers the policymaking aspects of judicial process by investigating the current state of the law, the extent of court involvement in policy change, the responses of other governmental entities and outside actors, and the factors which influenced the degree of implementation and impact of the relevant court decisions. Throughout the book, Howard and Steigerwalt examine and analyze the literature on judicial policymaking as well as evaluate existing measures of judicial ideology, judicial activism, court and legal policy formation, policy change and policy impact. This unique text offers new insights and areas to research in this important field of American politics.

Robert M. Howard is Professor of Political Science at Georgia State University and editor of *Justice System Journal*.

Amy Steigerwalt is Assistant Professor of Political Science at Georgia State University.

JUDGING LAW AND POLICY

Courts and Policymaking in the American Political System

Robert M. Howard
Professor of Political Science
Georgia State University

Amy Steigerwalt
Assistant Professor of Political Science
Georgia State University

Routledge
Taylor & Francis Group

NEW YORK AND LONDON

First published 2012
by Routledge
711 Third Avenue, New York, NY 10017

Simultaneously published in the UK
by Routledge
2 Park Square, Milton Park, Abingdon, Oxon OX14 4RN

Routledge is an imprint of the Taylor & Francis Group, an informa business

© 2012 Taylor & Francis

The right of Robert M. Howard and Amy Steigerwalt to be identified as authors of this work has been asserted by them in accordance with sections 77 and 78 of the Copyright, Designs and Patents Act 1988.

Library of Congress Cataloging in Publication Data
Howard, Robert M., 1956–
    Judging law and policy : courts and policymaking in the American political system /
    Robert M. Howard, Amy Steigerwalt.
    p. cm.
    1. Political questions and judicial power—United States. I. Steigerwalt, Amy, 1976– II.
    Title.
    KF5130.H69 2011
    347.73'1—dc22
    2011009564

ISBN13: 978-0-415-88524-9 (hbk)
ISBN 13: 978-0-415-88525-6 (pbk)
ISBN13: 978-0-203-83986-7 (ebk)

Typeset in Garamond
by EvS Communication Networx, Inc.

Robert M. Howard dedicates this book to the loving memory of his grandparents, William and Anna Horowitz and Ivan and Rachel Skura

Amy Steigerwalt dedicates this book to her grandparents, Nathan and Gladys Steigerwalt, and in loving memory of her grandparents, Irving and Rose Wainstein

TABLE OF CONTENTS

CONTENTS

LIST OF FIGURES AND TABLES

Figures

Tables

ACKNOWLEDGMENTS

The genesis of this book arose from an initial meeting with Mike Kerns to review books that would work in undergraduate and graduate classes in judicial politics and process; in particular Mike asked us what book would give a complete overview of courts, law and policy. As we discussed the various options, we came to realize that, although there were several books discussing judicial process and courts and policy, there was no book that specifically focused on the impact and influence of courts and the law on the dominant, controversial and important social and public policy issues of the day. There were many wonderful books on judicial politics and process with chapters or sections discussing courts and policymaking, but no specific volume on why courts make and change policy.

Hence this book on judges and judging that we sincerely believe makes a contribution both to undergraduate and graduate learning and to the literature on the nature of judging and how and why courts can and should impact public and social policy in the United States. We think the book will aid a student's understanding of courts and policymaking. At the same time, the book has a point of view. The book enters the debate on the efficacy of courts and their ability to move social and public policy—an action we firmly believe they regularly perform. However, we do accept that there are limits to this ability. The reader is free to argue with our evidence and conclusions throughout the book.

We would like to thank our research assistants, Shenita Brazelton, Clarissa Dias, Jessica Burke and Devian Harris for their assistance in gathering data. We would not have been able to complete this book without their invaluable aid. We would also like to thank Taryn Howard, our personal Excel guru. She could truly make a second career showing academics how to use and manipulate data and charts. All the charts and figures in the book are the result of her aid and expertise. Any errors or problems with them are, of course, our own.

We also thank our contacts at Routledge, Mike Kerns and Mary Altman. We thank Mike for his encouragement from the inception of the idea for the project through its completion. He assisted us in formulating the outline, the major ideas, theories and chapters. He did such a good job that the final proposed outline of chapters, subsections, tables, and figures and the completed project are astonishingly similar. That is truly a remarkable achievement. We thank Mary for her so gentle prodding that at times we did not even realize that we were getting a slight kick to encourage us to finish. But, her methods were wonderfully effective.

We finally thank Harold J. Spaeth, who has throughout the years been a supporter and mentor to us both. He has consistently given us encouragement and advice on matters both small and large, and we thank him for being willing to share his time, expertise and wisdom with us. Without Harold's encouragement to Amy to apply to the open Georgia State position we would not have had the opportunity to collaborate on this project and have such an enjoyable and collegial working relationship.

Bob Howard would like to thank his family for their love and support. To my wonderful children, Courtney and Jordan—you have both grown up to be as wonderful adults as I could have ever wished for all those years watching you both mature and develop. I also want to thank Dave Hodapp who has made me realize that the statement, "you aren't losing a daughter you are gaining a son" is actually true. To my parents, Amy and Bernie Howard, and my father-in-law Hans Merz, I thank you for all the years of love and support. Finally, to Taryn— somehow thank you is a very inadequate term for the more than thirty years of love and listening to my almost constant kvetching.

Amy Steigerwalt would like to thank her family as well. To my parents, Arnold and Ronna Steigerwalt, and my mother-in-law, Maureen Butler Smith, thank you for all of your support, love and guidance through the years. I can only hope that I am as great a parent to your soon-to-be-arriving grandson as you all have been to me. And, to Greg, who lovingly and willingly put up with a spouse facing an advancing pregnancy and a pressing book deadline, and did so with love, generosity and many, many biscuits—thank you, from the bottom of my heart.

INTRODUCTION
Judges, Law and Policy

1. The Myth of the Neutral Judge

This book examines the impact and influence of judges and judging on the development of law and policy in the United States. We examine the causes and effects of rulings, cases and judicial opinions on the development of public and social policy for the federal government and, to a more limited extent, in the U.S. states. Our purpose is to examine and analyze what courts can and cannot do in terms of policy development, policy change and policy implementation. We see policy as a plan or course of action by the government intended to influence and determine decisions, actions and other matters. By the term "public policy" we mean who gets what, when and how. So far as the term "social policy" is concerned, it is a matter of who is allowed to do what, when and how. To paraphrase a bit from political scientist David Easton's famous axiom, public and social policy is the allocation of society's values and resources.

We assess the effect of courts on policy development through the lens of examining court action and behavior, which in many ways upends a central myth of American democracy and the role of courts in our democracy. This myth maintains that policy development, change and implementation are the province of the elected branches of government. The courts, as described in Hamilton's argument in *The Federalist Papers*, are the "least dangerous" branch (cited in Rossiter 1961). Courts interpret but do not make the law. As Chief Justice John Marshall stated in *Marbury v. Madison* (1803), "It is emphatically the province and duty of the judicial department to say what the law is" (177). He noted in the same opinion that "Questions, in their nature political ... can never be made in this Court" (170; see Table of Cases for full citation on all court cases).

Furthermore, courts do not decide questions of policy. For us, this remains one of the great and enduring myths of American public life. There are always persistent and enduring myths in American public life, and these myths pervade the American political system. Some are merely stories about historical figures that impart some lesson or involve some morality tale, such as George Washington never telling a lie in response to his father's questioning him about chopping down a cherry tree, Betsy Ross sewing the first American flag or Paul

Revere actually yelling "The British are coming." There might be some marginal element of truth to these stories, but on the whole each lacks specific evidence as to any of these events actually having taken place. While these stories provide moral lessons for young Americans, they do not have any impact on American political life other than perhaps to promote the causes or candidacies of past events or long gone political figures or even to enrich the pocketbooks of the authors who wrote the stories.

Other myths move beyond mere story, however, and are ingrained into the consciousness of American political thought. These myths have many defenders, espousers and hard core believers. For example, the myth of American individualism (see Shain 1996), or the myth of American exceptionalism or even the myth that unfettered markets are the most efficient way to produce the greatest good for the greatest number of Americans (Bookman 2008). These myths matter. They inform policy decisions and policy deliberations. Political parties enshrine these myths into their party platforms, candidates run on promises to enforce these myths and policy decisions are made by political leaders often to no or even bad effect because of the persistence of myth.

One of those myths, and the myth that is the subject of this book, is the fable of the neutral, rule enforcing judge. Ironically, while Marshall wrote his pronouncement about the proper, but limited, role of the judiciary, his opinion and statements in *Marbury v. Madison* bolstered the power of the fledgling and fragile third branch of government. In the early days of the republic, the judiciary was weak, having no building to call its own, residing in a new, undeveloped and uninteresting federal city and dependent for its budget on a politically hostile legislature and executive that reinstituted the onerous burden of riding circuit. The mostly federalist judiciary was marked for a reduced role in the rebirth of democracy brought about the election of Thomas Jefferson in 1800.

John Marshall, aware of the inherent weaknesses of the courts, carved out a specific role for the judiciary—that of primary interpreter of the law—and in particular reinforced the ability of the Supreme Court to act as a constitutional court by establishing the power of judicial review. The early decisions of the Marshall Court reinforced the authority of the federal courts and did much to make their rulings and policy pronouncements an accepted development in American political life. The Supreme Court, and by extension, the lower federal courts, became important components of the American political system and public life.

Courts, of course, have always done more than merely rule on the meaning of law. However, the notion of the judicial branch being above politics and ruling solely on the law remains a powerful force in the public arena. This idea was reinforced by Chief Justice John Roberts's statement at his confirmation hearing that a judge is nothing more than a referee or umpire, merely enforcing the rules:

Judges and justices are servants of the law, not the other way around. Judges are like umpires. Umpires don't make the rules; they apply them. The role of an umpire and a judge is critical. They make sure everybody plays by the rules. But it is a limited role. Nobody ever went to a ball game to see the umpire. Judges have to have the humility to recognize that they operate within a system of precedent, shaped by other judges equally striving to live up to the judicial oath. (Roberts 2005)

Implicit in this statement is the idea that judges enforce the rules as determined by other parties. The job of judging is limited to interpreting the meaning of those rules. Roberts explicitly argues that "Judges have to have to humility to... operate within a system of precedent, shaped by other judges."

Thus, the myth: Judges interpret the rules of the game fashioned by others and do so in a system in which they are bound by what was previously written. Judges do not make the rules of the game, or for the purposes of this book, *judges do not make policy*. Policy is made by the elected officials: at the federal level by Congress and the president of the United States and at the state level by the governors and the various state legislatures.

This is certainly not the first, nor the last statement that judges are or should be neutral arbiters. Twenty years before Chief Justice Roberts's testimony, then Attorney General Edwin Meese articulated the views of the Reagan administration and a growing conservative legal scholarship movement condemning what they saw as improper political and policy interpretations of the law. Meese argued, "In considering these areas of adjudication ... it seems fair to conclude that far too many of the Court's opinions were, on the whole, more policy choices than articulations of constitutional principle" (Meese 1985). Specifically Meese argued for a mode of constitutional interpretation premised on finding and then adhering to the intent of the Framers. The assumption behind such a statement is that adherence to the intent of the Framers, or originalism, prevents judges from imposing their own policy preferences and prevents courts from creating policy. Under this view, all judges should do is interpret the law.

Not all agreed with the interpretive portion of Meese's statements. Associate Justice William Brennan replied, "There are those who find legitimacy in fidelity to what they call 'the intentions of the Framers'.... It is a view that feigns self-effacing deference to the specific judgments of those who forged our original social compact. But in truth it is little more than arrogance cloaked as humility" (Brennan 1985). Several Democratic senators challenged Roberts's assertion as to the ability of a judge to remain a neutral arbiter and merely find the law.

To Meese and supporters of his position, Brennan represented the apotheosis of the "activist judge." Generally synonymous with liberal political ideology, the activist judge is the judge who ignores precedent, ignores the intent of the Framers and in fact eschews all standards of law and judging in order to create law and policy they prefer, often in defiance of the will of the electorate.

3

While Meese and others bemoan judicial activism, a strong line of scholarly literature argues that judges might want to impose policy preferences, but because of constraints inherent within the political system, they are incapable of actually doing so. This view achieved prominence in the work of Gerald Rosenberg, who, in his seminal work *The Hollow Hope* (1991, 2008), argues that the ability of courts to bring about social change amounts to nothing more than a "Hollow Hope." To Rosenberg, American courts are ineffective and weak in comparison to the president and Congress. Two of Rosenberg's key chapters dealt with civil rights following the unanimous decision of the Supreme Court striking down school segregation in *Brown v. Board of Education I* (1954), and abortion in the aftermath of the controversial *Roe v. Wade* (1973) decision. Rosenberg finds that Congress, the White House and the civil rights movement did more than *Brown* to break down the vestiges of segregation, and he concludes that the famous *Brown* decision itself had little or no impact. As for abortion, while the decision in *Roe* eliminated restrictive abortion laws still in place in forty-six states, it curtailed pro-choice activism. Those promoting a woman's right to an abortion relied on *Roe* instead of continuing to increase political mobilization and enact pro-choice legislation. Arguing against both the myth of judicial activism and judicial neutrality, Rosenberg argues that courts might not be neutral decision makers, but they lack the ability to influence public and social policy to the degree feared by Meese and others.

Several scholars reacted with books and articles arguing against Rosenberg's position (see e.g., McCann 1994; Van Dyk 1998) and finding that courts have a greater impact on public and social policy than Rosenberg acknowledges. We argue with Rosenberg's contention as well. It is our position, and the argument of this book, that all judges, conservative or liberal, Republican or Democrat, originalist or adherents to a "living constitution," promote and make policy and create policy changes. Judges throughout the judicial hierarchy make policy, including the trial judges of the federal system, the federal district courts, and the appellate judiciary, including the U.S. circuit courts of appeal and the Supreme Court of the United States. We will also show that state level courts, particularly the state courts of last resort, usually known as state supreme courts, also make and change public and social policy. We assume judges have some freedom within our political system to make these policy rulings, and we argue that as important and as influential as these rulings are, they are but one part of the overall decisional calculus of public and social policy. We make no argument that courts are more important than other policy makers and, in fact, we acknowledge that courts generally have less of an impact on social and public policy than presidents and the Congress or governors and state legislatures. However, saying that does not lessen the importance of judges in policymaking nor make their influence and impact unimportant.

In the rest of this chapter we lay out our argument concerning judicial policy impact. We first examine the literature on the political and ideological nature of judging. Next, we examine the potential impact of courts. Specifically, we offer a theoretical explanation of when courts can influence policy and the extent of that influence relative to the other branches of government. Finally, we use this chapter to provide an overview of some important cases and opinions that moved and changed social policy before we examine in subsequent chapters several specific policy domains and the influence of courts on policy development of these areas.

2. Judging Judges: The Politics of Judging

One of our primary assumptions is that judges are political. Judges have beliefs, ideologies and attitudes, and, within the constraints of law and politics, judges will try to craft an opinion or ruling in accordance with those preferences. We think those rulings matter a lot to the social and public policy that is implemented in the United States.

The notion that judges rule according to their attitudes dates back to the Legal Realism movement in the first third of the twentieth century. Legal realism argued against the idea that courts simply "found" law. The Legal Realists, prominent among them Karl Llewelyn (1930, 1962) and Jerome Frank (1930, 1949), argued that discretion is inherent in judicial decision making and that there are no truly unbiased decisions. The values and beliefs of judges form some of the bases of judicial decisions, and, in fact, it is impossible to rid judicial decision making of bias. One outgrowth of the legal realism movement was a much greater emphasis on statutory codification—the Restatement of Laws movement. The idea was that greater codification of the law would lead to less discretion in judging, and less bias among judges.

Building on the assumptions of the legal realism movement, social scientific examinations of the effect of judicial attitudes began with pioneering works such as Herman Pritchett's (1948) *The Roosevelt Court* and the writings of Glendon Schubert (1959) and Harold Spaeth (1964, see Rohde and Spaeth 1976).[1] Pritchett offered the first quantitative analysis of voting behavior on the Supreme Court. Pritchett believed that the justices' positions could be explained primarily, but not entirely, by their attitudes. He used vote coding as a means to measure the rate of agreement among pairs of justices, and then in turn used these vote codes to identify justices who agreed most often. These were the first tentative steps in developing a model of judicial ideology, and Pritchett supplemented his initial quantitative study with extensive qualitative analysis. Glendon Schubert was the first to fully develop the attitudinal model. His early certiorari research revolutionized the study of decision on the merits, creating the so-called attitudinal model.

Harold Spaeth then expanded this work. First, he adopted the views of psychologist Milton Rokeach, who defined attitudes as an enduring "interrelated set of beliefs about an object or situation. For social action to occur, at least two interacting attitudes, one concerning the attitude object and the other concerning the attitude situation must occur" (quoted in Spaeth 1972, 65). What are the objects in these situations? The objects are the direct and indirect parties to the action (for example, a defendant or prosecutor and the police) and the situations which become the dominant legal issues in the case, which are the facts, or the level of intrusiveness for a Fourth Amendment search and seizure issue. The theory assumes that there will be similar attitudes to similar situations so that issue areas will provoke attitudes.

In a 1976 work, political scientist David Rohde along with Spaeth, provided a rationale for policy-motivated behavior by judges. To do so, they borrowed from the rational person standard used in economic research. The assumption of the rational person model is that people rationally and purposefully pursue goals. The goals for Supreme Court justices are to see their policy preferences inscribed in law. The institutional structure and rules of the Supreme Court allow the justices sincerely and with few constraints to follow their policy preferences. Among other things, the justices have almost complete and total control over their docket, they are unelected and serve for life terms, and so there is no electoral or political accountability (see for example, *Bush v. Gore* 2000) and little desire to seek a higher office. It is almost impossible to overrule their constitutional decisions, short of the cumbersome and rarely used amendment process.

Throughout the 1960s, while there was widespread theoretical support for the attitudinal model, there was little available empirical evidence. Schubert and even Spaeth attempted to measure the justices' attitudes primarily based on votes. However, votes are not the same thing as personal policy preferences. There is a significant problem with circularity since how a justice votes in the past is, with this measurement scheme, the predictor of how he or she will vote in the future; in other words, attitudes are determined by votes and votes then determine attitudes. Moreover, what is liberal and what is conservative? In 1989, Segal and Cover utilized newspaper editorials to assemble an ideological indicator not based on votes. They used four newspapers and examined the editorials written at the time of a Supreme Court justice's appointment/confirmation: two liberal, the *New York Times* and the *Washington Post*, and two conservative, the *Los Angeles Times*, and the *Chicago Tribune*. Based on each editorial's assessment of the relative conservatism or liberalism of the nominee, they created a single score reflecting these combined assessments of the nominee's ideology. They then correlated these values to votes. By and large, they work very well: Segal–Cover scores explain about 57% of voting behavior in Fourth Amendment search and seizure cases. The enormous benefit is that these scores provide an indirect measure of ideology that escapes the problem of circularity by avoiding pegging ideology to voting outcomes.

One problem with this measure, however, is that it remains constant throughout the tenure of the Supreme Court justice because it is based solely on assessments at the time of the justice's nomination to the Court. It therefore assumes that the justices' attitudes do not change over time. On its face, this assumption is reasonable: Supreme Court justices serve with life tenure and are typically appointed after serving in other political or judicial roles. However, it is also possible that the worldviews, and thus the policy positions, of justices evolve through the course of their careers.

More recent work measuring attitudes has challenged this assumption of time invariance. Segal and his colleagues (1995) find that certain justices do become more conservative or more liberal over time. For example, Justice Hugo Black became more conservative, while Justice Harry Blackmun voted much more liberally over the course of his judicial career. This time variant evidence has found its way into more recent measures of judicial ideology. At the Supreme Court level, political scientists Andrew Martin and Kevin Quinn (2002) created a model of Supreme Court ideology using Bayesian inference via computer modeling to update Supreme Court justices' ideology by locating them in a one-dimensional policy space over time. A later (2007) article provides evidence that the assumption of time invariant policy preferences is flawed. In another work, authored by Martin and other colleagues (2007), the Martin–Quinn scores for the justices are related to the common space measures developed by Poole and Rosenthal for Congress and the presidency. These so-called judicial common space scores allow the ideologies of the justices to be directly compared to the ideologies of actors in the other branches of government.

Unlike the Supreme Court, there is no generally accepted measure of lower court ideology. A judge's own partisan affiliation and the ideology of a judge's appointing president have often been employed as useful surrogates for judicial attitudes. But focusing on the partisanship of judges restricts possible ideology indicators to one of two values that fail to account for the subtlety and diversity of attitudes on the bench. Tate and Handberg (1991) proposed an ordinal measure based on the ideology of the appointing president: −1 for ideologically conservative presidents, 0 for nonideological presidents, and 1 for ideologically liberal presidents. This measure may be attributed to every lower federal court judge, but the range is not much better—it still provides only three possible values of ideology. Segal, Timpone and Howard (2000) improved on the Tate–Handberg ranking of presidential ideology by surveying presidential scholars and establishing an interval scale for each president since FDR. The Segal–Howard economic liberalism scores for judges range from 17.6 (for appointees of Reagan, the most conservative president) to 82.5 (for appointees of FDR, the most liberal president).[2] Using this approach, the data range for judge ideology is at least theoretically better, but no rankings are available for presidents (and their appointees) prior to FDR, and all judges appointed by the same president receive the same score.

A number of scholars have suggested that existing measures of ideology be combined. For example, Songer constructed a differentiated measure of judicial ideology based on a logit analysis of judicial voting in economic cases, with a North–South dummy and the Tate–Handberg measure of an appointing president's ideology as predictors (Humphries and Songer 1999). These scores range from 0 (conservative) to 1 (liberal), and can be computed for every appeals judge who has ever served on the modern circuit bench.[3] In practice, however, judges are assigned only one of six possible scores. Giles, Hettinger and Peppers (2001) created the most widely used measure of lower court ideology. They take into account both presidential preferences and the tradition of senatorial courtesy and utilize the Poole and Rosenthal common space scores, which again measure ideology on a single dimension. Absent senatorial courtesy, they use the nominating president's score. If senatorial courtesy is present, meaning that one or both of the nominee's home-state senators are from the president's party, they use the mean of the two senators' scores if both are from the president's party or the score for the single home-state senator who is a member of the president's party. These scores capture variations even among judges nominated by the same president; the judges' scores do not, however, vary over time. By basing these scores on the Poole and Rosenthal common space scores, the resultant judicial ideology scores are comparable to the ideology scores of members of Congress and the president.

Howard and Nixon (2003) also developed a measure of judicial ideology that is compatible with the Poole and Rosenthal scores. Nixon (n.d.) first assembled ninety-five executive appointees who had also served in Congress since 1938, and demonstrated that their common space scores were predicted well by separation of powers considerations at the time of their appointment. Howard and Nixon then extended Nixon's insight by collecting data on all sixty-three federal judicial appointees who had served in Congress since 1938 and created a predictive model of judicial ideology based on factors identifiable for any federal judge such as party identification, party of appointing president and other factors. These scores are quite finely differentiated, based on the political circumstances surrounding the judge's appointment.

State court scholars have devised their own measures of judicial ideology. It is a bit more complex to try and determine the ideologies of judges in state judicial systems than it is for those in the federal system because of the variety of the appointment processes, including merit plans, gubernatorial appointments, legislative appointments, partisan and nonpartisan elections and appointments subject to retention elections.

The most widely accepted measure of state judicial ideology was developed by political scientists Paul Brace, Laura Langer and Melinda Gann Hall. Their measure, the party adjusted ideology score (PAJID; 2000), is a composite measure premised on state measures of elite and citizen ideologies that were developed by William Berry and colleagues (Berry, Ringquist, Fording and Hanson 1998). The PAJID measures use voting for president and governor and union strength in each state as a proxy for judicial ideology. It is not solely based on partisanship because the authors note the problems of using partisanship and region because for many years Southern Democrats were much more conservative than Northern Republicans, particularly Republicans in the Northeast. Their measure can vary for courts over time as older judges depart and new judges take their place, thus capturing the dynamic nature of both judicial ideology and changes in the political and partisan composition of states. These state high court ideology scores can range from 0, most conservative, to 100, most liberal. In practice, the average scores for these state courts of last resort range from about 5 through the high 70s with occasional outlying scores in either direction. Similar to the Martin–Quinn measures, these ideology scores also vary over time.

Throughout our substantive policy chapters we will refer to these various measures of ideology and use them to demonstrate how ideology and judicial attitudes lead to policy choices made by judges at the state and federal level.

3. Constraining Judges—How Judges and Courts Can Make Policy

Given the attitudinal preferences of judges throughout the federal and state courts, we next want to examine how judges make policy; that is, how they operate within the American political system. As we previously noted, we make no argument that courts are more important than elected officials in making policy, but we do argue that they perform an important and influential role. In this section, we offer a theory of how courts make policy that borrows from Hammond and Knott's (1996) articulation of agency control which we expand to the concept of policy control. For our purposes, we examine national, regional (appellate and trial) and state courts.

In Hammond and Knott's formulation, courts exogenously establish a "legal set" through a decision making process that those authors left unmodeled. The legal set may or may not overlap with what is termed the "legislative–executive core." The legislative–executive core is the critical veto point over executive action; in other words, policies falling within this core are supported by both the legislature and the executive, while policies falling outside the core are those that run the risk of being vetoed by the president or overridden by the Congress. One assumes therefore that this core point on a liberal–conservative continuum is where most policy will be set at the national level, or at the state level if one substitutes a governor for the president. We present this situation in Figure 1.1.

Figure 1.1 implies that the majority of public and social policies will fall within the legislative–executive core, because such policies are highly unlikely to be overturned through statutory means (Hammond and Knott 1996). If the president, P, is relatively extreme, one boundary of the legislative–executive core is defined by the median House member, H_m, or the median senator, S_m, whichever is furthest from the president. The crucial veto-override legislator in the House, H_{vo}, or Senate, S_{vo}, whichever is closer to the president, defines the other boundary of the core. It is the views captured within these boundary lines that reflect the policy preferences of the dominant national coalition.

If the legal set does not fully subsume the legislative–executive core, then judicial review presents additional constraints on policy development and change. In such a situation, policy will not be established at the boundary of the legislative–executive core, because it will be overturned in the courts and then a court-ordered policy will be substituted for the elected preferences anywhere

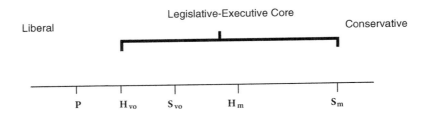

P — President
H_{vo} — 290th Most Liberal House Member (key veto override representative)
S_{vo} — 67th Most Liberal Senator (key veto override senator)
H_m — Median Representative
S_m — Median Senator

Figure 1.1 Policy Domain without Courts

within the legal set. Alternatively, if the court's policy preference falls outside of the preferences of the legislative–executive core, then there is the possibility of a legislative override of the court-ordered policy. Statutory interpretation policies established by the courts are easier for the legislature to override than constitutional interpretations. Thus, it was easier for the Congress to override the Lilly Ledbetter decision on equal pay and when the right to sue begins, because it merely interpreted a federal statute with the passage of the Lilly Ledbetter Fair Pay Act of 2009, than it is for abortion opponents to override the decision of the Supreme Court in *Roe v. Wade* (1973), which established that the fundamental right to privacy found in the Fourteenth Amendment of the U.S. Constitution extends to the right of a woman to choose to have an abortion.

The same holds true for regionally specific courts and even trial courts. Courts, most of which are regionally specific, may induce regional variation in policy if the policy announced falls within the legislative–executive core; such a policy will then survive any legislative efforts to overturn it and will also pass judicial review if it falls within the legal sets of higher ranking appellate courts. This new policy thus represents the best policy the political process can obtain under these conditions. We show this added legal set for trial courts, the appellate courts and the Supreme Court in Figure 1.2.

How does an appellate court establish a range of permissible agency policy outcomes? For example, consider Figure 1.3's illustration of a small appellate court of five judges, J_{1-5}, whose ideological preferences are arrayed on a liberal–conservative scale.

The legal set here would be established as the range between J_2 and J_4. To understand this, it is necessary to recognize that federal appellate court judges typically hear cases in randomly assigned three-judge panels.[4] The random assignment of three judges may be thought of as a permutation problem. To consider the situation generically, imagine that there are k judges serving on an appellate court.

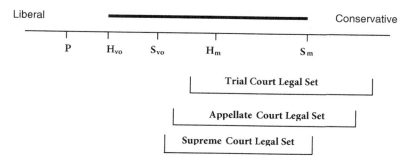

P – President

H$_{vo}$ – 290th Most Liberal House Member (key veto override representative)

S$_{vo}$ – 67th Most Liberal Senator (key veto override senator)

H$_m$ – Median Representative

S$_m$ – Median Senator

Figure 1.2 Policy Domain with Courts

There are then (k3) distinct three-member panels, and the median judge on the appellate court as a whole is more likely than any other judge to be the median judge on any particular panel. This result is shown in Table 1.1.

The extension of these theories highlights how, even within a system of constraints judicial decisions can still substantially impact policy. And, the more the views of the judges are in line with those of elected officials, the more power judges possess to substantially alter policy with little fear of oversight or backlash.

Furthermore, these models do not take into account the numerous instances when legislatures and executives decide to cede power over certain issue areas to the courts, thus increasing the courts' ability to influence state and national policy. In particular, legislatures might defer to the courts, thus transferring power to make important policy choices to the courts on certain issues (see e.g., Graber 1993; Lovell 2003). For example, legislatures might pass laws which are intentionally vague in order to reach legislative compromise and, just as importantly, shift the blame for necessary difficult decisions to the courts. As Katzmann explains, "ambiguity [in statutes] is a deliberate strategy to secure a majority coalition in support of the legislation" (1997, 61). However, when those ambiguities inevitably lead to questions that must be resolved, courts are

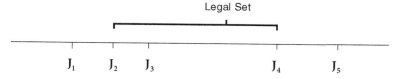

Figure 1.3 Policy Range of Courts

Table 1.1 Three-Member Permutations for a Five-Member Appellate Court

Panel Members	J_1, J_2, J_3	J_1, J_2, J_4	J_1, J_2, J_5
	J_1, J_3, J_4	J_1, J_3, J_5	J_2, J_3, J_5
	J_2, J_3, J_4	J_1, J_4, J_5	J_2, J_4, J_5
		J_3, J_4, J_5	
Panel Median	J_2	J_3	J_4

forced to answer the questions, even if the legislature has provided relatively little guidance, because courts *must* answer all legal claims properly brought before them.

On the other hand, legislatures may also deliberately pass legislation in order to provoke a reaction from the courts. Take, for example, the debates surrounding the passage of the Flag Protection Act in 1989. The Supreme Court in the case of *Texas v. Johnson* (1989) struck down a Texas law prohibiting flag burning as a violation of the First Amendment. While a majority of senators and representatives voted for this law, a majority of them also recognized that the law was likely unconstitutional. However, many members supported the law for strategic purposes: they wanted the Supreme Court to strike down the law, and thus hopefully mobilize the necessary support to pass a constitutional amendment. As Senator Robert Kasten stated,

> The matter before us tonight is an attempt to provide by statute, the protection our flag deserves. Given the decision of five Supreme Court Justices that the statute in *Texas v. Johnson* violated the Constitution, I don't believe this vehicle will work. But I will support this effort until the Senate considers the constitutional amendment which will provide the protection the flag deserves.[5]

Finally, it is not uncommon for legislatures to pass laws which deliberately increase the ability of individuals to bring lawsuits and thus increase the possibility of ceding policymaking power to the courts. One of the fundamental provisions of the Civil Rights Act of 1964 was that it enabled individuals to file discrimination claims against public and private employers who failed to follow the Act's directives. Congress and the states have passed similar laws which increase the ability of individuals to gain access to the courts and resolve legal disputes, and to consequently further the legislature's policy goals. And, by increasing the propensity of the courts to have to address questions of statutory (and potentially constitutional) interpretation, these legislative actions directly affect the level of influence courts are able to exert over the content of policy in the United States. Thus, while legislatures, and especially the U.S. Congress, have the power to reduce the influence of the judiciary, they also many times act deliberately to increase this influence for a variety of reasons.

4. Judging and Making Policy Choices:
The Supreme Court and Judicial Review

Even within the constraints of the political system, judges make choices and those choices make and change policy. However, few assertions of judicial power have remained as troubling or as controversial as the power of judicial review. The most gripping examples of judicial policymaking are decisions to declare unconstitutional laws of Congress and the state legislatures. The conflict between elected representatives and the appointed judiciary is most pronounced in these situations, and the Court's decision is usually final.

The ability to declare laws enacted by duly elected officials unconstitutional has provoked scholarly inquiry, academic debate, and even political outcry. Constitutional scholars have long argued over the propriety of this countermajoritarian power, with most normative theorists (e.g., Hand 1952; Wechsler 1961), empirical researchers (e.g. Segal and Spaeth 1993, 299), and even leading political figures asserting that, in general, courts should defer to the will of the democratic majority as expressed through their elected representatives. Normatively, judicial restraint is considered appropriate because judges are insulated from public opinion and electoral accountability (Allen 1996; Commager 1943; Franck 1996; Thayer 1893; Waldron 1993, 1998). Of course, as Baum notes, "positions on activism and restraint have served chiefly as justifications of policy choices rather than determining those choices themselves" (2001, 158).

Despite the normative outcry, as we have shown in the previous section, courts can impose their preferences on the legal system through judicial review as long as the legal set and legislative–executive core within which they operate cannot overturn the decision. The Supreme Court's freedom to make decisions declaring federal, state or municipal law unconstitutional has had a significant impact on public and social policy. However, although these examples are dramatic, they occur far less frequently than many suppose.

Judicial review was established in the early days of the Republic, but initially the Supreme Court used this power over federal legislation rather sparingly.[6] The practice of striking down laws became more prevalent after the Civil War and, in particular, in reaction to the rise of the regulatory state (Hall, Finkelman and Ely Jr. 2005, 363–66). State and federal governments increasingly asserted their power to regulate and control market forces. With increased immigration and the subsequent growth of the population, there was a greater demand for government involvement in the redistribution of goods and services and the need to ensure employee safety in the marketplace, with states initially in the forefront of regulation and the federal government later seeking to control wages and working conditions.

Initial reaction by the Supreme Court was mixed, upholding some state regulations, such as mandatory vaccinations (*Jacobson v. Massachusetts* 1905) and a cap on grain elevator rates (*Munn v. Illinois* 1877). However, as the membership on the Court began to change, so too did its views on government regulation. The Court became increasingly skeptical of attempts by state and federal governments to regulate the economy. Led by Supreme Court justices David Brewer and Joseph Field, and relying on theories developed by Cooley (1868) and Tiedeman (1886) among others, the Court began to overturn efforts to impose mandatory minimum wage requirements and to regulate employee hours and working conditions. If the effort came from the federal government, the Court would overturn the legislation on Tenth Amendment grounds. For example, the Court severely restricted the reach of the Sherman Anti-Trust law (*United States v. E.C. Knight* 1895), overturned an attempt to regulate child labor (*Bailey v. Drexel Furniture Co.* 1922) and even struck down Congress's attempt to institute an income tax through statutory means (*Pollock v. Farmer's Loan and Trust Co.* 1895)

If a state attempted to regulate the economy, defenders of this view of the economy sought refuge in the Fourteenth Amendment, developing a doctrine known as substantive due process. The Fourteenth Amendment states, "[N]or shall any State deprive any person of life, liberty, or property, without due process of law...." Due process usually refers to a procedure, a way of doing things. The guarantee is that if the state acts fairly and not in an arbitrary manner, then it may do things like regulate conduct and even put people in jail (hence, depriving them of their liberty). However, advocates of greater economic freedom turned their attention to the word "liberty" in the Fourteenth Amendment. They gave it a specific meaning of liberty or "right of contract," although the phrase "liberty of contract" is nowhere to be found in the Constitution. Premised on this interpretation of the Constitution, the Court overturned numerous state attempts to regulate the economy and employee working conditions in cases such as *Allgeyer v. Louisiana* (1897) and *Lochner v. New York* (1905).

The Supreme Court's imposition of economic policy preferences reached a critical juncture following the election in 1932 of Franklin D. Roosevelt and his efforts to implement the New Deal. In particular, Henry Steele Commager and other pre-World War II scholars critical of an "activist" Court criticized the *Lochner* decision and early Roosevelt era courts that struck down liberal and progressive state and federal legislation. For example, early New Deal legislation was hampered by a conservative Court with many holdovers from earlier Republican administrations. Several important pieces of legislation championed by Franklin D. Roosevelt that sought to regulate the national economy were overturned. Prominent cases included Panama Refining Co. v. Ryan (1935; the Hot Oil case), *Schechter Poultry Corp. v.* United States (1935; the Sick Chicken case), *Railroad Retirement Board v. Alton Railway Co.* (1935), *Louisville Joint Stock Land Bank v. Radford* (1935), *United States v. Butler* (1936) and *Carter v. Carter Coal Co.* (1936).

In all of these cases, the Supreme Court restrained the Roosevelt administration from implementing, among other things, wage and price controls and regulating various industries through the meaning and definition of the commerce clause and the tax and spending power of the U.S. government. However, Roosevelt was eventually able to replace this Court with his own appointees. The Court's policy preferences eventually moved more in alignment with national political preferences, and gradually the Court retreated from overturning economic legislation. The fate of the notion of liberty of contract was sealed in 1937 with the case of *West Coast Hotel v. Parrish* where the Court overturned its previous precedents and declared that no such constitutional right existed.

However, claims of judicial activism rose again as the Supreme Court invalidated a number of state and federal laws during Chief Justice Earl Warren's tenure. The Warren Court continued the "rights revolution" of Roosevelt era courts by expanding the constitutional rights of criminal defendants in several controversial decisions including imposing warrant requirements on the states (*Mapp v. Ohio* 1961), mandating counsel for almost all criminal defendants (*Gideon v. Wainwright* 1963) and perhaps most controversially, limiting the rights of the police and prosecutors to question a criminal defendant (*Escobedo v. Illinois* 1964; *Miranda v. Arizona* 1966). With the alleged activism of the Warren Court, many scholars made arguments similar to those raised during the *Lochner* era that when liberal courts overturn democratically enacted laws in favor of liberal, activist constitutional interpretations, they destroy citizens' rights to democratic participation and self-government (Bork 1971).

In addition to their rulings in the criminal justice area, the Warren Court (as well as the early Burger Court) significantly expanded individuals' civil rights and civil liberties. Most notable in the civil rights area was the famous *Brown v. Board of Education I* (1954) decision banning segregation in schools. The Warren Court did not stop with school desegregation: eventually the Warren Court overturned almost all state-sanctioned segregation, opening up beaches, buses, golf courses, parks, municipal restaurants and overturning laws banning interracial marriage (*Loving v. Virginia* 1967). By 1963, the Court declared, "It is no longer open to question that a state may not constitutionally require segregation of public facilities" (*Johnson v. Virginia*, disallowing a judge's sectioning off a section of a courtroom for blacks). The Burger Court continued this trend by sanctioning busing as an appropriate remedy for school desegregation (*Swann v. Charlotte Mecklenburg Board of Education*, 1971) and allowing colleges and universities to continue affirmative action programs, albeit for reasons beyond mere racial balance (*Regents of the University of California v. Bakke*, 1978).

The Warren Court also revived the notion of substantive due process, although this time it was for social, not economic liberty. In *Griswold v. Connecticut* (1965), the Court struck down a Connecticut law which prohibited using or dispensing contraceptives. The Court initially limited the ruling to married couples, premising its decision on the notion of a right to privacy for married couples over procreation decisions. Although the right to privacy was not specifically mentioned in the U.S. Constitution, the Court determined that various guarantees within the Bill of Rights created penumbras, or zones, that established a more general right to privacy. Eventually, the Court would adopt the decision that, much like the ill-fated right to contract, the right to privacy was protected under the due process clause of the Fourteenth Amendment.

Following the same reasoning, the Burger Court later expanded the right to privacy to cover unmarried couples' right to purchase contraceptives (Eisenstadt v. Baird *1972*) and minors (*Carey v. Population Services* 1977), and, most controversially, to abortion in *Roe v. Wade* (1973). *Roe v. Wade* forbade state regulation of abortion in the first trimester of a woman's pregnancy and limited interference during the second trimester. Subsequent Court decisions affirmed the basis of a woman's abortion rights under the right to privacy, although the Rehnquist Court abandoned the trimester approach of *Roe* in *Planned Parenthood of Southeastern Pennsylvania v. Casey* (1992).

Recently, several theorists have criticized the more conservative Rehnquist Court as an activist court, particularly after recent decisions regarding state sovereignty and the Court's decision concerning the outcome of the 2000 presidential election, *Bush v. Gore* (2000; see e.g., Balkin 2001; Kairys 2001; Keck 2004; Noonan 2002). However, the fact that the Supreme Court regularly issues high profile, important cases that overturn state or federal law in itself does not justify the label of activism. For example, Segal and Spaeth (1993) note that in terms of the raw numbers of laws struck down, all courts may be called restraintist in that only a minute proportion of laws passed are ever overturned (see also Howard and Segal 2004).

Is the Supreme Court a restraintist institution? To answer this question, we used the U.S. Supreme Court database (2010 v.2) to examine every instance of when the Court overturned a federal, state or municipal law as compared to the overall docket of the Court. The database runs from 1953 through 2010, which means we miss the Roosevelt era, but include the Warren Court and the Rehnquist Court, as well as the current Roberts Court. We present our results in Table 1.2 and in Figure 1. 4.

Table 1.2 breaks down the Supreme Court's activism by decade, with 1953 to 1959 counting as the first decade and continuing thereafter from 1960 onward. Figure 1.4 displays this information in graphical form. Both break

Table 1.2 Declarations of Unconstitutionality by Supreme Court, 1950s–2000s

Decade	Constitutional	Federal Uncon	Muni Uncon	State Uncon	Total
1950s	96.34%	0.71%	0.95%	2.01%	100.00%
1960s	91.98%	1.07%	0.47%	6.48%	100.00%
1970s	91.31%	0.78%	0.78%	7.13%	100.00%
1980s	93.52%	0.62%	0.62%	5.24%	100.00%
1990s	92.95%	2.15%	0.69%	4.21%	100.00%
2000s	96.35%	1.58%	0.73%	1.34%	100.00%
Total	93.27%	1.07%	0.68%	4.97%	100.00%

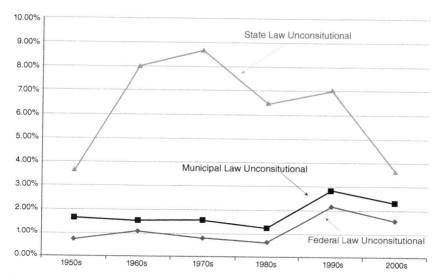

Figure 1.4 Declaration of Unconstitutionality by Decade

down laws overturned over time by the categories of federal law, state law and municipal law. A few interesting findings emerge. First, in terms of overturning federal law, the almost 60 years of data show that the Supreme Court is indeed restrained. The so-called activist Warren Court rarely overturned federal law, while the Rehnquist Court was indeed the "most activist court" if one examines only federal law, as it overturned federal laws at twice the rate of the Warren Court. The Warren Court, however, did overturn state laws at a higher rate than subsequent courts, but again, the rate of overturning state laws amounted to less than one in every ten cases the Court decided.

To buttress these conclusions, we show this same information about declarations of unconstitutionality but arranged by Chief Justice during the same period. This information is presented in Table 1.3.

If analyzed solely by total declarations of unconstitutionality, the Warren Court deserves the label of most activist court and the Burger Court as the least activist court. However, if one examines federal law, then the Rehnquist Court

Table 1.3 Declarations of Unconstitutionality by Chief Justice, 1953–2000

	Burger	*Rehnquist*	*Roberts*	*Warren*	*Grand Total*
Constitutional	92.02%	94.07%	96.33%	93.55%	93.27%
Federal Law	0.78%	1.57%	1.47%	0.91%	1.07%
Muni Law	0.64%	0.69%	0.98%	0.68%	0.68%
State Law	6.56%	3.67%	1.22%	4.86%	4.97%
Total	100.00%	100.00%	100.00%	100.00%	100.00%

and the Roberts Court are the most activist, each overturning federal law in about 1.5% of cases decided, which translates to about one time per year. This might not sound like much, but it is a much higher rate than the two earlier courts.

Overall, these results suggest that the label of "activism" is many times a function of whether one agrees with the policy changes implemented by these courts. On the one hand, critics of the Warren Court decry the vast advances in rights for criminal defendants, arguing that such decisions as *Miranda* undercut the ability of law enforcement to prevent crime and ensure those who break laws are punished. Not surprisingly, Warren Court supporters argue that the Court's decisions ensured the protection of innocent persons from police abuses and granted important civil rights to all persons in the United States. On the other hand, critics of the Rehnquist and Roberts Courts claim that these justices have systematically undercut protections needed for the most powerless in society, while granting more and more protections for the states and large corporations. Once again, however, advocates of these decisions maintain that they were necessary to ensure fairness for all, rather than for some favored groups, and to stop the federal government from encroaching on the states' constitutionally protected powers. One wonders then if, in the end, all courts run the risk of being labeled "activist" by their detractors and by those unwilling to recognize the crucial role the courts play in both interpreting and making law and policy.

5. Law and Policy

In later chapters we will examine the impact and influence of courts on public and social policy. We will examine when the legal set is outside the political set and what that means for the direction of public and social policy. We will examine the myth of the neutral judge and how judicial preferences can, within the limits described herein, change public and social policy. We will also examine the reactions of state and federal governments, as well as the public, to court decisions. In some cases, legislatures and executives worked to overturn the policies established by the courts, while in others, legislation actually served to further the aims of the courts' decisions or to grant additional power to the courts to influence policy on a broad scale.

In Chapter 2 we examine the influence of courts on taxes and tax policy. In particular, we demonstrate the power and influence of trial courts, including the U.S. district courts and, most importantly, the U.S. Tax Court. We focus on the influence of these courts on Internal Revenue Service (IRS) policy decisions.

In Chapter 3 we move to environmental policy and, in particular, the policies of the Environmental Protection Agency (EPA). Here we focus on environmental litigation and how the EPA responds to court pressure and court influence as well as how the original legislation of Congress has ceded significant influence to the federal courts in this area.

Chapter 4 shifts our focus to social policy and policymaking. This chapter examines the effort to ensure equality between the genders through the courts. We show that, in the aftermath of the failure of the Equal Rights Amendment to the U.S. Constitution, litigation strategies focused on securing gender equality through court decisions. We show both how the Supreme Court aided these efforts by requiring governments to meet a heightened standard to justify discrimination based on gender, as well as how state and federal governments have passed legislation to try to aid these efforts.

Chapter 5 continues our presentation of social issues by moving to the controversial subject of reproductive rights and abortion. We provide greater detail on the all-important cases of *Griswold v. Connecticut* and *Roe v. Wade* which established these constitutional rights and then examine the notable backlash that resulted. In particular, we detail how states have passed laws relating to birth control as well as criminal laws aimed at pregnant women and doctors who perform abortions in order to try and legislatively curtail the broad right to privacy established by the Supreme Court. We end by offering our assessment on the current state of abortion rights and our prediction on likely Supreme Court outcomes.

Chapter 6 focuses on the modern civil rights contests and the courts' influence, and specifically the remedy of affirmative action for education. We begin with an overview of the critical civil rights decisions and then we review *Regents v. Bakke* (1978) and the more recent cases of *Grutter v. Bollinger* and *Gratz v. Bollinger* (2003) as well as their implications. We also assess the efforts of some states to limit the use of educational affirmative action programs, such as the passage of California's Proposition 209. We examine the impact of the relative ideologies of the major political actors and institutions and see how the courts' determinations fit in with dominant political core sentiments.

In the final two substantive chapters we examine state courts and policymaking. In Chapter 7, we analyze educational finance and educational finance reform. Public school funding is in large part determined by the local tax and property base, leading to significant disparities across and within states. Due to unequal funding mechanisms, wealthier areas generally have greater resources to spend on public schools than areas with a lower property tax base. The Supreme Court in *San Antonio Independent School District v. Rodriguez* (1973) held that there is no federal constitutional right to equalized school funding. This decision consequently left further developments in this area up to the states and state courts. We examine the relevant state court decisions in this area and the vast differences between the rulings in the several states, as well as the reactions of state legislatures to these decisions.

Chapter 8, our final substantive chapter, continues our examination of state court policymaking in the area of same-sex marriage. To date, it has been state court and state legislative activity that has been in the forefront of the issue of same-sex marriage. We examine the initial state court rulings in Vermont, Hawaii and Massachusetts, legislative responses to these rulings, and the subsequent court actions and legislative responses in other states as well as by the federal government.

In Chapter 9, we conclude with our thoughts on judging judges, courts and judicial policymaking. Through the substantive chapters, we hope to show that despite the persistent myth that judges simply apply the law, the reality is that judges are not neutral and detached arbiters of the law. Rather, they exert a strong impact on the development of policy in the United States, and they do so as a crucial part of the American political system.

Part 1

FEDERAL COURT POLICYMAKING

2

FEDERAL COURT POLICYMAKING

Courts and Taxes

1. Introduction

Taxes and tax policy have been among the most dominant domestic federal public policy issues of the past twenty-five years, taking a back seat perhaps only to post-9/11 national security concerns. Legislation concerning tax policy is debated constantly in Congress, and individuals, outside groups and corporations spend countless hours and dollars attempting to convince legislators to alter the tax codes in their favor. As one respected policy analyst noted, throughout the 1980s there were more frequent and detailed changes to the tax code than in any other period in U.S. history (Steuerle 2008), and the pace of tax legislation has not diminished in succeeding decades. Both Presidents Clinton and George W. Bush's initial major domestic policy proposals dealt with taxes. Similarly, President Obama's stimulus plan contained significant tax relief for certain income classes. Taxes and tax policy continue as a major focus of campaigns, policy debates and legislation.

Courts play a vital and important role in the determination of tax policy. Like any other law or regulation, tax policy is subject to debate, interpretation and revision as litigants and the government pursue their disputes. Given the importance of taxes to both the federal government as well as individual taxpayers, there exists a complex legal system with competing federal trial courts that taxpayers can access to fight tax assessments. The Internal Revenue Service (IRS) is unique among federal agencies in that it is subject to the jurisdiction of specialized trial courts which are tasked with interpreting the numerous and complex—and many times, contradictory—legislative and regulatory provisions that govern federal tax policy. Almost every day, these specialized federal courts make decisions favoring either the IRS or the taxpayer, as they revise and reinterpret the law. Prominent individual cases and the cumulative impact of court rulings that favor classes of taxpayers can significantly change the meaning and interpretation of law. The end result is that courts have an important and substantial impact on tax law and policy.

Over thirty thousand cases are filed annually by taxpayers who are challenging tax assessments. How do taxpayers fare in these cases? Do the courts protect the rights of the individual, particularly the low-income taxpayer, or do they enforce dominant policy preferences? Do these court decisions influence the IRS to change its audit behavior and focus less attention on the lowest income group of taxpayers? Finally, is there a difference between specific courts in their decisions and in their relative influence on the IRS?

While fairness before the law might be a laudable goal, the federal judicial appointment process ensures that tax policy and tax enforcement rulings by the courts reflect the politics of the day (see e.g., Dahl 1957; Martinek, Kemper and Van Winkle 2002; Scherer, Bartels and Steigerwalt 2008; Steigerwalt 2010). Conservative courts nominated and confirmed by conservative presidents and Senates generally issue rulings that reflect conservative political preferences by the particular Senate and president. Liberal courts nominated and confirmed by liberal presidents and Senates likewise usually issue rulings that reflect liberal preferences (see e.g., Songer and Ginn 2002).

2. Taxes and Tax Policy

Taxes and the courts have always been intimately intertwined. It is unrealistic to think that potentially divergent judicial attitudes are meaningless when it comes to judicial rulings on taxes and tax policy, and it is unrealistic to think that judicial attitudes have not played an important role in the formation and development of tax policy since the inception of the income tax.

The first income tax laws were enacted in 1861 and 1862 to fund the Civil War; however, these statutes expired in 1872.[1] These same acts created the Internal Revenue Service.[2] However, the story of the interaction between courts, national politics and taxation really begins in 1894. Responding to dissatisfaction with high tariff rates and the need to raise revenue, Congress relied on the powers granted by Section 8 of Article I of the U.S. Constitution and established a federal income tax for the first time since the end of the Civil War. The arguments for and against the income tax echo many of the arguments heard today concerning taxation, with similar ideological and partisan filters. Prior to the creation of this federal income tax, the primary means of raising revenue in the United States was the tariff—a tax on imports. Progressive advocates and Democratic politicians attacked these tariffs as regressive and hurting the poor and lower classes by increasing the costs of goods. Democrats viewed the income tax as a more equitable and fair way to raise revenue, while Republicans argued that the income tax amounted to a socialist redistribution of income.

Democratic President Grover Cleveland personally opposed the imposition of the income tax on individuals (Witte 1985). However, because of the favorable and politically popular tariff relief provisions attached to the legislation, Cleveland reluctantly signed the income tax into law (Whittington 2005; Witte 1985). As part of the income tax legislation, banks were required to pay a 2% tax on income in excess of $4,000. One such bank that had to pay this income tax was the Farmer's Loan Bank located in Massachusetts. In a contrived case, Charles

Pollock, a shareholder in the Farmer's Loan Bank, sued to enjoin the bank from paying the required income tax. Eventually the lawsuit, *Pollock v. Farmers' Loan & Trust Co.* (1895), reached the U.S. Supreme Court.

After two separate oral arguments, Chief Justice Fuller, writing for a minimum 5-4 majority, struck down the income tax as an unconstitutional direct tax. Among other reasons, the Court focused on the part of the statute that included rents from real estate as income. Land is subject only to direct taxation, the opinion stated, and you cannot separate income from the land itself. Therefore, the Court held, this provision violated the apportionment provisions of the U.S. Constitution. One cannot apportion tax on land because such a tax must be in proportion to the population.

Of course, these bare and very questionable legal rationalizations hid the underlying emotions of the case and the conflicting views of the social desirability of the income tax. Despite Chief Justice Fuller's admonition in his majority opinion that "we are not concerned with the question whether an income tax be or be not desirable," Joseph Choate, the lead attorney for the plaintiff, attacked the law as "communistic" and "socialistic" (Hall, Finkelman and Ely 2005, 385). Certainly the other justices on both sides viewed the decision in ideological terms far outside of the majority opinion's bare-bones legal reasoning. In fact, the case also contained one concurrence and two dissents, and in these separate opinions, the authoring justices commented on the emotions and lack of logic in the respective opinions of those with whom they disagreed.

Called the "most controversial case of its era" (Beth 1999, 241), the *Pollock* case provides a strong example of how courts can alter policy, often with the tacit approval of elected officials. In this particular set of circumstances, because of the complications and unpopularity of high tariffs, President Cleveland and the legislators in Congress opposed to the income tax were forced into supporting compromise legislation that created a federal income tax because this was the only political avenue open to these elected officials that would lead to a reduction in tariffs. Unhappy with the bundled income tax part of the legislation, President Cleveland and the legislators opposed to the income tax supported the effort to overturn it through the courts as an unconstitutional tax. Thus, an attempt at progressive taxation was stymied by the courts with the approval of the president.

The Court's decision was met with great criticism, and even though the tariff provisions were upheld, dissatisfaction with tariffs as a primary source of revenue continued. Consequently, a coalition of newly elected liberal Republicans and progressive Democrats began to seek legislative reenactment of an income tax. Under the guidance of President William Howard Taft, who was fearful of a constitutional crisis between Congress and the Supreme Court, Congress agreed to another compromise. The Congress would propose a constitutional amendment specifically allowing an income tax without direct apportionment based on population as well as pass legislation placing an excise tax on corporate profits but no tax on individual incomes. As a result of this compromise, in 1909 the Congress overwhelmingly passed a resolution proposing an amendment to the

U.S. Constitution that would permit an income tax without apportionment with a near unanimous vote in the House and a unanimous vote in the Senate. The proposed amendment was then sent to the states; ratification by three-fourths of the states was necessary for the amendment to become law. State ratification was slow, with mostly Southern states supporting the measure and many Eastern states reluctant to support an amendment permitting income taxation. Eventually, in 1913, the necessary thirty-sixth state ratified the Sixteenth Amendment, providing the legitimate constitutional power for the Congress to authorize the collection of a federal income tax.[3] Importantly, this amendment successfully overturned the 1895 *Pollock* decision, and remains one of the few times that a constitutional amendment has overturned a constitutional ruling of the Supreme Court.[4] The ratification coincided with major Democratic election victories in the 1912 election, including the election of President Woodrow Wilson, the first Democratic president since Grover Cleveland. This new, more progressive Congress then enacted income tax legislation in the same year as the ratification of the Sixteenth Amendment.

However, numerous questions would remain to be argued about and ruled upon over the coming decades, such as how to determine the top and bottom rates, whether and to what extent income tax provisions should apply to corporations, whether and when excess profits should be taxed, whether estates would be taxed, and what constitutes "income" for purposes of taxation. In fact, just nine years after the passage of the Sixteenth Amendment and the subsequent constitutionally permissible income tax legislation, the first book to help taxpayers avoid excess taxation was published. It was titled *Minimizing Taxes*, written by Wall Street lawyer John Sears and offered advice on how to minimize taxes legally, which in Sears's view amounted to the patriotic goal of "hasten[ing] legislative correction of evils, or hasten[ing] fair economic adjustment thereto" (1922, v).[5]

In a typical year, taxpayers file over 100 million individual tax returns. The line between legitimate tax avoidance, as advocated by John Sears and others through the years, and illegal tax evasion is not always clearly defined. Conflict between the IRS and taxpayers is therefore unavoidable. Tax evasion and cheating creates severe problems. By 1986, Roth, Scholz and Witte (1989) note that the IRS estimated that individuals failed to report between $70 and $79 billion in income received, and that the true figure might in fact be closer to $100 billion. Philip Brand, the IRS's chief compliance officer, verified the $100 billion figure for the tax year 1994, which amounts to nearly 20% of all reported income.[6]

Evasion impacts all of us. Lack of compliance represents a severe loss of revenue for the U.S. government, meaning less money to spend on defense and social programs and increases in budget deficits. To attack evasion and noncompliance, the IRS scrutinizes certain returns in an audit process. Trained IRS officials conduct the audits out of district offices located throughout the fifty states. If the audit results in a claim for additional revenue, the audited taxpayer can contest the finding and eventually the matter can end up in the courts.

26

In resolving individual disputes, courts have become major players in the formation and enforcement of U.S. tax policy. Some cases, particularly at the Supreme Court level, have ramifications for tax policy beyond just the IRS and the audited parties. However, even in cases without major tax policy implications, the impact of a series of rulings for or against the IRS can cause the IRS to shift its audit policy by, for example, moving from auditing corporations to individuals or moving from auditing high income individuals to more low income taxpayers.

3. The Supreme Court and Appellate Courts

The Supreme Court has ruled on more than two hundred major tax disputes since the beginning of the Warren Court in 1953 (Epstein, Segal, Spaeth and Walker 2003), more than any other domestic policy domain. The greatest percentage of Supreme Court cases during the Warren Court years involved controversies over the Internal Revenue Code (IRC). During the Burger and Rehnquist Courts, IRC controversies accounted for the third and second highest percentage of cases, respectively (Epstein et al. 2003). This heavy Supreme Court docket of tax cases is remarkable considering that the Court is many times reluctant to take such cases because of the justices' lack of interest and the issue's complexity (Perry 1991).

We have already discussed the *Pollock* case, which took place right before the turn of the twentieth century. Following that case, the Supreme Court issued several significant tax rulings. For example, the Court determined what constitutes income (*Commissioner v. Glenshaw Glass Co.* 1955), what are acceptable business and personal deductions (*Welch v. Helvering* 1933) and the taxable consequences of divorce (*United States v. Davis* 1962). *Tax Stories* (Caron 2003), an edited volume of leading twentieth century tax cases, lists the cases reported in Table 2.1 as ten of the major Supreme Court tax cases. Table 2.1 notes the principle established and the prevailing party in each case.

While several of these cases seem dry and esoteric, the implications for the revenue collected by the government have been enormous. Interestingly, in all but one of these cases, the Supreme Court sided with the IRS. All of these cases represent appeals by the IRS following postaudit assessments, and the response of the Court has significantly shaped and determined the state of federal tax law and tax policy.

Tax cases also represent a very large part of the docket of the U.S. courts of appeal. For example, the courts of appeal handle, on average, more than 220 new tax case appeals per year. Federal appellate courts often interact with the IRS in a regionally specific manner. Appeals from district courts are heard by the appeals court from the state within which the district court is located, while the relevant appellate jurisdiction of tax court cases is premised on the residence of the taxpayer (M. Taylor, Simonson, Winter and Seery 1990).[7] In 1997 alone, federal appeals courts handled two hundred and forty-eight civil tax appeals by

Table 2.1 Leading Supreme Court Tax Cases

	Case	Year	Principle Established	Prevailing Party
1.	*Commissioner v. Glenshaw Glass*	1955	Modern concept of gross income	IRS
2.	*Eisner v. Macomber*	1920	Timing of income realization	Taxpayer
3.	*U.S. v. Kirby Lumber*	1931	Cancellation of debt is taxable income	IRS
4.	*U.S v. Davis*	1962	Transfers pursuant to divorce	IRS
5.	*Welch v. Helvering*	1933	Deducting business expenses	IRS
6.	*INDOPCO v. Commissioner*	1992	Deducting business expenses	IRS
7.	*Crane v. Commissioner*	1947	Tax shelters	IRS
8.	*Schlude v. Commissioner*	1963	Tax accounting procedures	IRS
9.	*Lucas v. Earl*	1930	Income assignment (led to creation of joint returns)	IRS
10.	*Knetsch v. U.S.*	1960	Impermissible tax avoidance	IRS

plaintiffs against the United States. In contrast, according to the Supreme Court compendium, from 1953 until 1994, the U.S. Supreme Court decided only one hundred and thirty-one federal tax cases with the United States as a party.

Control of IRS behavior and policy has been subject to intense study during the past few decades, and many of these studies have shown how courts fit into this policy domain. Initially, many of the studies focused on the amount of presidential or congressional control. Scholz and Wood (1998) show that the IRS changed its corporate to individual audit ratio in response to political change, particularly changes in presidential administrations and congressional committee membership. President Reagan's election, for example, led to an increase in individual audits and a decrease in corporate audits.

In a later study, the two show that federal and state partisan composition affects audit rates, with Republicans initially seeking efficiency over tax fairness or equity, and Democrats favoring equity (Scholz and Wood 1999). Howard (2001) and Howard and Nixon (2002, 2003) add to these initial studies by examining the level of federal appellate courts' IRS responsiveness in the areas under the jurisdiction of these circuit courts of appeal. They find that regional variation in audit policy is explained in part by ideological differences in these courts. That is, liberal courts favor low income and individual taxpayers while conservative courts favor high income and corporate taxpayers. They further

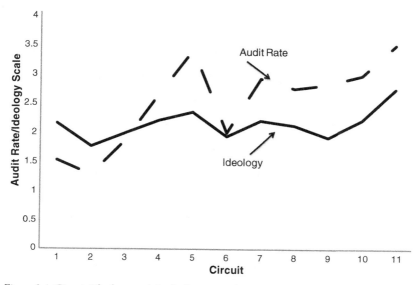

Figure 2.1 Circuit Ideology and Audit Rates, 1994–2000

find that the IRS responds to the ideology of each circuit by lowering the audits of low income and individual taxpayers in more liberal circuits and increasing the number of audits of these taxpayers in more conservative circuits (Howard and Nixon 2002, 2003). Figure 2.1, which tracks circuit court ideology and the audit ratio of low income and high income taxpayer audits, demonstrates this relationship.

The audit rate represents the average number of low income audits as compared to high income audits per circuit from 1994 through 2000. The ideology score is a common space measure normally ranging from -1 (most liberal) to 1 (most conservative) that is rescaled for ease of comparison from 1 (most liberal) to 5 (most conservative). The chart shows that in more conservative courts, there are more audits of low income taxpayers as compared to high income taxpayers. Thus, in states within the jurisdiction of the First Circuit Court of Appeals, there were, on average, 1.5 audits of low income individuals for every one audit of high income taxpayers, while in states within the jurisdiction of the Fifth Circuit Court of Appeals, the ratio was three to one. These results reflect that the Fifth Circuit was more conservative during these years than the First Circuit. The ideology scores of the other circuits and the low/high audit rates track closely.

4. Tax Trial Courts

Despite these important Supreme Court cases and the demonstrated importance of the circuit courts, most tax-related matters are disposed of at the trial level.

Tax cases also often involve technically complex issues calling for significant judicial discretion in interpretation, and the evaluation of such claims usually demands expertise in the area of tax policy. Regarding the degree of complexity in the tax codes, one former IRS revenue agent and the author of tax preparation manuals urged his readers not to examine the over 2000 pages of the Internal Revenue Code as a reference source for tax law because of its sheer complexity and lack of accessibility for nonspecialists (Wade 1986).

Furthermore, there are competing courts that litigants of all income levels may utilize. These courts are the federal district courts, the trial courts of general jurisdiction within the federal court system; the U.S. Tax Court, a specialized trial court created under the Article I legislative power of Congress (and the Tax Court has a low cost option); and the U.S. Court of Federal Claims.

While the Supreme Court handles a few tax cases each year, and the circuit courts of appeals a bit less than two hundred and fifty, the trial courts render almost more than twice that number of tax decisions per year, and this number does not reflect all of the settlements that preclude the courts issuing a judicial decision. For example, in the 2000 calendar year there were seven hundred total decisions rendered by the U.S. federal district courts and U.S. Tax Court. Trial courts are thus the principal courts through which taxpayers interact with the federal legal system. One would expect that these competing federal tax trial courts would induce regional and yearly variations in IRS policy because the agency must continually interact and deal with these competing courts to a much greater extent than they interact with any appellate-level court.

Because there are different courts, there are also different ways to measure and examine the confluence of law and policy. For example, why do tax litigants choose to sue in one forum as opposed to another? Are there differences in the decision making processes of these courts and are there differences in the impact on tax policy from these courts?

There are several important structural and institutional differences between these courts. For example, federal district court judges are given full judicial independence with lifetime tenure, and their salaries are guaranteed for life. In contrast, the judges of the U.S. Tax Court and the U.S. Court of Federal Claims have fixed terms and lack this salary guarantee.

Tax Court

By far the most common forum to litigate in is the Tax Court, a specialized tribunal designed to handle deficiency claims. After the passage of the Sixteenth Amendment, the federal district courts were the sole venue for challenging tax assessments. However, in 1924, nine years after the passage of the amendment, Congress created the Board of Tax Appeals to handle taxpayer litigation. It was renamed the Tax Court in 1942. Originally an independent part of the executive branch of government, in 1969 Congress passed legislation removing the Tax Court from the executive branch and establishing its independence as an Article

1 court.[8] In 1974, the Tax Court moved out of the space it shared with the IRS and into its own building.

The Tax Court is an example of a court with limited jurisdiction and limited independence, which was created through the legislative power of Congress under Article I. There are nineteen full-time judges appointed by the president and subject to confirmation by the Senate. Each judge serves for fifteen years, although as a practical matter, if they so desire, they may be reappointed either to an additional term or allowed to remain on the court to decide cases on senior status. There are also seven special judges appointed by the Chief Judge of the Tax Court. The special judges have full authority over all matters not exceeding $50,000. For matters exceeding $50,000, the report of the special judge is forwarded to the Chief Judge who then assigns the report to a regular judge for approval (U.S. Tax Court Rules 182 and 183). The full-time judges enjoy full federal pension and retirement benefits and draw the same salary as federal district court judges (see generally Dubroff 1979, part 1).

To sue in Tax Court, a taxpayer files a claim with the Tax Court clerk in Washington, DC, and then either a judge can request the assignment, or the Chief Judge will assign the case to one of the judges. The judge then tries the case in the area designated by the taxpayer, often in the taxpayer's local area or as close to the taxpayer's local area as is possible. No prepayment of the disputed funds is required, and all cases are tried without a jury (i.e., through a bench trial). The losing party can appeal the decision to the appellate circuit within which the claim was initially filed; however, this right of appeal only applies, as discussed below, to non-small-claims cases. The proceedings are conducted under the federal rules of civil procedure and the federal rules of evidence. Under the rule established in *Golson v. Commissioner* (1970), the Tax Court follows the law of the particular circuit, if the circuit has ruled on that issue (Dubroff 1979, 387–94). The IRS is defended by attorneys from the Office of the Chief Counsel of the Internal Revenue Service.

If the claim is for less than $50,000, the proceeding is classified as a small claims or "S" case. The taxpayer files a claim stating her reasons for protesting the assessment, serves it upon the IRS and is then notified of a trial date. Costs are at a minimum with low filing fees, limited discovery and usually *pro se* (the taxpayer representing himself or herself without counsel) litigants. Trial dates typically occur within six months of filing, and decisions are rendered within a year. The average trial lasts less than two hours (Daily 1992, 104–105). Procedural and evidentiary rules are simplified, and the rules mandate that the trial judge "ensure substantial justice." There is no right of appeal, and the decisions rendered by the court in these cases have no precedential value.

If the matter concerns more than $50,000, the taxpayer still does not pay the disputed amount, but the backlog to hear such cases is significant. It can take much longer than one year for a decision to be rendered. Each side also preserves the right of appeal. Since formal procedural and evidentiary rules are used, effective presentation of the taxpayer's case almost always demands the services of a skilled advocate. The trial can take several days, although presumably since the Tax Court judge is tax specialist, and there is no jury, the parties will need to spend less time educating the judge about the particular tax issue. Because of the specialized knowledge of these judges, there is less information asymmetry between the parties and the court in the Tax Court than in a court of general jurisdiction.

Federal District Court

Alternatively, the taxpayer can pay the disputed amount, and then sue and file a claim for a refund in the federal district courts. The pay and prestige of the district court judges are greater than those of the Tax Court judges. Their salary is guaranteed and their tenure is for life, dependent only upon good behavior. The taxpayer files the claim and the case is tried in either Washington, DC, or as close as possible to the taxpayer's local district, depending upon the request of the taxpayer. One judge presides over the case from the onset of the pleadings through trial. The taxpayer can also request a jury trial. Decisions of these courts can be appealed to the circuit court within which the district court is located.

In addition to its powers to try civil cases involving tax refunds, the district court also tries criminal tax cases and has equity power, which allows the district court to order certain behaviors. For example, the IRS can use the district court to enforce a subpoena seeking information about a taxpayer which is in the possession of a third party such as a bank. The IRS is represented by the U.S. Attorney's office. The cases are usually important, skillfully argued and have precedential value. Thus, although only 5% of all taxpayer suits (Daily 1992, 5–12) are initiated in the District Court, its prestige, precedential value, equity and criminal case power make it an important part of the tax justice system.

The United States Court of Federal Claims

The Federal Courts Improvement Act established the U.S. Court of Federal Claims, formerly called the U.S. Claims Court, in 1982 as the successor to the trial division of the Court of Claims. The Court of Claims had been in existence since 1855. Like the Tax Court, the Court of Federal Claims is an Article I court. The president, with the advice and consent of the Senate, appoints judges to the Court of Claims for terms of fifteen years. The court's headquarters are in Washington, DC, but cases are also heard at other locations convenient to the parties involved. The Court of Claims has nationwide jurisdiction over a variety of subject areas, including tax refunds, the federal taking of private property for public use, the constitutional and statutory rights of military personnel and their dependents, back-pay demands from civil servants claiming unjust dismissal, persons injured by childhood vaccines and federal government contractors alleging breach of contract. Approximately one-quarter of the currently pending twenty-two-hundred-plus cases are tax refund cases. Similar to claims filed with the district courts, the taxpayer pays the disputed assessment and sues for a refund. However, like the Tax Court, there are no jury trials in the Court of Claims. Most often the case will be tried in Washington, DC, and appeals are heard by the U.S. Court of Appeals for the Federal Circuit.

Decisions to sue in these different courts present varying costs and benefits. In almost one half of the cases filed in the Tax Court, the taxpayer obtained a reduction in taxes (Daily 1992, 95). Of the specific options, the "S" option is the quickest and least costly, but presents the most information asymmetries; the taxpayer also lacks expert advice and protection. A decision to litigate in the Tax Court does entail substantial costs, even if the litigant does not have to pay the contested amount in order to begin proceedings. Pretrial pleadings and discovery, as well as the trial itself and posttrial planning and maneuvering, take considerable time and money, and decisions by a Tax Court judge are often delayed for more than one year. Expert advice and protection, however, are available, and information asymmetries are lessened.

In district courts and the Court of Claims, taxpayers have to pay first, but according to some, win more cases than in Tax Court (see Daily 1992, 105). Both of these options are expensive, with high expertise, communication, opportunity and time costs. However, perhaps paradoxically, swift discovery rules and strict time schedules, lead to a shorter decision time than for Tax Court cases.[9] But because of the lack of issue area specialization, greater opportunity exists for both information asymmetries and perverse incentives, particularly when the fact finders are jury members. Table 2.2 presents the strengths and weaknesses of these different forum choices.

Having different courts with different costs and benefits promotes equity because the taxpayer can choose the forum most appropriate to the level of the claim involved. Simple matters can be resolved swiftly and inexpensively. More complex matters get a full hearing with the choice of an expert arbiter or a jury trial. Thus, even if the rate of success is low, the taxpayer at least gets the appearance of justice, and specifically what is termed "procedural justice." In other words, the system design appears fair. As Tyler (1984, 1988, 1990) notes, the fairness of the process itself is often more important than the outcome, and fairness is the yardstick by which courts are usually evaluated.

While the appearance of fairness is important, this still begs the question of what these courts mean for tax policy. It is possible that one type of court favors a certain type of taxpayer, for example, low income or individual taxpayers as opposed to high income or corporate taxpayers, more than the other types of courts, and that this difference in decisional outcomes is due to structural differences in the appointment or tenure process. It is also possible that one court has a stronger impact on policy. In the following section we analyze whether distinctions among the three types of courts with jurisdiction over tax cases lead to measurable differences on these issues.

Table 2.2 Comparing Tax Trial Courts

	"S" Cases	Claims Court	Tax Court	District Court
Benefits	Specialized Arbiter Speed Low Communication Opportunity & Time Costs No Expertise Costs Few Information Asymmetries Lack of Perverse Incentives	Specialized Arbiter Speed Low Communication Opportunity & Time Costs No Expertise Costs Few Information Asymmetries Lack of Perverse Incentives	Specialized Arbiter Fewer Information Asymmetries Fewer Opportunities for Perverse Incentives Right of Appeal Precedential and Policy Value to Decisions	Right to Jury Level Playing Field Right of Appeal Precedential and Policy Value to Decisions Faster Decisions Greater Chance of Winning Prestigious Court
Costs	No Right of Appeal $10,000 Jurisdictional Limit Low Chance of Winning Nonlevel Playing Field Often Confront Skilled IRS Attorney Lack of Formal Rules Inhibits Complete Disclosure Lower Court Prestige	No Right of Appeal $10,000 Jurisdictional Limit Low Chance of Winning Nonlevel Playing Field Often Confront Skilled IRS Attorney Lack of Formal Rules Inhibits Complete Disclosure	Entails Time, Communication and Opportunity Costs Expertise Cost Long Wait for a Decision Low Chance of Winning Lower Court Prestige	Significant Information Asymmetries and Negotiation and Strategy Costs Significant Communication & Opportunity Costs Expertise Cost Greater Opportunity for Perverse Incentives Lack of Specialized Arbiter

5. The Specialized Court versus the General Jurisdiction Court

The Tax Court is a specialized court, meaning that the judges serving on this court only hear cases dealing with federal income tax statutes and regulations. Those who study specialized courts note that they are generally created for policy-neutral goals, such as when there is the need for discretion or judgment in interpretation of intricate issues in specific subject areas (Hansen, Johnson and Unah 1995; Legomsky 1990), the subject matter involves significant technical complexity (Legomsky 1990), or the caseload would overwhelm courts of general jurisdiction (Baum 1990; Hansen et al. 1995). Technical expertise is a significant benefit of a specialized court as opposed to a general jurisdiction court. Familiarity with the policy area allows specialized courts to offer expertise and skill in the subject matter (Unah 1997), and a specialized court decision confers judicial legitimacy on the result, something that decisions by an administrative law judge (not technically a judge in the traditional sense of the word) might not confer.

Despite these benefits, many have argued that specialized courts are little better than the agency they supposedly review; that is, critics contend that these tribunals are captured by the agency or under the control of industry interests (see Posner 1973). Critics assail specialized courts as more biased than general jurisdiction courts and afflicted with a narrow outlook (Unah 1997), and this concern has prevented the creation of a specialized Tax Court of Appeals (Geier 1991; Posner 1996).

Empirical scholarship has shown that specialized federal courts in other areas such as the Court of International Trade, the former Court of Customs and Patent Appeals and its successor the Court of Appeals for the Federal Circuit, do not necessarily behave as critics assert. For example, the creation of the U.S. Court of Appeals for the Federal Circuit seems to have brought about consensus in patent law and an end to forum shopping (Posner 1996, 253). Specialized courts are also many times less deferential to agencies than the nonspecialized federal courts of general jurisdiction (Hansen et al. 1995; Unah 1997). Due to their expertise in these areas of law, specialized court judges do not have to rely as heavily on agency interpretations as do generalized court judges. This may further extend to their relationship with hierarchically superior courts. Examining the Court of Customs and Patent Appeals, Baum (1994) found that this court was significantly less likely than the general jurisdiction courts of appeal to rely on Supreme Court authority when making decisions.

The question thus becomes whether the taxpayer faces a more favorable environment in the specialized court or the general jurisdiction courts. An examination of raw numbers reveals that the taxpayer does better in the general jurisdiction district court than in the specialized Tax Court. Some studies show that the taxpayer wins only 5% of the time in Tax Court as compared to winning 20 to 30% of the time in the district courts. Other studies acknowledge at least a 20% differential (Geier 1991, 1998). Data used for this study show taxpayers winning 20% of the time in Tax Court and 32% of the time in the district courts, a 12% differential. These differential rates have led some scholars to argue that the Tax Court is biased in favor of the IRS (Kroll 1996; but see Maule 1999), with this potential for bias leading Congress to resist creating other specialized courts (Baum 1990).

However, as we have noted, taxes are an issue with a significant ideological dimension. Republicans and conservatives have sought to portray tax collection and the IRS as dangerous and out of control (see e.g., Stevenson 1997; Wiseman 1997). Arguably, these contentions reflect the antigovernment posture adopted by conservatives and the progovernment posture adopted by liberals during this time period. Government spending depends on tax collection; therefore, opposition to government spending necessarily means opposition to the collection of revenue that supports such spending, while support for government spending consequently requires support for the collection of revenue. One study finds a significant positive correlation between judicial liberalism and support for the IRS (Howard and Nixon 2002).

Given that judges of the Tax Court are appointed by the president and confirmed by the Senate, there is no obvious reason, save for institutional structure and design, that this court should be any less ideological in its decision making than the district courts, even though the Tax Court has structural differences and is a tribunal comprised of tax experts. One could argue that the Tax Court, given its expertise, is as much if not more ideological in its decisions because the judges know the law and do not have to rely on hierarchically superior courts, the IRS or tax lawyers for guidance as to interpretation and meaning. Rather, they know the law and can structure results that are consistent with both the law and their personal ideological preferences.

However, because it is an Article I court, the Tax Court does not enjoy the same prestige, independence and salary guarantees given to Article III courts. This lack of independence and increased institutional constraints might lead to a greater willingness by Tax Court judges to defer to agency goals (see Unah 1997), and thus lead to a bias in favor of the IRS. However, this constraint is not obvious in practice, with the difference said to be "largely theoretical" (Posner 1996, 268; see also Easterbrook 1990). Because Tax Court judges enjoy full pension protection, are usually reappointed or assume senior status, and have the same salary as district court judges, in actuality they do enjoy the same protections as the Article III judges (see Dubroff 1979; Maule 1999).

In fact, our data show a different picture from what one would imagine for a specialized court (see also Howard 2005, 2009). We find that the Tax Court, free from any practical structural constraints, allows its judges a much freer hand in rendering decisions based on their policy preferences. The Tax Court, contrary to expectations, seems to be both more expert and more ideological in its decision making than the district courts. As expected, the more liberal the judge, the greater the likelihood of support for the IRS, while the more conservative the judge, the greater the likelihood of support for the taxpayer. Moreover, a

Table 2.3 Probability of IRS Winning*

Court	Tax Court	U.S. D. Ct.
Ideology	−.19**	.04
Income* Ideology	.10	.007
Deduction* Ideology	.14**	−.05

*The probability represents an increase of one standard deviation below the mean to one standard deviation above the mean.
** p < .05

Tax Court judge is *more* likely to rely on his or her ideological preferences in deciding a tax case than a comparable district court judge. In Table 2.3, below, we show this by calculating the probability of the Tax Court favoring the IRS when the ideology of the average Tax Court judge becomes more conservative by a standard measure of variation within the range of normal, specifically, one standard deviation above the mean. We do this by determining if the judge is more likely to favor the IRS or the taxpayer. We assume a decision favoring the IRS is a more liberal decision, while a decision favoring the taxpayer is a more conservative decision.

Table 2.3 specifically examines decisions showing the probability of a decision favoring the IRS premised on the ideology of the judge alone and using ideology in two particular factual tax claim circumstances. The first is when the IRS makes a claim that the taxpayer has underreported income, while the second is when the IRS challenges a deduction taken by the taxpayer. The results show that in no circumstances were the district court decisions premised on ideology by accepted measures of statistical significance. In contrast, as a tax court judge becomes more conservative, the probability of a decision favoring the IRS drops by a statistically significant 20%. Interestingly, if the taxpayer was accused of failing to report income, the more conservative judge, in that circumstance, was more likely to favor the IRS. Hidden income is a form of noncompliance that borders on cheating. Perhaps conservative judges do not like tax cheats and differentiate between legal tax avoidance as opposed to illegal tax evasion.

6. Policy Impacts

We have previously discussed the impact of the U.S. Supreme Court on tax policy. The decisions of the Supreme Court, although much fewer than the decisions of the tax trial courts, have a profound influence on tax policy. However, that begs the question of the influence of the trial courts on tax policy. Following our discussion of the ideological nature of tax decisions, we now examine the extent to which the IRS changes its audit rates of low income and high income taxpayers in response to the ideology of the Tax Court and the district courts. In a similar study about the link between lower federal court composition and permit decisions by the Army Corps of Engineers, Canes-Wrone (2003) finds that variations in the ideological composition of the lower federal courts directly influences the likelihood of the Corps granting a permit, even when no lawsuit is pending. Using our data, we can also compare the influence of these courts to the influence of the elected branches of the federal government, that is, the president and the Congress, on the IRS's actions.

As we previously noted in our discussion of the federal appellate courts, no enforcement tool used by the IRS produces more attention than the audit, and the degree to which audits focus on various groups of taxpayers based on their earnings is politically relevant to competing concerns along a liberal–conservative continuum. One would expect more liberal executives and legislatures and more liberal courts to want the IRS to audit fewer low income individuals and audit more high income taxpayers, while one would expect more conservative political actors to favor greater attention to audits of the poor, particularly if that shifts attention away from the wealthy. In Table 2.4 we examine the relative influence of the trial courts and elected branches of government on IRS audit patterns. Our measure for the legislative–executive coalition calculates the relative ideologies of the president, the House and the Senate and uses the veto override points for each chamber of Congress to arrive at a single distinct measure of ideology (Howard 2009; Howard and Nixon 2002, 2003). Again, we use a standard measure for observing variation in statistical measurement, one standard deviation from the mean. Thus, we compare the ideologies of the Tax Court, the District Court and this national political coalition in Table 2.4.

The two trial courts and the national political coalition all have a significant and powerful influence on IRS auditing policy. As shown in Table 2.4, as each court and the national political coalition become more conservative, audits on low income taxpayers' increase, and correspondingly, audits on high income taxpayers decrease. The results suggest that the Tax Court has a more powerful influence than the district courts, more than doubling the district courts' impact on the shift from high income to low income audits. However, the effect of both pales when compared to the influence of the national political coalition. For example, if we change from the Clinton presidency and the Democratic-controlled Congress of 1993 through 1994 to the George W. Bush presidency and the Republican-controlled Congress of 2003 through 2006, we witness a profound change in the relative number of audits of low income and high income taxpayers—a shift of 171%.

Table 2.4 National and Local Influence on IRS Low-Income Audits*

Tax Court Ideology	+ 40.0%**
Dist. Court Ideology	+ 22.5%**
Political System	+ 171.0%**

*The probability represents an increase of one standard deviation below the mean to one standard deviation above the mean.
** p < .01

Of course, change in the national political coalition can be rapid—potentially every two years for Congress and every four years for the presidency. Judges, including Article I judges, have a much longer tenure. The impact of the national political coalition can thus be quite fleeting. Perhaps the most long lasting impact of the contemporary political coalition is the ability to appoint the judiciary— the Tax Court, the District Court, the Federal Circuits and the Supreme Court. While the influence of court ideology—and thus judicial appointments—is not as dramatic, its effect can last much longer.

7. Conclusion

Courts and taxes are intimately intertwined and courts have a deep and long-lasting influence on the direction of tax policy in this country. It is not just the Supreme Court and appellate courts that determine the course of tax policy, but also the numerous lawsuits at the trial level that lead to a series of decisions favoring one party over another or one type of taxpayer as compared to another. While their influence might be less than that of the federal elected officials, their influence is substantial, enduring and difficult to change.

3

FEDERAL COURT POLICYMAKING
The Air We Breathe and the Water We Drink—
Courts, Law and Environmental Policy

1. Introduction

The environment and environmental concerns have played a major role in American political life for much of the latter part of the twentieth century and through the first decade of the twenty-first century. Undoubtedly, courts have played a crucial role in the development of environmental policy. Curiously, though, much of the scholarly literature is mixed on both the extent and direction of the courts' influence on policy. Some scholars assert that judicial activism has altered environmental policy in a very negative way beyond congressional intent and statutory mandate. Others assert that the courts have been hostile to the environment, and have left control of it to the political branches of government.

One of the striking aspects to environmental policy, and the related question of the judiciary's influence on environmental policy, is how relatively recently it has become a national issue. Its genesis was in the middle of the last century, and it began influencing the national consciousness only some forty years ago. Following World War II, the United States experienced a vast increase in throwaway packaging—cans, bottles, plastics and paper products—and the introduction into the marketplace of thousands of new synthetic organic chemicals. As a result, there was a significant increase in solid waste and toxic materials. This increase in the production of potential pollutants, along with a recognition that air and water conditions were deteriorating, led to a growing environmental movement in the post-World War II years. The movement was spurred in part by books like Rachel Carson's *Silent Spring* (1962), and in part due to a growing awareness of the risks to individual health and to industries and businesses dependent upon clean air and water.

Foundations, institutes, clubs, college curricula and corporate departments were formed and state-level environmental agencies were created or given added responsibilities to try and stem the tide of pollution and its growing threat to the environment. In recognition of these dangers, an "Earth Day" was declared in April of 1970 in order to create additional public awareness of increasing environmental risks.

The concern over the environment has not been misplaced. Even today, for example, air pollution contaminants kill 60,000 to100,000 Americans each year (Davis, 2002). Those living in cities where industries pump out impurities and car emissions exist in great numbers confront a greater load of air pollutants than those in rural, less industrialized areas. An estimated 120 million Americans live where the air is harmful (Natural Resources Defense Council 2008). This is also not just a U.S. phenomenon; it is worldwide. The World Health Organization estimates that 800,000 people die each year worldwide because of urban air pollution (Natural Resources Defense Council 2007).

Against this background, Congress created the U.S. Environmental Protection Agency (EPA) in 1970, a national agency dedicated to protecting environmental resources. The EPA was, by Executive Order, "reorganized" from parts of the executive branch by transferring units from existing organizations into a new independent agency. Control of air quality, among other things, was transferred from the Department of Health, Education and Welfare, while control of water quality came from the Interior Department; radiation protection standards were transferred from the Atomic Energy Commission and the Federal Radiation Council.

In addition to the creation of the EPA, Congress also responded with two major pieces of legislation in the 1970s, the Clean Air Act (CAA; 1970) and the Clean Water Act (CWA; 1977). The Clean Air Act regulates air emissions from area, stationary and mobile sources, and authorized the EPA to establish National Ambient Air Quality Standards (NAAQS) to protect public health and the environment. The Act was amended in 1977 primarily to set new dates for achieving attainment of NAAQS because many areas of the country had failed to meet the deadlines established in the original statute. The subsequent 1990 amendments to the Clean Air Act in large part were intended to meet unaddressed or insufficiently addressed problems such as acid rain, ground level ozone, stratospheric ozone depletion and air toxins.

The Clean Water Act is a 1977 amendment to the Federal Water Pollution Control Act of 1972, which set the basic structure for regulating discharges of pollutants into U.S. waters. This law gave the EPA the authority to set effluent standards on an industry-by-industry basis (technology-based) and continued its authority to set water quality standards for all contaminants in surface waters. The CWA makes it unlawful for any person to discharge any pollutant from a point source into navigable waters unless a permit (NPDES) is obtained under the Act. The 1977 amendments focused on toxic pollutants. In 1987, the CWA was reauthorized and again focused on toxic substances, as well as authorizing citizen suit provisions and funding sewage treatment plants (POTWs) under the Construction Grants Program.

With all new laws and new programs, courts are asked to determine statutory meaning and congressional intent. Thus, from the beginning of the environmental movement, from its nascence to its maturity, courts have played a significant role in the development and scope of environmental policy. The EPA was given oversight over numerous environmental concerns—from air and water to hazardous material to land management—and courts have ruled and pushed policy in these and other areas. We will review some of these issues; however, the primary focus of this chapter is the influence of federal courts on air and water policy in the aftermath of the creation of the EPA and the legislation on clean air and water enacted by Congress since the early 1970s.

Similar to tax policy, which was discussed in Chapter 2, environmental policy provides a particularly good opportunity to demonstrate the Supreme Court and regional appellate courts' approaches to public policy through an analysis and examination of the courts' oversight of the EPA. Much of the ideological decision making by the courts on environmental cases comes in the form of standing, deference and even federalism decisions. By limiting standing, which is the legal concept that one must have a sufficient connection to a case to be a party to the proceedings and seek some sort of redress, courts can limit who has the right to challenge perceived environmental dangers. By increasing the standard for agency deference (*Chevron v. National Resources Defense Council* 1984; *Vermont Yankee Nuclear Power Corp. v. National Resources Defense Council* 1978; see also Schuck and Elliott 1990), the Supreme Court made it difficult for a court to substitute its judgment for that of an agency. Finally, a federalism decision, such as whether states can act independently or whether federal law supersedes state action, can limit or expand the authority of the state or the federal government to respond to or deal with environmental issues.

Table 3.1 lists the important environmental policy cases decided from 1972 through 2009. The table lists the cases by the name of the case, by the reviewing court—Supreme Court or court of appeals—by the year and citation, specific issue area and whether or not the court issued a pro- or antienvironmental decision.

Courts are important policymakers in the area of environmental law. In particular, almost all environmental cases ask courts to determine the meaning of specific statutes, and thus engage in the process of statutory interpretation. With so many important environmental laws passed in response to the growing environmental movement, the courts had to step in and determine the meaning and intent of this legislation. In reviewing the cases listed in Table 3.1, the majority of which are Supreme Court cases, it is difficult to ascertain any clear pro- or antienvironmental bias. Several decisions are in favor of the EPA, and some of the most important and influential of the Supreme Court decisions, as we note above, are in favor of deference to the administrative agency. However, deference also means that courts are blocked from substituting their judgment for that of the agency, meaning a more liberal court and one potentially with a more proenvironmental bias cannot substitute its preferences for the EPA's decisions.

In examining the table, out of thirty-two critical decisions, seventeen can be classified as proenvironment decisions, while fifteen can be considered antienvironment. Twenty-three of the decisions are from the Supreme Court and nine

Table 3.1 Prominent Environmental Cases, 1972–2009

Case	Court	Year	Citation	Issue Area	Pro/Anti Environ.
Sierra Club v. Morton	S.Ct	1972	405 US 727	Standing	Anti
U.S. v. Maine	S.Ct	1975	420 US 515	Preservation	Pro
Reserve Mining v. EPA	8th Cir	1975	514 F2d 492	Hazardous material	Pro
Kleppe v. New Mexico	S.Ct	1976	426 US 529	Federalism	Pro
Cappeart v. U.S.	S.Ct	1976	426 US 128	Preservation	Pro
Union Electric Co. v EPA	S.Ct	1976	427 US 246	Air Quality	Pro
Vermont Yankee v. NRDC	S.Ct	1978	435 US 519	Agency Deference	Anti
TVA v. Hill	S.Ct	1978	437 US 128	Preservation	Pro
Philadelphia v. New Jersey	S.Ct	1978	437 US 617	Federalism	Anti
Strykcer's Bay v. Karlen	S.Ct	1980	460 US 766	NEPA	Anti
AFL-CIO v. Amer. Pet. Inst.	S.Ct	1980	448 US 607	Hazardous Material	Anti
Hodel v. VA Surface Mining	S.Ct	1981	452 US 264	Federalism	Pro
Edison Co. v. People Against	S.Ct	1983	460 US 766	NEPA	Pro
Chevron v. NRDC	S.Ct	1984	467 US 837	Agency Deference	Anti
U.S. v. Waste Industries, Inc	4th Cir	1984	734 F2d 159	Hazardous Waste	Pro
U.S. v. NE Pharmaceuticals	8th Cir	1986	810 F2d 726	Hazardous Waste	Pro
U.S. v. Monsanto Co.	4th Cir	1988	858 F2d 160	Hazardous Waste	Pro
Lujan v. Nat. Wildlife Fed.	S.Ct	1990	497 US 149	Standing	Anti
Corrosion Proof v. EPA	5th Cir	1991	947 F2d 1201	Hazardous Waste	Anti
U.S. v. McDonald & Watson	1st Cir	1991	933F2d 35	Hazardous Waste	Anti
U.S. v. Laughlin	2d Cir	1993	10 F3d 961	Hazardous Waste	Anti
Babbitt v. Sweet Home	S.Ct	1995	515 US 678	Preservation	Pro
U.S. v. Hanousek	9th Cir	1999	176 F3d 894	Hazardous Waste	Pro
Harmon Ind v. Browner	8th Cir	1999	191 F3d 1116	Hazardous Waste	Anti
Earth, Inc. v. Laidlaw Serv.	S.Ct	2000	528 US 167	Standing	Pro
Solid Waste v. Army Corps.	S.Ct	2001	531 US 159	Preservation	Anti
Whitman v. Amer. Trucking	S.Ct	2001	531 US 457	Pollution	Pro
Rapanos v. U.S.	S.Ct	2006	547 US 715	Preservation	Anti
MA v. EPA	S.Ct	2007	127 SCT 1438	Standing	Pro
U.S. v. Atlantic Research	S.Ct	2007	127 SCT 2331	Hazardous Waste	Pro
Energy Corp. v. Riverkeeper	S.Ct	2009	129 SCT 1498	Pollution	Anti
Burlington Northern v. U.S.	S.Ct	2009	129 SCT 1870	Hazardous Waste	Anti

stem from the circuit courts. Three of the circuit court decisions are from the Eighth Circuit. The circuit decisions are as split as the Supreme Court, with five proenvironment decisions and four antienvironment decisions.

Our next table, Table 3.2, examines these same cases, but this time with the median ideology of the respective court at the time of the decision listed in column three. We use the same ideology measures that we used in previous chapters, the Martin-Quinn scores. Lower (negative) values mean the court is more liberal, while higher (positive) values mean the court is more conservative. In this table we omit citation and issue area.

As one can see from Table 3.2, for most of the time, the median ideology of the Supreme Court did not vary that much, centering almost on 0, the moderate midpoint, which might be one explanation for the wide variation we can observe in environmental rulings. A court dominated by a moderate ideology should produce both pro- and antienvironmental rulings, with neither a conservative nor a liberal block gaining control of the decisional outcome. However, when we group the cases as either proenvironment or antienvironment, some ideological differences emerge. First, the average ideology for all the cases that resulted in a proenvironment decision was .05, or very slightly right of center. On the other hand, the cases that were antienvironment had an average median ideology score of .18, a bit more conservative. If we examine only the nine courts of appeals cases, the difference is even starker with a .08 mean ideology for the proenvironment cases as compared to .20 for the antienvironment cases. So again, ideology seems to matter in assessing the likelihood of a particular court handing down a pro- or antienvironment ruling, though the effect is not as strong as we find in other issue areas discussed in other chapters.

Again, as we have focused on in other chapters, the courts do not stand in isolation from other branches of government. In Table 3.3 below we list each EPA administrator and the corresponding common space ideology of the agency administrator, as well as the ideology scores for the House, the Senate and the Supreme Court since the beginning of the EPA through 2010. For the House, Senate and Supreme Court, we use the median scores for all members serving in a particular year. For reasons we will explain later on in the chapter, we assume that the director of the EPA has the same ideology as the appointing president.

Utilizing the information presented in Table 3.3, we can examine these years and label the legal set as either constrained or unconstrained—it is constrained if an ideologically liberal or conservative court confronts a Congress, president and agency that are ideologically unified, meaning all three are liberal or all are conservative. Those situations present the theoretically easiest circumstances for an adverse court decision to be overturned. A statutory interpretation case that results in a more conservative decision could be overturned when the agency, House and Senate are all liberal. Conversely, a statutory interpretation case that results in a more liberal decision could be overturned when the agency, House and Senate are all more conservative.

Table 3.2 Prominent Environmental Cases, 1972–2009 with Median Court Ideology

Case	Court	Year	Median Ideology	Pro/Anti Environ.
Sierra Club v. Morton	S.Ct	1972	0.126	Anti
U.S. v. Maine	S.Ct	1975	0.078	Pro
Reserve Mining v. EPA	8th Cir	1975	0.006	Pro
Kleppe v. New Mexico	S.Ct	1976	0.056	Pro
Cappeart v. U.S.	S.Ct	1976	0.056	Pro
Union Electric Co. v EPA	S.Ct	1976	0.056	Pro
Vermont Yankee v. NRDC	S.Ct	1978	−0.024	Anti
TVA v. Hill	S.Ct	1978	−0.024	Pro
Philadelphia v. New Jersey	S.Ct	1978	−0.024	Anti
Strykcer's Bay v. Karlen	S.Ct	1980	−0.062	Anti
AFL-CIO v. Amer. Pet. Inst.	S.Ct	1980	−0.062	Anti
Hodel v. VA Surface Mining	S.Ct	1981	−0.085	Pro
Edison Co. v. People Against	S.Ct	1983	0.034	Pro
Chevron v. NRDC	S.Ct	1984	0.118	Anti
U.S. v. Waste Industries, Inc	4th Cir	1984	0.234	Pro
U.S. v. NE Pharmaceuticals	8th Cir	1986	0.112	Pro
U.S. v. Monsanto Co.	4th Cir	1988	0.234	Pro
Lujan v. Nat. Wildlife Fed.	S.Ct	1990	0.132	Anti
Corrosion Proof v. EPA	5th Cir	1991	0.458	Anti
U.S. v. McDonald & Watson	1st Cir	1991	0.009	Anti
U.S. v. Laughlin	2d Cir	1993	0.135	Anti
Babbitt v. Sweet Home	S.Ct	1995	0.093	Pro
U.S. v. Hanousek	9th Cir	1999	−0.209	Pro
Harmon Ind v. Browner	8th Cir	1999	0.178	Anti
Earth, Inc. v. Laidlaw Serv.	S.Ct	2000	0.113	Pro
Solid Waste v. Army Corps.	S.Ct	2001	0.040	Anti
Whitman v. Amer. Trucking	S.Ct	2001	0.040	Pro
Rapanos v. U.S.	S.Ct	2006	−0.052	Anti
MA v. EPA	S.Ct	2007	−0.002	Pro
U.S. v. Atlantic Research	S.Ct	2007	−0.002	Pro
Energy Corp. v. Riverkeeper	S.Ct	2009	0.848	Anti
Burlington Northern v. U.S.	S.Ct	2009	0.848	Anti

Table 3.3 Comparing Ideology: EPA, Congress and Court, 1971–2010

No	Administrator	Year	President(s)	Agency	Senate	House	Sup. Court
1.	William D. Ruckelshaus	1971	Richard Nixon	0.396	-0.045	-0.013	0.068
	William D. Ruckelshaus	1972	Richard Nixon	1.396	-0.045	-0.013	0.129
2.	Russell E. Train	1973	Richard Nixon	0.396	-0.125	-0.010	0.210
	Russell E. Train	1974	Gerald Ford	0.377	-0.125	-0.010	0.077
	Russell E. Train	1975	Gerald Ford	0.377	-0.178	-0.163	0.079
	Russell E. Train	1976	Gerald Ford	0.377	-0.178	-0.163	0.055
3.	Douglas M. Costle	1977	Jimmy Carter	-0.512	-0.174	-0.148	0.041
	Douglas M. Costle	1978	Jimmy Carter	-0.512	-0.174	-0.148	-0.030
	Douglas M. Costle	1979	Jimmy Carter	-0.512	-0.118	-0.127	-0.079
	Douglas M. Costle	1980	Jimmy Carter	-0.512	-0.118	-0.127	-0.066
4.	Anne M. Gorsuch Burford	1981	Ronald Reagan	0.552	0.017	-0.024	-0.089
	Anne M. Gorsuch Burford	1982	Ronald Reagan	0.552	0.017	-0.024	-0.106
5.	William D. Ruckelshaus	1983	Ronald Reagan	0.552	0.017	-0.102	0.033
	William D. Ruckelshaus	1984	Ronald Reagan	0.552	0.017	-0.102	0.120
6.	Lee M. Thomas	1985	Ronald Reagan	0.552	0.017	-0.075	0.096
	Lee M. Thomas	1986	Ronald Reagan	0.552	0.017	-0.075	0.132
	Lee M. Thomas	1987	Ronald Reagan	0.552	-0.072	-0.092	0.122
	Lee M. Thomas	1988	Ronald Reagan	0.552	-0.072	-0.092	0.179
7.	William K. Reilly	1989	George H. W. Bush	0.524	-0.096	-0.092	0.201
	William K. Reilly	1990	George H. W. Bush	0.524	-0.096	-0.092	0.133

	Name	Year	President				
	William K. Reilly	1991	George H. W. Bush	0.524	-0.128	-0.107	0.183
	William K. Reilly	1992	George H. W. Bush	0.524	-0.128	-0.107	0.065
8.	Carol M. Browner	1993	Bill Clinton	-0.438	-0.125	-0.112	0.103
	Carol M. Browner	1994	Bill Clinton	-0.438	-0.125	-0.112	0.115
	Carol M. Browner	1995	Bill Clinton	-0.438	0.029	0.182	0.090
	Carol M. Browner	1996	Bill Clinton	-0.438	0.029	0.182	0.063
	Carol M. Browner	1997	Bill Clinton	-0.438	0.122	0.174	0.100
	Carol M. Browner	1998	Bill Clinton	-0.438	0.122	0.174	0.084
	Carol M. Browner	1999	Bill Clinton	-0.438	0.111	0.149	0.116
	Carol M. Browner	2000	Bill Clinton	0.562	0.111	0.149	0.112
9.	Christine Todd Whitman	2001	George W. Bush	0.399	-0.010	0.172	0.037
	Christine Todd Whitman	2002	George W. Bush	0.399	-0.010	0.172	-0.019
10.	Michael O. Leavitt	2003	George W. Bush	0.399	0.057	0.216	-0.044
	Michael O. Leavitt	2004	George W. Bush	0.399	0.057	0.216	-0.058
11.	Stephen L. Johnson	2005	George W. Bush	0.399	0.189	0.233	-0.087
	Stephen L. Johnson	2006	George W. Bush	0.399	0.189	0.233	-0.050
	Stephen L. Johnson	2007	George W. Bush	0.399	0.001	-0.135	-0.002
	Stephen L. Johnson	2008	George W. Bush	0.399	0.001	-0.135	-0.064
12.	Lisa P. Jackson	2009	Barack Obama	-0.322			0.848
	Lisa P. Jackson	2010	Barack Obama	-0.322			0.848

A court will have considerably more freedom, however, when the ideology of the agency, House and Senate is in conflict. That is, a conservative court will have greater leeway to impose policy preferences if either the agency (president), House or Senate is in ideological alignment with the deciding court. Either a presidential veto or the inability to persuade one chamber of Congress to approve a change in the law to override a Supreme Court interpretation would allow the Court ruling to stand.

Of course, the reality is a bit more complicated than just described. For example, the Senate and House could have enough votes to override the veto of a president. For example, Richard Nixon's veto of the Clean Water Act was overridden by Congress. In addition, the relevant committee or committee chair can block legislation or move legislation forward in such a way as to circumvent the median ideology. Nonetheless, Table 3.3 still allows some insight into the process.

In examining Table 3.3, one thing that becomes apparent is how much leeway the Supreme Court has had during this time period because many years have been characterized by divided government, whereby the Congress and the presidency are controlled by different parties (or one chamber of Congress is controlled by a different party). In this forty-year period, there are only seven years when the Court, by the above definition, could be considered "constrained." The first occurred in the first two years of the Carter presidency when a more liberal agency and Congress confronted a more conservative Court; an identical pattern emerged in the first two years of the Clinton presidency. During Carter's final two years, the Supreme Court median shifted to a more liberal position, while the Republicans took control of the House and Senate for the final six years of Clinton's presidency. And, for much of this time the Court was moderately conservative and thus unlikely to deviate much from conservative congressional preferences or from conservative agency preferences.

This still begs the question of the actual *extent* of court influence over environmental policy. While it is clear that courts have had a pivotal role in shaping environmental policy from the onset of the EPA and the passage of early environmental laws, there has been a debate as to the extent and meaning of court influence over environmental policy. As some of the cases listed above in Table 3.1 show, the Supreme Court was reluctant to intervene in certain cases. The Court cited federalism or standing as reasons to decline getting involved in certain environmental issue areas. Although not specifically meant to be a ruling on the merits, the result was to leave standing agency decisions considered antienvironment.

Perhaps these Supreme Court cases came in response to a significant increase in lower court oversight of environmental policy. One scholar argues that in the case of the Clean Air Act, the courts became so involved in the environmental process that judges became more like regulators, assuming expertise over a vastly complex area and significantly changing the meaning and purpose of the original act and amendments (Melnick 1983, 2004). For Melnick, this increased activism had adverse consequences for environmental policy because judges lacked the expertise of the bureaucratic and policy officials and thus their interference led to inefficiency and inequity in environmental policy. Regulators, on the other hand, began to act more like judges by anticipating court rulings, in effect changing the plain meaning of the law to avoid being second guessed and having their decisions challenged and changed. Expertise became secondary to legal considerations. From this perspective, deference to the EPA and standing rulings make sense if one considers that for much of this period the lower federal courts were often more liberal than the Supreme Court.

Melnick's argument implies that the courts were involved in judicial activism writ large, interpreting environmental laws and regulations with regard to their own particular policy preferences—and with adverse consequences. Despite Melnick's assertions, however, some initial concerns of the role of courts and the environment were raised by scholars who thought courts had *too little* a role to play in shaping environmental policy. For example, Oakes (1977) notes that increased federal regulation of the environment presented the courts with unique and difficult questions of policy that were not always amenable to resolution by traditional legal tools. The novelty of those questions, coupled with the technical complexity and social importance of environmental matters, caused some courts to exercise considerable restraint in the interpretation and application of legislative standards. This argument is echoed by Leventhal (1974), who posits that courts no longer had a major role in the direction of the formulation of the pertinent legal rules regarding the environment. The enactment of environmental laws such as the Clean Air Act, the Water Pollution Control Act and the National Environmental Policy Act (NEPA) removed from courts the primary role of dealing with environmental issues.

This view was buttressed by others. Stewart (1976) concludes that environmental concerns did not receive exceptional protection by reviewing courts and that court decisions that appear to reflect special judicial solicitude for environmental interests must be understood as part of a more general judicial effort to curb perceived agency biases and ensure consideration of the full range of interests affected by agency decisions. In fact, in a 1990 article, David Shilton examines decisions on NEPA cases brought before the U.S. Supreme Court and finds that the Court decided every NEPA case in favor of the government, leading to an appearance of hostility to environmental concerns. Stewart (1976) argues, however, that procedural deference to the government does not mean outright hostility to the environment, and, given the information reported in Table 3.2, the basic data seem to support Stewart's assertions.

However, Stewart's view of a lack of hostility by the Supreme Court to the environment in the mid-1970s is challenged by other, more recent scholarly analyses. Two leading articles, written a decade apart, both substantiate the notion of Supreme Court hostility to environmental law. Levy and Glicksman (1989) and Lazarus (2000) argue that post-1976 the Supreme Court was actively hostile to the environment. Levy and Glicksman (1989) argue that a consistent prodevelopment pattern has prevailed in the Supreme Court's environmental law decisions since 1976. To Levy and Glicksman, these decisions reflect policy activism by the Court. They suggest that in a number of cases, the Court's exercise of institutional restraint seems inconsistent with statutory language or legislative history.

Lazarus (2000) posits that the Supreme Court's apparent apathy or even antipathy toward environmental law during that time results from the justices' failure to appreciate environmental law as a distinct area of law. The justices have instead tended to view environmental protection as merely an incidental factual context for the presentation of legal issues that share no unique environmental dimension.

How do we reconcile Melnick's argument with both the data and the scholarly analyses that show the Supreme Court did little to actively promote environmental causes? One way to draw and understand the distinction is to realize the importance of lower courts to environmental policy. Much of the scholarly literature, and many of the cases listed in Tables 3.1 and 3.2, focus on the Supreme Court and the Supreme Court's rulings on the environment and environmental law. This concentration properly reflects the national scope and national interest in environmental policy. However, much of environmental law and policy occurs at a regional, not national level. Failure to recognize or account for regional court influences on environmental policy leaves a very incomplete picture.

The EPA itself is organized around regions, and each state has been assigned to a specific region. To facilitate implementation of environmental regulations, the EPA delegates much of the responsibility to its ten regional offices. In addition, the EPA allows state agencies to implement their own regulations as long as the state's regulations are at least as stringent as the federal rules. Thus, the EPA is an agency that operates within a national framework, yet allows significant local control over much of its policy outputs.

Data and scholarly analyses bear out these claims of regional variation (e.g., Hunter and Waterman 1992; Ringquist 1993a; Ringquist and Emmert 1999). There are significant enforcement differences from states and regions that seem driven by the idiosyncrasies of regional EPA personnel. For example, the number of Clean Water Act inspections in Arkansas ranged from a low of one in 1985 to a high of a hundred and one in 1992. During the same period, inspections in Kansas ranged from a low of five hundred and eighty-four in 1982 to a high of a thousand and sixty-one in 1992.

Hunter and Waterman (1992) reinforce these bare findings by showing that there are "considerable differences in the enforcement vigor of EPA's 10 regional offices" (415). While each region has its own "political culture, political environment and water related problems" (Hunter and Waterman 1992, 407), an additional explanation for these regional variations is that the regions are subject to different interpretations of environmental laws by the different federal appellate courts, and that this regional control by these courts is more influential than national political control. The variation is therefore plausibly the result of the differing ideologies and policy preferences of the various federal appellate courts, and the subsequent response by the regional EPA offices to these differences.

The appellate courts are often overlooked as key players in examining the EPA. In a typical year, the federal appeals courts will handle more cases involving the environment than the U.S. Supreme Court will decide over a thirty-five-year period.

Many studies also show significant political responsiveness by the EPA to the political control of Congress and the presidency (Ringquist 1995; Ringquist and Emmert 1999; Wood and Waterman 1994). This marks the EPA as comparable to other agencies (Scholz and Wood 1998, 1999; Wood and Waterman 1994). For example, Wood and Waterman (1994) find significant changes in Clean Air enforcement due to changes in presidential administrations. The Reagan administration and subsequent budgets led to a decline in both monitoring and abatement actions (1994, 117–26). Evan Ringquist shows in a series of studies (1993a, 1993b, 1995) that political control of environmental policy is highly dependent upon regional and local policy as established by regional and local policy actors. Interestingly, Ringquist did not find any actual change in agency culture, goals or values of those who work for the EPA—officials remain committed to vigorous enforcement of environmental laws. Nonetheless, legislative and executive control was able to alter and change regional agency outputs, particularly for water policy. Thus, EPA officials, regardless of their preferences or the preferences of the president, must and do respond to other political actors. In a later study with Craig Emmert, Ringquist and Emmert (1999) find that environmental cases were to some extent a function of lower court preferences as well as broader institutional preferences.

However, very few of these studies have examined how agencies carry out regionally specific policy given demands by both the executive and legislative branches (Howard and Nixon 2002, 2003; Shipan 1998), and even fewer have shown how regional courts fit into this separation of powers dynamic of determining agency policy (Howard and Nixon 2002, 2003). Thus, an examination of the EPA provides another opportunity to examine the impact of courts on policy through the imposition of the legal set of policy preferences.

2. A Model to Compare Influences

To determine the relative influence of regional courts on the EPA as a way of testing the influence of lower courts vis-à-vis the Supreme Court and other national institutions, we tested a model to determine the impact of appellate court ideology on EPA policy choice in a legal set context that allows for regional variation and allows us to compare the relative impact of the appellate courts and the political actors in the system—the president and the Congress. We use a measure developed by David Nixon (Howard and Nixon 2003; Nixon n.d.) that is strictly comparable to the common space and Martin-Quinn scores used throughout the book. We calculated the median ideology of each relevant circuit court of appeals using the Nixon measure for each appropriate EPA region. This measure allows us to directly test the influence of the median ideology on enforcement policy.

We also use an interaction of ideology and the standard deviation of the median ideology of each circuit court. The standard deviation measures the ideological concordance of the circuit court. The greater the standard deviation, the greater is the variation in ideology within the circuit. A small standard deviation means either a more coherently conservative circuit or a more coherently liberal circuit court. Utilizing this interaction allows us to examine how the agency reacts to the lack of an identifiable ideology. To measure national political influence, we use a measure of national political preferences that we call the "core." This is the key veto override point of Congress on presidential preferences. We assume that an agency, faithful to the president, would aim its policy preferences directly at the "core" to avoid any override of those preferences.

Using the Freedom of Information Act, we created a dataset of EPA notices of water violations. The dataset we constructed features one observation for each state for each year between 1981 and 1995, with the exception of one missing data point (N = 799). Following the approach used by Scholz and Wood (1998, 1999) and Howard and Nixon (2002, 2003), we examine state variation as a method of testing for local or regional control. We investigate the causal effect of national and local institutions, including the appellate courts, on the number of notices of violations of the Clean Water Act per state per year for the period of this study. Recent studies have focused on both the Clean Air Act and the Clean Water Act (Hunter and Waterman 1992; Ringquist 1995; Wood and Waterman 1993). We specifically focus on the Clean Water Act because the enforcement system is highly decentralized among the regions, with the level of national influence curtailed in some states. However, because the EPA is in constant contact with the regional offices and the states, especially with regard to bringing initial notices of violations of the Clean Water Act, notices of violations provide an ideal measure of competing national and regional influences.

To determine the relative influence of local and regional control, we use measures suggested by previous studies that might have an impact on water enforcement independent of political control. For example, things such as per capita income, urbanization, population density, manufacturing activity, agricultural activity and state government might all have an influence on environmental policy. Per capita income is a measure of state wealth. One would assume that greater wealth usually means greater industrialization. Greater industrialization usually means a greater potential for pollution and therefore a greater potential for pollution violations. Urbanization and population density are also indicators of greater industrialization. So by the same logic, we expect a positive relationship between the existence of these factors and notices of water violations. For one additional measure of industrialization, we use state manufacturing income as an additional control for nonpolitical reasons for pollution and pollution control. One would assume that the greater the state's manufacturing income, the greater the level of industrialization, and therefore the greater the number of notices of violation.

As Ringquist notes, industrialization activity is not the only factor that affects water quality (1993b, 185). Agricultural activity can also significantly lead to greater clean water violations. Therefore, as an additional measure, we examine the agricultural income of each state. We expect a positive relationship between agricultural income and notice of water violations. For our last control measure, we want to examine the influence of state political actors. For this we look at the liberalism of the state government. Such a measure, as discussed in Chapter 1, was developed by Berry and colleagues (1998). It is a measure of the summed proportion of Democratic representatives in the state legislature and Democratic control of the governor's office, and has been used in previous studies of agency policy. Given the involvement of states in Clean Water Act enforcement (Hunter and Waterman 1993; Ringquist 1993a), local variation might be a result of responsiveness to local as well as national political officials.

Given the time dependent nature of our data and the potential for some methodological problems (Beck and Katz 1995, 636; Greene 1997), we use some other measures to account for differences over time and between the states. For example, we use a lagged dependent variable to control for any additional variation, and used time point dummy variables.

3. Results

We present the key results in Figure 3.1 and Figure 3.2. The results, as shown by the figures, strongly support our predictions, and show that, on average, regional control by the courts results in a much greater change in behavior of the EPA than do changes in the ideological or partisan balance of the electoral system.

The virtue of our measurement of judicial ideology is that the influence of national versus regional control may be compared directly. That is, the impact of a .20 shift in a circuit judge median may also be calculated and compared to the impact of the .20 shift in the legislative–executive core. We see that the court ideology measure and the core variable both support the proposed hypotheses, but

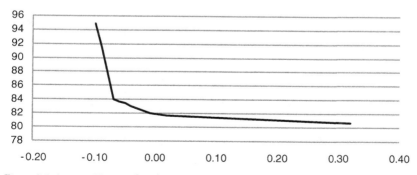

Figure 3.1 Average Notice of Violations per Circuit, 1981–1995 by Political System Ideology

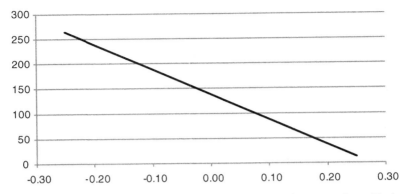

Figure 3.2 Average Notice of Violation per Circuit, 1981–1995 by Circuit Court Ideology

the impact of the courts is much stronger. The political system has an undeniable influence, but it is most dramatic when the system is in a very liberal position. After that, the impact of changes in ideology diminishes. The difference between an extremely conservative president and Congress and a Congress and president operating in the middle of the ideological spectrum is only about two notices of violations per EPA region per circuit.

In contrast, the influence of the courts of appeal is particularly dramatic and presents almost a monotonic relationship of ideology and notice violations. A similar shift to what we observed in the "core" change shows that moving from a moderate to a conservative circuit court results in approximately one hundred fewer notices of violations.

Of course, one thing to note is that the political system's ideology can change much more rapidly than a circuit court's ideology. An election can switch control of the House or Senate or both from one party to another party every two years. Change of partisan control has recently occurred in 1994, 2006 and 2010. In 1994 and 2006 both houses of Congress switched control, while in 2010 the House of Representatives changed from Democratic to Republican control. The presidency can switch every four years. Even without a switch in the control of either chamber, one party or another can dominate an election cycle, moving the core ideology in a more liberal or a more conservative direction. In 2008, for example, the Democrats solidified their control of both houses of Congress and, with the election of Barack Obama, the core switched to a much more liberal point. However, the subsequent midterm elections of 2010 resulted in a Republican takeover of the House of Representatives, and so the ideological pendulum has swung back again toward the conservative spectrum.

Palpable changes in court ideology take place over a much longer time period than national political shifts. Lifetime appointments insure that ideological change in the judiciary is rarely a rapid occurrence, and ongoing battles over federal judicial appointments also decrease the rate of change (see e.g., Steigerwalt

2010). Thus, although the impact of ideological change is dramatic, one has to view the differences with some caution given the difference in the time it takes for ideological change to occur in courts as compared to elected political officials.

4. Conclusion

Our examination in this chapter highlights that lower federal courts exert a great deal of influence on EPA policy. Just as the Supreme Court establishes a legal set, so too do the regional federal courts. Our results suggest that changes in the national executive and legislative balance, together with changes in the regional ideological balance on the benches of the circuit courts of appeals, can influence EPA behavior. For certain policy domains, and perhaps especially for environmental policy, these regional courts might have greater influence than the Supreme Court or national political actors. Those who focus purely on the Supreme Court in determining judicial influence over policy thus miss the true picture of court influence and impact.

Again, there is no neutral judge. More than many policy domains, environmental policy is a function of statutory interpretation. Many believe that statutory interpretation decisions are merely a function of legislative intent and the plain meaning of the text of the statute. However, even in this relatively straightforward area of statutory interpretation, legal policy preferences influence environmental policy outcomes. Liberal judges lead to greater enforcement of environmental violations while more conservative judges suggest less agency enforcement. It is thus only by exploring both the influence of different types of courts, as well as variations among these courts, both as to level and regional jurisdiction, that we can truly understand how the federal judiciary significantly influences the development of national environmental policy.

4

FEDERAL COURT POLICYMAKING
The Status of Women

1. Introduction

In 1967, Richard Reed, a minor and the only son of Sally and Cecil Reed, died in Idaho. Richard died without a will, and so an executor for his estate needed to be named. Both Sally and Cecil Reed, who had previously divorced, applied to be the executor of Richard's estate. Based on Idaho law, the probate court declared Cecil Reed the executor of the estate. This case became the starting point for an evolution in the developing standard for gender discrimination cases promulgated by the U.S. Supreme Court. Along with the growing women's rights movement and congressional passage of the Equal Rights Amendment in 1972, major legal, political and social changes concerning the status of women began to take place in the United States. These events allow us to examine the role of the legal set and the importance of courts in moving policy forward, provided the courts' policies fit into the available and supportable policy domain.

Two provisions of the Idaho Code were used to make this determination. Section 15-312 explicated what persons were entitled to administer the estate of those who died intestate. It listed eleven classes of persons, and ranked them in order of preference. One of the classes is "[t]he father or mother" of the deceased, and so, under this provision, both were equally entitled to administer their son's estate. Section 15-314, however, stated that "[o]f several persons claiming and equally entitled [under §15-312] to administer, males must be preferred to females, and relatives of the whole to those of the half blood." The probate judge thus ruled that since both Sally and Cecil Reed were "equally entitled" to be administrators of the deceased's estate, Cecil Reed was the preferred candidate under Idaho law since he was male. The probate judge also made clear that he had not attempted to determine whether one of the parties was more or less capable to perform the functions necessary to execute an estate.

The U.S. Supreme Court was asked to determine whether §15-314 violated the equal protection clause of the Fourteenth Amendment of the U.S. Constitution since it required a mandatory preference for males over females, regardless of their individual qualifications. Idaho in part argued that the law served to reduce the workload of the courts, which would otherwise have to hold hearings when two "equally entitled" persons petitioned to be executor of someone's estate. The Supreme Court unanimously disagreed, ruling that "[t]o give a mandatory preference to members of either sex over members of the other, merely to accomplish the elimination of hearings on the merits, is to make the very kind of arbitrary legislative choice forbidden by the Equal Protection Clause of the Fourteenth Amendment" (1971, 76).

While today the decision in *Reed v. Reed* seems rather mundane, at the time it was incredibly radical. Never to that point had the Supreme Court struck down a law which treated males and females differently. Instead, the Supreme Court's previous decisions had, many times in rather stark terms, upheld the notion that the sexes could be treated differently simply due to their sex (see Table 4.1 for a listing of major Supreme Court cases dealing with equality between the sexes). For example, in 1873 in *Bradwell v. Illinois*, the Supreme Court denied Myra Bradwell a license to practice law, stating, "The natural and proper timidity and delicacy which belongs to the female sex evidently unfits it for many of the occupations of civil life. The constitution of the family organization, which is founded in the divine ordinance, as well as in the nature of things, indicates the domestic sphere as that which properly belongs to the domain and functions of womanhood" (141). Similarly, in 1908 in the case of *Muller v. Oregon*, the Supreme Court upheld a law which placed a maximum on the number of hours women— but not men—could work, explaining that "woman's physical structure and the performance of maternal functions place her at a disadvantage in the struggle for subsistence ... as healthy mothers are essential to vigorous offspring, the physical well-being of women becomes an object of public interest and care in order to preserve the strength and vigor of the race" (421). And, as late as 1961, the Supreme Court upheld a Florida law which categorically exempted women from serving on juries unless they made a specific request to be placed on the jury list. In *Hoyt v. Florida* (1961), the Court explained why it was okay to provide women with an absolute exemption from jury service due solely to their sex: "Despite the enlightened emancipation of women from the restrictions and protections of bygone years, and their entry into many parts of community life formerly considered to be reserved to men, woman is still regarded as the center of home and family life" and so may be relieved from jury service "unless she herself determines that such service is consistent with her own special responsibilities" (61–62). In all of these cases, the Supreme Court relied in part on the notion that women were more likely to be the primary caretakers of children and the home, and this difference meant that women could be exempted—if not outright excluded—from participation in public and civic life.

As of 1971, when the Supreme Court handed down its landmark decision in *Reed v. Reed*, numerous states as well as the federal government had laws which treated men and women differently based simply on their sex. In many ways, in terms of legal and political equality, women were still viewed as the weaker sex, unfit for many of the obstacles and hardships related to public life. Additionally, many laws placed men at a disadvantage when the issue of child rearing

Table 4.1 Major Supreme Court Sex Equality Cases

Case	Year	Principal Established
Bradwell v. Illinois (83 U.S. 130)	1873	Upheld the decision by the state of Illinois to prohibit Myra Bradwell from admittance to the practice of law due solely to her gender
Minor v. Happersett (88 U.S. 162)	1875	Upheld Missouri law prohibiting women from voting, based solely due to their gender
Muller v. Oregon (208 U.S. 412)	1908	Upheld an Oregon law placing a limit on the number of hours women, but not men, could work
Hoyt v. Florida (368 U.S. 57)	1961	Upheld a Florida statute that excused all women from jury service unless they requested to serve, arguing that it was reasonable given that women are regarded as the "center of home and family life"
Reed v. Reed (404 U.S. 71)	1971	Struck down an Idaho law which established a preference for males in terms of appointing executors for estates. First case in which a sex-based classification was declared unconstitutional
Frontiero v. Richardson (411 U.S. 677)	1973	Struck down a federal law which required female military personnel to prove their spouse's financial dependence while presuming the financial dependence of spouses of male military personnel
Weinberger v. Wiesenfeld (420 U.S. 636)	1975	Struck down a provision of the federal Social Security Act which permitted widows but not widowers to collect special benefits while caring for minor children
Craig v. Boren (429 U.S. 190)	1976	Struck down an Oklahoma statute which established different drinking ages for men and women. Established the principle that sex-based classifications would be subjected to "Heightened Scrutiny" under the Equal Protection Clause
Califano v. Goldfarb (430 U.S. 199)	1977	Struck down a provision of the federal Social Security Act which required husbands whose wives passed away to prove that they received half of their support from their wives at the time of her death in order to receive survivor's benefits, but did not impose the same requirement on widows
Orr v. Orr (440 U.S. 268)	1979	Struck down an Alabama statute which required husbands, but not wives, to pay alimony
Michael M. v. Superior Court of Sonoma County (450 U.S. 464)	1981	Upheld a California statutory rape statute which only criminalized sexual relations with a minor female on the basis of men and women being "dissimilarly situated" with regards to reproduction

Case	Year	Principal Established
Rostker v. Goldberg (453 U.S. 57)	1981	Since women are restricted from combat, only men could be subjected to the draft
Automobile Workers v. Johnson Controls, Inc. (499 U.S. 187)	1991	Held that a company policy barring all female employees from working in jobs that exposed them to lead in excess of OSHA safety standards due to concerns about fetal health constituted sex discrimination under Title VII of the Civil Rights Act of 1964
J.E.B. v. Alabama ex rel T.B. (511 U.S. 127)	1994	The Equal Protection Clause prohibits the exclusion of jurors based solely on their sex
United States v. Virginia (518 U.S. 515)	1996	Male-only admissions policy to the Virginia Military Institute was unconstitutional, and the creation of a women-only school did not provide women with the same opportunities provided by VMI
Tuan Anh Nguyen v. INS (533 U.S. 53)	2001	Upheld a federal statute mandating different requirements for attaining citizenship by children born abroad and out of wedlock depending on the sex of the parent with American citizenship

was at stake. Thus, laws served to reinforce the notion of men as the dominant force in public life, while women retained control over the private sphere. For example, states such as North Carolina and Louisiana had laws which designated the husband "head and master" of the household and so entitled to unilateral control over even property jointly owned by the husband and wife. Oklahoma law established that since the husband was the head of the household, he had exclusive legal rights to select where the couple would live and their style of living, and his wife must conform to those wishes; Georgia state law stipulated that wives were "subject to" their husbands as "head of the family." States also had laws which either resulted in women being fired from certain jobs once they became pregnant, or being forced to take maternity leave given concerns about their physical ability to carry out their job requirements. Maximum work hour laws for certain jobs that pertained only to women existed in Mississippi and New Hampshire, and laws in Arkansas, Missouri, Ohio and the Federal Code entirely prohibited women from working in some fields. Title VII of the Civil Rights Act also allowed sex to be considered "a bona fide occupational qualification" for certain jobs, leading the Supreme Court in *Dothard v. Rawlinson* (1977) to hold that women could be denied jobs as prison guards because of their "very womanhood" (335).

However, a burgeoning women's rights movement was seeking policy and legislative change at the state and federal level, which included introducing an Equal Rights Amendment (ERA) in every Congress since 1923. We discuss the ERA in greater detail later in the chapter. Advocates for gender equality also simultaneously sought changes through the federal courts during this same period. Beginning in 1971, a series of important cases attacking legally mandated sex-based classifications systematically chipped away at these long-standing barriers to gender equality. What had been accepted conventions concerning sex differences became signs of blatant misogyny, and the resulting court decisions undermined traditional notions of the proper roles of men versus women and helped usher in fundamental differences in society concerning the two sexes. However, the courts have also had to grapple with the reality that women and men *are* different, at least in terms of reproduction, and that this difference may mean that the sexes at times should be, or at least can be, treated in a dissimilar fashion. And, this same struggle has concerned society as well, as legislatures and the public have wrestled with the question of whether men and women should be treated at all times as legally equivalent beings. The end result is a still ongoing battle over gender equality, a battle where the federal courts have played a central role.

2. Gender Equality in the Courts: From Rational Basis to Intermediate Scrutiny

Under equal protection analysis, courts generally defer to the legislature. Even though the equal protection clause of the Fourteenth Amendment mandates that "no state shall … deny to any person within its jurisdiction the equal protection of the laws," the reality is that the central purpose of laws is to classify people on the basis of certain characteristics and then treat them accordingly. Criminal laws classify people according to whether or not they have broken a certain law, and it is only those who have broken those laws who will be subject to the punishments specified under the law. More broadly, many laws treat people differently in order to achieve certain policy goals. For example, many social welfare programs, such as Medicaid or Transitional Assistance for Needy Families, provide benefits and resources only to those who meet certain income-based criteria. The rationale is that in order to ensure that everyone in our society receives the most basic of requirements for subsistence, these resources are reserved for those who are in most need of them. The courts have traditionally deferred to the legislatures in such instances, arguing that states should be given the latitude to determine public policy in the absence of invidious discrimination. "In short, the judiciary may not sit as a superlegislature to judge the wisdom or desirability of legislative policy determinations made in areas that neither affect fundamental rights nor proceed along suspect lines" (*New Orleans v. Dukes* 1976, at 304). As a result, in most instances, the Court applies the rational basis test, requiring the state to show that the law has a legitimate governmental purpose, and that the law is rationally related to achieving that purpose.

However, if the classification the law is based upon is itself considered "suspect," then the Court reserves the right to give the law a more searching inquiry as to its constitutionality. The Court has generally reserved such scrutiny for those classifications which are "suspect" due to the fact that they cover immutable traits for which there is a long, detailed history of discrimination, and which generally serve as bad proxies for obtaining the legislation's ultimate goal. As of the end of the 1960s, the Court had reserved the category of suspect for laws which classified on the basis of race, alienage or nationality. If a law is determined to rely upon one of these suspect classifications, then the Supreme Court will judge the law under what is known as the strict scrutiny test. This test subjects the state to a much higher burden of proof for showing the relation between the law's purpose and the chosen classification; the state must now show that the law serves a compelling governmental interest and that it is narrowly tailored to achieving that interest. In other words, while the judiciary will generally defer to the legislature in the making of public policy, it will not do so when the legislature seems to be engaging in invidious discrimination.

As we previously stated, beginning in 1971 the Supreme Court began to question the propriety of laws which classified persons on the basis of sex. The Court was particularly troubled by laws which treated men and women in arbitrary ways, and seemed to be furthering traditional—and generally stereotypical—notions of the proper roles for males and females. A number of lawsuits alleging sex discrimination were filed by the American Civil Liberty Union's (ACLU) Women's Rights Project and its lead lawyer, Ruth Bader Ginsburg. In each of these lawsuits, Ginsburg argued against laws which fostered sex-based stereotypes. The Supreme Court issued a strong rebuke of such laws in the case of *Frontiero v. Richardson* in 1973. Sharon Frontiero was a full-time lieutenant in the U.S. Air Force who applied for spousal benefits for her husband. Under federal law, if members of the uniformed services claimed their spouse as a "dependent," they were then eligible to obtain higher living allowances and medical and dental benefits. However, the law distinguished between males and females in terms of the process of establishing one's spouse as a dependent. The wives of servicemen were automatically assumed to be dependent on their husbands, regardless of their actual finances. Alternatively, a servicewoman must prove that her husband was dependent on her for over one-half of his financial support. Frontiero challenged the law as a violation of the due process clause of the Fifth Amendment. The Supreme Court, in an 8-1 decision, struck down the law as unconstitutional, arguing that the United States had not presented a persuasive justification for why two similarly situated members of the armed forces were treated differently due solely to their sex. Using surprisingly strong language, the majority took aim at the nation's "long and unfortunate history of sex discrimination" which "was rationalized by an attitude of 'romantic paternalism' which, in practical effect, put women, not on a pedestal, but in a cage" (684). The Court also signaled its suspicion of laws which "often have the effect of invidiously relegating the entire class of females to inferior legal status without regard to the actual capability of its individual members" (687).

However, the members of the majority coalition in *Frontiero* also disagreed over the correct standard that should be used to judge laws which were found to classify persons on the basis of sex. Justice Brennan's majority opinion argued that, like racial classifications, sex-based classifications are "inherently suspect and must therefore be subjected to close judicial scrutiny" (682). Alternatively, Justice Powell, joined by Chief Justice Burger and Justice Blackmun, concurred that the law was unconstitutional, but wrote separately to emphasize their concern with adopting this higher standard of scrutiny for sex discrimination cases. In part, these justices noted that the Equal Rights Amendment had been approved by Congress and ratification by the states was pending, and they expressed concern about the Court preempting an ongoing, highly salient political debate:

> There are times when this Court, under our system, cannot avoid a constitutional decision on issues which normally should be resolved by the elected representatives of the people. But democratic institutions are weakened, and confidence in the restraint of the Court is impaired, when we appear unnecessarily to decide sensitive issues of broad social and political importance at the very time they are under consideration within the prescribed constitutional processes. (693)

Similarly, in *Weinberger v. Wiesenfeld* (1975), the Court unanimously struck down a provision of the Social Security Act which denied a father "mother's benefits" after his wife, the family's primary breadwinner, died in childbirth, because fathers were ineligible to receive benefits for caretaking roles that were normally the province of mothers. The Court, however, noted that this statute reinforced and reified traditional social roles by pushing women out of the workforce and into the home and pushing men out of caregiving roles and into the workforce by undervaluing the contributions of female workers.

The Court again faced the question of the proper standard to be used for cases involving legislatively mandated sex discrimination in *Craig v. Boren* in 1976. Oklahoma law stipulated that low-alcohol beer could not be sold to males under the age of twenty-one, but could be sold to females between the ages of eighteen and twenty-one. The question was the constitutionality of such sex-based differences. Oklahoma argued that such differential treatment was justified by arrest statistics showing that males between the ages of eighteen and twenty-one were more likely to be arrested for drinking and driving than females in the same age group. The majority disagreed, however, holding that "the relationship between gender and traffic safety [is] far too tenuous to satisfy Reed's requirement that the gender-based difference be substantially related to achievement of the statutory objective." Brennan's majority opinion also stipulated that "classifications by gender must serve important governmental objectives and must be substantially related to the achievement of those objectives" (197). This statement of how sex-based statutes would be judged represented a break from the Court's earlier determinations that sex discrimination was subject to the rational basis test. Instead, the Court would now scrutinize such statutes under what eventually became known as the intermediate scrutiny test. The implication was that much less deference would be given from this point on to laws which treated people differently based solely upon their sex.

3. The Question of Biological Differences versus "Similarly Situated"

While the Court's decision in *Craig v. Boren* held that sex-based legal classifications would be subject to more scrutiny than other classifications, the Court did not decide that sex-based classifications were "suspect" in the same manner as racial classifications. The simple explanation for this conclusion is that sex is different from race: the very real biological differences between the sexes in terms of reproduction mean that in some instances, sex-based classifications are permissible, if not necessary. While the Court rejected the notion that because women bear offspring they are incapable of participating in public life, the Court did not dismiss the reality that reproductive distinctions may create strong reasons to treat men and women differently in certain situations.

The difficulty comes in determining whether a law reflects these real biological differences, or whether the law uses these differences to further outdated stereotypes about the two sexes. During the 1970s and 1980s, the vast majority of laws which clearly discriminated against women—or men—were struck down or repealed by state and federal legislatures. What remained, however, were laws which claimed to treat the sexes differently due to biological necessity. Thus, the next series of sex discrimination cases included those in which the Court had to assess the constitutionality of laws in which men and women were viewed as "dissimilarly situated."

The Court addressed this question head-on in the case of *Michael M. v. Sonoma County Superior Court* in 1981. Two teenagers engaged in sexual relations, and the male minor, Michael M., was eventually charged under California's statutory rape law.[1] Distinct from traditional rape statutes, statutory rape statutes criminalize behavior based solely on the age of the victim. They are justified by the argument that those under the legal age of consent are unable to consent and thus must be protected; as a consequence, unlike with rape cases, whether the victim gave "consent" is not a potential defense since the victim is considered unable to legally provide consent. Section 261.5 defined unlawful sexual intercourse as "an act of sexual intercourse accomplished with a female not the wife of the perpetrator, where the female is under the age of 18 years." In other words, men were legally barred from engaging in sexual relations with a minor female, but women were not similarly restricted from engaging in sexual relations with a minor male.

California argued that the statute was necessary to help prevent illegitimate teenage pregnancies. Since only females can become pregnant, the state argued that it is reasonable to prohibit males from having sexual intercourse with minor females, and potentially impregnating them. The Supreme Court agreed: "Because virtually all of the significant harmful and inescapably identifiable consequences of teenage pregnancy fall on the young female, a legislature acts well within its authority when it elects to punish only the participant who, by nature, suffers few of the consequences of his conduct.... Moreover, the risk of pregnancy itself constitutes a substantial deterrence to young females. No similar natural sanctions deter males. A criminal sanction imposed solely on males thus serves to roughly 'equalize' the deterrents on the sexes" (473). Justice Stewart concurred, writing, "In short, the Equal Protection Clause does not mean that the physiological differences between men and women must be disregarded.... The Constitution surely does not require a State to pretend that demonstrable differences between men and women do not really exist" (481).

The dissenting justices took a very different view. Justice Brennan explained that the statute originally was predicated on the belief that minor females, and not minor males, were incapable of consenting to sexual intercourse, and thus needed to be protected by the state. Alternatively, minor males were presumed to be able to make such decisions themselves. Brennan thus concluded that the reliance on such "outmoded sexual stereotypes" hindered California's ability to demonstrate a substantial relationship between the law at issue and the state's goal of reducing teenage pregnancies (496). The dissenters were thus concerned that the law made assumptions based on stereotypes stemming from the biological differences between the sexes. Furthermore, the dissenters questioned why a gender neutral version of the law would not better serve the state's goals. As Justice Stevens rhetorically asked, "Would a rational parent making rules for the conduct of twin children of opposite sex simultaneously forbid the son and authorize the daughter to engage in conduct that is especially harmful to the daughter? That is the effect of this statutory classification" (499).

In a more recent case, *Tuan Anh Nguyen v. INS* (2001), the Supreme Court confronted a similar question concerning the establishment of U.S. citizenship for children born to unmarried parents only one of whom was a U.S. citizen. Nguyen was born in Saigon, Vietnam; his mother was a Vietnamese citizen while his father was a citizen of the United States. When Nguyen was six years old, he came to the United States where he became a lawful permanent resident and was raised by his father. At the age of twenty-two, based on his alien status Nguyen was facing deportation after pleading guilty to criminal charges. He appealed, and attempted to obtain U.S. citizenship. However, under 8 U.S.C. §1409, Nguyen was denied citizenship due to the fact that he had not completed the necessary statutory requirements prior to his eighteenth birthday. The statute stipulates that if a child is born outside the United States to unmarried parents, and the father is the citizen parent, the paternity of the father must be established prior to the child's eighteenth birthday. If the mother is the citizen parent, however, the child automatically acquires the mother's nationality status upon birth.

The Supreme Court, in a 5-4 decision, ruled that two important considerations stemming from the reality of birth justified this sex-based difference in requirements for claiming citizenship. First, the Court agreed that the relationship between the mother and child is verifiable, indeed able to be witnessed, at birth. Alternatively, even the presence of the father at the birth "is not incontro-vertible proof of fatherhood.... Fathers and mothers are not similarly situated with regard to the proof of biological parenthood" (62–63). Second, the Court argued that there needed to be evidence of a "real" relationship or bond: "In the case of a citizen mother and a child born overseas, the opportunity for a mean-ingful relationship between citizen parent and child inheres in the very event of birth.... The same opportunity does not result from the event of birth, as a mat-ter of biological inevitability, in the case of the unwed father" (65).

The four dissenting justices, in an opinion written by the first woman to serve on the U.S. Supreme Court, Sandra Day O'Connor, strongly disputed these arguments. Instead, the dissenters viewed this law as emblematic of the types of pervasive stereotypes about traditional sex roles that serve to undermine efforts to achieve equality. For example, they argued that the law was originally passed under "a historic regime that left women with responsibility, and freed men from responsibility, for nonmarital children" (92). They also questioned the majority's reliance on the stereotype that mothers are more likely than fathers to develop "real" relationships with their children; this argument seemed particularly apt here, as Nguyen was raised by his father, but had relatively little contact or rela-tionship with his mother. Much like the dissenters in *Michael M.*, the major question raised was why these governmental interests were not better accom-plished through a sex-neutral, as opposed to a sex-based, law.

The Court did, however, recognize that discrimination against pregnant women is a form of sex discrimination, regardless of the fact that only women can become pregnant. In *Nevada Department of Human Resources v. Hibbs* (2003), the Court upheld the Family and Medical Leave Act and highlighted how discrimination against pregnant women reinforces the notion that women are "mothers first, and workers second" (736). Thus, even though pregnancy con-stitutes an important way in which men and women are not similarly situated, the Court was willing to realize that discrimination on the basis of this trait is itself discrimination on the basis of sex.

4. The Response and Effect of Gender Equality Cases

The implications of these cases is that in many instances, the Supreme Court has struck down statutes that can be easily categorized as invidiously discrimi-nating against one sex but has also been willing to uphold sex-based statutes on the premise that men and women are simply not "similarly situated" due to their differing roles in reproduction. However, the Court has also been strongly divided in virtually all of these cases, with the dissenting justices arguing that the furtherance of such laws many times serve simply to reinforce outdated ste-reotypes concerning men and women. As O'Connor's dissent in *Nguyen* argued, "Sex-based statutes, even when accurately reflecting the way most women or men behave, deny individual opportunity" (2001, 74). This divide is perhaps why, as shown in Table 4.2, while important advancements have been made by women

Table 4.2 Timeline of Legal and Social Advancements by Women, 1848–2010

1848	The world's first women's rights convention is held in Seneca Falls, NY, July 19–20. A Declaration of Sentiments and Resolutions is debated and signed by 68 women and 32 men, setting the agenda for the women's rights movement that followed
1849	Elizabeth Blackwell becomes the first woman in the United States to be awarded a medical degree
1850	Quaker physicians establish the Female Medical College of Pennsylvania, PA. The first women graduated under police guard
1855	Lucy Stone becomes first woman on record to keep her own name after marriage
1855	The University of Iowa becomes the first state school to admit women
1859	American Medical Association announces opposition to abortion. In 1860, Connecticut is the first state to prohibit all abortions, both before and after quickening
1868	14th Amendment is passed ratified, the first time "citizens" and "voters" are defined as "male" in the Constitution. Elizabeth Cady Stanton becomes the first woman to run for a seat in the U.S. House of Representatives
1870	For the first time in the history of jurisprudence, women serve on juries in the Wyoming Territory
1870	Iowa becomes the first state to admit a woman to the bar: Arabella Mansfield
1872	Through the efforts of lawyer Belva Lockwood, Congress passes a law to give women federal employees equal pay for equal work
1872	Charlotte E. Ray, a Howard University law school graduate, becomes first African American woman admitted to the bar in the U.S.
1872	Victoria Woodhull becomes the first woman to run for president of the U.S. on the Equal Rights Party ticket
1873	Congress passes the Comstock Law, defining contraceptive information as "obscene material"
1877	Helen Magill becomes the first woman to receive a Ph.D. in the U.S., in Greek from Boston University
1878	The Susan B. Anthony Amendment, to grant women the vote, is first introduced in the U.S. Congress
1887	Susanna Salter becomes the first woman elected mayor in Argonia, Kansas
1896	Martha Hughes Cannon becomes the first woman elected as a state senator to the Utah State Senate
1900	Frances Warren of Wyoming becomes the first female delegate to a Republican National Convention, while Elizabeth Cohen of Utah became the first woman delegate to a Democratic National Convention
1916	Jeannette Rankin of Montana becomes the first woman elected to the U.S. Congress
1919	The House of Representatives passes the women's suffrage amendment, 304 to 89; the Senate passes it with just two votes to spare, 56 to 25. It was ratified the next year, becoming the 19th Amendment to the U.S. Constitution
1921	Margaret Sanger organizes the American Birth Control League, which becomes Federation of Planned Parenthood in 1942, while Edith Wharton becomes the first woman to win a Pulitzer Prize for fiction for her novel *The Age of Innocence*

1922 Rebecca Felton of Georgia becomes the first woman U.S. Senator after being appointed to fill a temporary vacancy. She served for only two days

1925 Nellie Taylor Ross is elected as the first woman governor in the U.S. for the state of Wyoming

1932 Hattie Wyatt Caraway, of Arkansas, is the first woman elected to serve in the U.S. Senate

1933 Frances Perkins, the first woman in a Presidential cabinet, serves as Secretary of Labor under FDR

1934 Lettie Pate Whitehead becomes the first American woman to serve as a director of a major corporation, the Coca-Cola Company

1941 A massive government and industry media campaign persuades women to take jobs during the war. Almost 7 million women respond, 2 million as industrial "Rosie the Riveters" and 400,000 join the military. However, the majority will lose their jobs when the war ends

1949 Eugenie M. Anderson becomes the first female U.S. Ambassador

1960 The Food and Drug Administration approves birth control pills

1963 The Equal Pay Act is passed, establishing equal pay for men and women performing the same job duties. It does not, however, cover domestics, agricultural workers, executives, administrators or professionals. Justice Lorna Lockwood of Arizona becomes the first woman Chief Justice of a state supreme court

1964 The Civil Rights Act of 1964 passes, barring employment discrimination by private employers, employment agencies, and unions based on sex, race and other grounds. To enforce the law, the Equal Employment Opportunity Commission (EEOC) is established, and receives 50,000 complaints of gender discrimination in its first five years.

1965 Phyllis Peterson and Julie Walsh become the first female members of the American Stock Exchange, while Patsy Takemoto Mink of Hawaii is the first Asian American woman elected to the U.S. Congress

1966 In response to EEOC inaction on employment discrimination complaints, twenty-eight women found the National Organization for Women (NOW) to function as a civil rights organization for women

1968 Shirley Chisholm (D-NY) becomes first Black woman elected to the U.S. Congress

1971 In *Reed v. Reed*, the Supreme Court strikes down for the first time a law for discriminating on the basis of sex

1973 In *Roe v. Wade*, the Supreme Court establishes a woman's right to obtain an abortion, effectively canceling the anti-abortion laws of 46 states

1974 Janet Gray Hayes becomes the first female mayor of a major U.S. city, San Jose, California

1978 For the first time in history, more women than men enter college. Nancy Landon Kassebaum from Kansas becomes the first female U.S. Senator who was not appointed to fill an unexpired term or succeeded her husband

1981 At the request of women's organizations, President Carter proclaims the first "National Women's History Week," incorporating March 8, International Women's Day

1981 Sandra Day O'Connor becomes the first woman ever appointed to the U.S. Supreme Court

(continued)

Table 4.2 Continued

1983 Dr. Sally K. Ride becomes the first female astronaut to ride in space

1984 Geraldine Ferraro is the first woman vice-presidential candidate of a major political party (Democratic Party). Kathryn Sullivan becomes the first female U.S. astronaut to walk in space

1989 Capt. Linda Bray becomes the first woman to lead American troops in combat, while Ileana Ros-Lehtinen of Florida becomes the first Hispanic woman elected to the U.S. Congress

1990 Dr. Antonia Novello becomes the first female (and first Hispanic) U.S. Surgeon General

1992 Carol Moseley-Braun of Illinois becomes the first black woman elected to the U.S. Senate

1993 Janet Reno is appointed as the first woman Attorney General, while Shiela Widnall is appointed Secretary of the Air Force, becoming the first female to head a branch of the U.S. military

1995 Lt. Col. Eileen Collins becomes the first American woman to pilot a space shuttle mission

1997 Madeline Albright becomes the first woman to serve as Secretary of State, and the highest-ranking woman in U.S. government to date

2001 Condoleezza Rice becomes the female National Security Advisor. She becomes the first black female U.S. Secretary of State in 2005

2007 Nancy Pelosi becomes the first female Speaker of the U.S. House of Representatives

2008 Sarah Palin becomes the first Republican vice-presidential candidate, while Hillary Clinton becomes the first woman to win a presidential primary contest (New Hampshire)

2010 Kathryn Bigelow becomes the first woman to win the Oscar for Best Director, for her movie *The Hurt Locker*

since the 1800s, the most notable part may be how many "firsts" have occurred in the past twenty years. And, these same disagreements that split the justices have divided elected officials and much of the public as well.

The Equal Rights Amendment

Between 1972 and 1982, ratification of the Equal Rights Amendment was pending in the states. The ERA simply stated, "Equality of rights under the law shall not be denied or abridged by the United States or by any State on account of sex." The Amendment was passed by the Congress by fairly large margins, 354-24 in the House, and 84-8 in the Senate. It was then sent to the states for ratification; three-quarters of states (38) were needed for the amendment to be adopted. President Richard Nixon immediately endorsed its ratification. By the original seven-year deadline for ratification in 1979, thirty-five states had ratified the amendment. The Congress thus passed a three-year extension in order to gain the remaining three needed states. However, by 1982, no new states ratified the amendment and five states (Idaho, Kentucky, Nebraska, Tennessee and South Dakota) actually decided to rescind their ratification.

Why did the ERA fail to be adopted? While numerous forces can be pointed to, one of the most important issues was opposition by women. Many women were concerned that sex-based laws which *benefitted* women would be found unconstitutional under the ERA, thus taking away many protections women, and especially mothers, depended upon. For example, it was widely accepted that passage of the ERA would result in the military draft applying to women as well as men, and lift prohibitions on women serving in combat. Given that the Vietnam War, which heavily utilized drafted forces, had recently ended, this issue was of real concern to many people. Furthermore, arguments were made that adoption of the ERA would require that sex-segregated places such as prisons, public bathrooms and (as of the mid-1970s) many schools and universities would become co-ed. Finally, many women were concerned that laws which protected wives and mothers, such as state laws which imposed on husbands the obligation to support their wives financially, would be struck down as unconstitutional (see e.g., Schlafly 1986). Part of these objections concerned the realities of women in the 1970s: most women did not work outside the home and were responsible for the majority of childcare and domestic chores. The concern was thus that legal protections women had won to protect them—such as ensuring that women would receive alimony payments in divorce settlements after having contributed to the marriage by raising children and keeping the home while the husband worked outside the house—would necessarily be taken away as illegal sex-based favoritism.

The fight over the ERA highlights the complexity of debates over gender equality. Even today, women are not subjected to the draft and are restricted from serving in combat. The idea of removing the restriction on women in combat has arisen rather frequently, however, especially as the United States has continued fighting in both Iraq and Afghanistan. And, during these debates, many women have forcefully spoken out against such changes. For example, Linda Chavez (2003) maintained, in response to the question of whether it was worse to lose a father or mother on the battlefield, "As tragic as the death of a father is in a young child's life, it simply can't compare to the loss of a mother."

The Equal Employment Opportunity Commission (EEOC) was created in 1964 to enforce the protections provided by the federal Equal Pay Act of 1963 and the Civil Rights Act of 1964. In the first five years, the EEOC received over five thousand sex discrimination complaints. In the face of what some saw as lax investigations of these complaints, and lax enforcement overall, the National Organization of Women (NOW) was founded in 1966.

In 1972, Title IX of the Education Amendments was passed, barring gender discrimination in classrooms and athletics. The results were strong almost immediately: within four years of implementation, female athletic participation increased by 600% (Shook 1996, 773).

Pregnancy Discrimination

A central issue stemming from the Supreme Court's jurisprudence that "dissimilarly situated" men and women can be treated differently concerns the treatment of pregnant women. Prior to 1976, employers routinely refused to hire pregnant women, required pregnant employees to take a leave of absence (or lose their jobs altogether) at certain points in their pregnancies, and denied pregnant employees insurance, disability coverage and leave. In the case of *Geduldig v. Aiello* (1974), the Supreme Court considered the constitutionality of California's disability insurance program which required private employees to contribute 1% of their salaries in return for disability coverage; however, the plan explicitly excluded pregnancy. The Court ruled that excluding pregnancy was not a sex-based classification, because "[t]he program divided potential recipients into two groups— pregnant women and nonpregnant persons. While the first group is exclusively female, the second includes members of both sexes. The fiscal and actuarial benefits of the program thus accrue to members of both sexes" (497, note 20). In other words, the classification reflected one's status vis-à-vis pregnancy, and not sex, regardless of the fact that only women can become pregnant. Two years later, the Supreme Court extended this interpretation in *General Electric Co. v. Gilbert* (1976) to statutory protections against sex-based discrimination, ruling that pregnancy discrimination was not actionable under Title VII's prohibition on sex discrimination. In response, Congress passed the Pregnancy Discrimination Act of 1978, and explicitly overruled *Gilbert* by amending Title VII to prohibit discrimination "because of sex *or pregnancy*" (emphasis added). While the Pregnancy Discrimination Act cannot supersede the Court's constitutional decision in *Geduldig*, since Title VII applies to all employers, private and governmental, the end result is that pregnant women are protected from clear discrimination based upon their pregnancy.[2]

Employment Discrimination and Lilly Ledbetter

At times, more recent Supreme Court cases have been detrimental to women's rights, leading the Congress to take action to reverse these decisions. For example, in *Ledbetter v. Goodyear Tire and Rubber Co.* (2007), the Supreme Court was faced with the question of when a Title VII pay discrimination claim must be filed for the claim to be considered timely. The Supreme Court rejected the argument that each paycheck represents a new "unlawful employment practice," holding instead that such a claim must be filed within one hundred and eighty days of when the original offense occurred. This ruling undercut Lilly Ledbetter's lawsuit that alleged discrimination against Goodyear. She was a supervisor at a plant in Gadsden, AL from 1979 until 1998. Over time, her salary in comparison to that of male managers with equal or less seniority slipped dramatically: by 1997, when Ledbetter was the only female manager, she was paid $3,727 per month while the lowest paid male manager was paid $4,286 and the highest paid $5,236. Under the Court's ruling, she would have needed to file her lawsuit within one hundred and eighty days of when the first pay disparity occurred. However, this ruling was complicated by the fact that she did not discover the pay disparity until 1997 (and only found out from an anonymous tip), and that it likely took some time before the pay disparity became both apparent and sizable.

As a result of this ruling, the U.S. Congress passed, and Barack Obama signed into law on January 29, 2009, the Lilly Ledbetter Fair Pay Act of 2009. This was the first act signed into law by the new president. The Act amends the Civil Rights Act of 1964 to state that the one hundred and eighty-day statute of limitations for filing pay discrimination lawsuits resets with each new discriminatory paycheck. This legislative enactment thus represents a strong illustration of what happens when the Supreme Court hands down a decision which is outside the preferences of the legislative–executive core.

Sex Discrimination and Class Actions

Perhaps the most ground-breaking ruling concerning sex discrimination in the past few decades is from a case still in its infancy. In April of 2010, the Ninth Circuit Court of Appeals upheld a federal district court ruling that a sex discrimination lawsuit against Wal-Mart could proceed as a class action lawsuit covering approximately 1.5 million women. The implication of this ruling is that companies can be sued en masse for systematic patterns of discrimination, rather than relying on individual plaintiffs to bring individual suits; the result will be to make it easier and less costly for individual allegations of employment discrimination to be heard by the courts.

5. The Supreme Court: Pushing Boundaries or Following the Crowd?

A major question concerning the role of the courts is whether court decisions can lead directly to social change. On the one hand, scholars such as Gerald Rosenberg (2008) argue that seemingly radical Supreme Court decisions are many times the logical reflection of changing social mores. For example, when it comes to the issue of gender equality, Rosenberg would point to the passage of the Equal Pay Act in 1963 and the Civil Rights Act of 1964—two major federal laws enacted well before the Supreme Court's 1971 decision in *Reed v. Reed* which prohibited the unequal treatment of men and women in the workforce—as evidence that the tide concerning the status of women had already begun to change. Similarly, the effort to pass the Equal Rights Amendment was well under way at this point, and so the Court's decision likely reflected the changing views of society. In other words, the Supreme Court's decisions were not necessarily the first step in knocking down sex-based discrimination but rather a reflection of the Court following the major changes beginning to be instituted by the federal and state governments.

On the other hand, scholars such as Michael McCann (1994) maintain that the Supreme Court's actions were a necessary, but not sufficient, condition for the advent of equality between the sexes. While Congress had enacted such laws as the ones noted above, the reality is that numerous laws at both the state and federal level still existed as of 1971—and, indeed, well into the 1980s—which treated men and women differently based solely on their sex. It was only by making clear that such laws violated the U.S. Constitution that real change could be made. Furthermore, the historical record suggests that the passage of those two laws was not so clear cut as it first appears. While the Equal Pay Act prohibited employers from paying men and women different salaries for performing the same jobs, it also allowed four affirmative defenses for pay disparities: (1) wages based on seniority systems; (2) wages based on merit systems; (3) wages based on productivity; and (4) wages based on differences unrelated to sex. Criterion number four has been used to justify paying men and women differential salaries in numerous cases and, critically, this defense does not require that the difference be job-related; rather, it just must not be related to the employee's sex. Furthermore, the Equal Pay Act does not prohibit employers from retaliating against employees who share salary and benefits information, which many times is the only way that an employee can discover the existence of pay differentials.

Similarly, the addition of "sex" to the Civil Rights Act of 1964 has a rather checkered history. As Wolfe (1991, 142) explains, "Representative Howard W. Smith initiated the addition of the word *sex* [to Title VII of the Act], believing it would make the bill seem ridiculous and divide liberals, thereby preventing passage of the legislation." His speech was mocking in tone, all of the men who spoke in support were Southerners who ultimately voted against passage of the final bill, and the resulting two-hour debate became known as "Ladies Day" in the House of Representatives (Skrentny 2002). As Congresswoman Martha Griffiths of Michigan noted, "[I]f there had been any necessity to have pointed out that women were a second-class sex, the laughter would have proved it" (quoted in Harriman 1996, 51).

Thus, the record suggests that the actions of Congress were not necessarily representative of changing public views concerning the traditional roles of men and women. Rather, an equal case can be made that the Supreme Court's decisions in cases like *Reed v. Reed* and *Frontiero v. Richardson* were necessary to combat the pervasive sex discrimination that imbued many local, state and national laws at the time. Figure 4.1 shows changes in the ideological positions of the median members of the Supreme Court and the two chambers of the U.S. Congress from 1971 through 2001. This covers the period of time from the Court's seminal decision in *Reed v. Reed* through its decision in *Tuan Anh Nguyen v. INS*.

A comparison of median ideology shows how courts can use the "legal set" to move policy within politically acceptable policy options. As one can see, the median ideology of the three institutions is highly correlated and moved over time in relative tandem. However, from 1975 through 1984, the Supreme Court's median ideology was notably more liberal than the Senate, and slightly

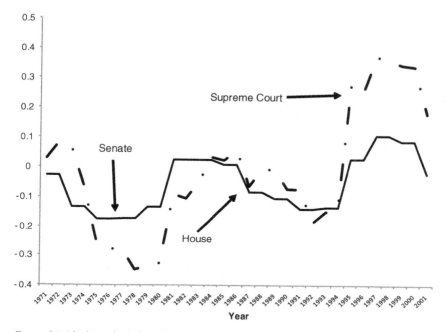

Figure 4.1 Ideological Medians Supreme Court and Congress, 1971–2001

more liberal than the House between 1977 and 1983. Importantly, these dates capture a lack of activity on the national stage with respect to gender equality: for example, 1977 was the last year a state voted to ratify the Equal Rights Amendment. Thus, during a period of retrenchment by political institutions, the Supreme Court issued several rulings expanding gender equality, including the initial establishment of the heightened scrutiny standard, which reflected the Supreme Court's relatively liberal position. However, as Figure 4.1 also shows, given that the Supreme Court's decisions were still generally within the boundaries of the political options (i.e., the legislative–executive core), and given the ideological divisions within Congress, the political institutions had no option but to accept the greater gender equality standards promulgated by the Supreme Court.

6. Conclusion

As of 2010, fights were still being waged concerning sex equality under the law. Even though the Equal Pay Act was passed by Congress in 1963, many argue that the reality is that women are still not paid the equivalent of men in similar jobs. In November of 2010, the Congress debated the passage of the Paycheck Fairness Act. The major change would be to limit the defenses employers can use to justify wage discrimination based on sex to reasons such as employees' education, training or experience. Currently, employers can justify wage differentials based on seniority systems and merit systems, both of which may reflect sex-based stereotypes or persistent discrimination. However, views about this Act were not uniform. Christina Hoff Sommers (2010) opposed the Act, writing in the *Wall Street Journal* that many times gendered pay gaps are explained by women's choices, such as the decision to leave the workplace to raise children or care for elderly parents or to take jobs which offer increased benefits (such as flexible-time policies or childcare services) in return for lower wages. In the end, passage of the bill failed, amid additional concerns that it would unnecessarily lead to an increase in litigation costs for employers.

Battles still continue in the courts as well. According to the EEOC, over 28,000 complaints alleging sex-based discrimination were filed in both FY 2008 and FY 2009, resulting in over $200 million worth of monetary damages, a number which does not include damages obtained through formal litigation.[2] In many ways, the newest battlefront for employment is over sexual harassment: growing numbers of women—and men—have filed suits alleging that they have been subject to sexual harassment in the workplace. Notably, the number of sexual harassment claims filed by men has jumped from 8% of all claims in 1990 to 16% of all claims in 2009. What is distinct about sexual harassment cases is that they represent a move beyond policies which overtly discriminate between the sexes to actions which individuals allege victimize them due to sex. And, such instances can be more difficult to both prohibit and secure legal relief for since the alleged violation is many times more esoteric in nature than, for example, clearly documented pay disparities.

In the end, the fight for legal equality between the sexes has succeeded on many fronts, yet important battles are still to be fought. Perhaps most notably, the number of "firsts" still occurring even today is rather pronounced: in 2006, Nancy Pelosi became the first female Speaker of the House. In 2008, Sarah Palin became the first female Republican Vice Presidential nominee (and only second woman ever) while Hillary Clinton became the first woman to win a presidential primary; to date, however, no woman has ever been a candidate for president nor served as president or vice president of the United States.

5

FEDERAL COURT POLICYMAKING
Reproductive Rights

1. Introduction

In April of 2010, the state of Oklahoma passed two abortion regulations that opponents contend unconstitutionally burden a woman's right to choose to have an abortion. The first law requires women seeking an abortion to undergo an ultrasound and listen to a detailed description of the fetus before they can obtain an abortion. The doctor must set up the monitor so that the woman can view the screen, and then describe the heart, limbs and organs of the fetus as seen. The law does not grant an exception for rape and incest victims. The second law prohibits women from suing a doctor postbirth who withheld information, or even provided incorrect information about birth defects or other fetal anomalies while the child was in the womb. Both laws were vetoed by the governor, but the Oklahoma state legislature voted to override both vetoes. In July of 2010, an Oklahoma judge granted an injunction blocking enforcement of the ultrasound law, a court challenge is still pending as of March, 2011.

Also in the summer of 2010, a new law, SB793, took effect in Missouri which requires women seeking an abortion to be counseled in person about their choice, and mandates that women receive a description of the "anatomical and physiological characteristics of the unborn child." Women must also be offered the opportunity to view an ultrasound or listen to the heartbeat of the fetus, and they must be given a state-produced brochure which states that "the life of each human being begins at conception. Abortion will terminate the life of a separate, unique living human being." One pro-life activist, Sam Lee of Campaign Life Missouri, explained: "We're hoping with that type of information, coupled with a 24-hour waiting period, that fewer women will have abortions in Missouri" (Lieb 2010). Finally, a new Nebraska law took effect on October 15, 2010, which prohibits all abortions after twenty weeks of pregnancy based on the claim that fetuses can feel pain after that point, rather than tying the limitation on late-term abortion availability to the achievement of viability, or the time when the fetus can exist outside the womb.

Numerous other state legislators and executives have announced their intentions to pass other abortion regulations in 2011, as well as laws dealing more broadly with reproduction and reproductive rights. The question with all of these laws, however, is whether they are constitutional under the U.S. Constitution, and so the ultimate decision about most of these laws will be made by the federal courts. Notably, these laws are judged under the right to privacy, an unenumerated right which the Supreme Court established in the case of *Griswold v. Connecticut* in 1965 and since located in the due process clause of the Fourteenth Amendment. As a result, the debate over the right to privacy and reproductive rights arguably provides the single best example of how the courts, and especially the federal courts, play an important and decisive role in making social policy on an issue of considerable importance.

This chapter traces how the U.S. Supreme Court determined both that individuals have a right to privacy and that this right of privacy extends to the right of women to choose to have an abortion, and how these landmark rulings launched a still ongoing battle between the federal courts and state and federal legislatures over the question of reproductive rights.

This chapter also encapsulates the myth of neutral judging and demonstrates both the power and limits of court policymaking and judging. Against the backdrop of *Roe v. Wade* (1973), and the legal debates over whether the right to privacy is mandated by the U.S. Constitution, political opposition coalesced against these court rulings, leading to the passage of numerous state laws seeking to restrict reproductive rights, if not eliminate them altogether. Finally, this chapter highlights how judicial decisions which fall outside the legislative–executive core, or broader public opinion, can be subjected to continuous backlash and attempts to undercut the courts' power and reach.

2. Establishing the Right to Privacy

In many ways, the right to privacy, and the attendant right to abortion, is the perfect example of how courts make and influence policy on a national scale. The right to privacy itself is a judicially created constitutional right. The right to privacy is unenumerated, meaning it is not literally written anywhere in the U.S. Constitution. Rather, the Supreme Court in the case of *Griswold v. Connecticut* (1965) determined that there was a "zone of privacy" surrounding the marriage relationship and this zone of privacy encompassed the right of married couples to choose whether to use contraceptives. As Justice Douglas asked, "Would we allow the police to search the sacred precincts of marital bedrooms for telltale signs of the use of contraceptives? The very idea is repulsive to the notions of privacy surrounding the marriage relationship" (485–86). The majority opinion of the Court compared the right to privacy to other, existing unenumerated rights, such as the right to association and the right to educate one's children as one chooses, both found in the First Amendment. The dissenting justices, however, argued simply that no such right was written in the Constitution, no matter how "uncommonly silly" Connecticut's ban on contraceptive use was (527). As Justice Stewart stated, "What provision of the Constitution, then does make this state

law invalid? The Court says it is the right of privacy 'created by several fundamental constitutional guarantees.' With all deference, I can find no such general
right of privacy in the Bill of Rights, in any other part of the Constitution, or
in any case ever before decided by this Court" (530). The decision in *Griswold*
thus resulted in the Supreme Court determining that a broad right to privacy,
encompassing the private decisions made by married couples as to their intimate
acts, was protected by the U.S. Constitution. In 1972, in the case of *Eisenstadt
v. Baird*, the Court extended this right to all individuals, married or unmarried.

The decisions in *Griswold* and *Eisenstadt*, both of which struck down laws
prohibiting the use of contraception, faced fairly little backlash. However, all
that changed with the Supreme Court's seminal decision in *Roe v. Wade* in 1973.
In *Roe*, the Court confronted the question of whether this new right to privacy
extended beyond decisions about contraceptive use, which prevents pregnancy
itself, to the decision to actively end a pregnancy. The case concerned a challenge
to a Texas law which outlawed abortions unless necessary to save the life of the
mother. The Supreme Court, in a 7-2 decision, declared the law unconstitutional
and extended the right to privacy to cover the decision by a woman (in consul-
tation with her doctor) to choose whether or not to obtain an abortion. In the
majority opinion, Blackmun argued that "the detriment that the State would
impose upon the pregnant woman by denying this choice altogether is apparent.
Specific and direct harm medically diagnosable even in early pregnancy may be
involved. Maternity, or additional offspring, may force upon the woman a dis-
tressful life and future. Psychological harm may be imminent" (153). However,
the Court's decision also recognized two compelling interests of the state: the
protection of the woman's safety and health and the protection of the "potential"
life. As a result, Blackmun designed the trimester system. In the first trimester,
abortion is safer than childbirth, and so the woman is free to decide whether to
obtain an abortion. In the second trimester, childbirth is safer than abortion and
so "a State may regulate the abortion procedure to the extent that the regulation
reasonably relates to the preservation and protection of maternal health" (163).
Finally, in the third trimester, the fetus reaches viability, and so a state may pro-
scribe abortion, so long as it also provides an exception for preserving the health
and life of the mother.

Justices White and Rehnquist dissented. White's dissent, in particular, out-
lined the arguments that would soon be heard in state legislative houses around
the country and in the public square: "The Court, for the most part, sustains
this position: during the period prior to the time the fetus becomes viable, the
Constitution of the United States values the convenience, whim or caprice of the
putative mother more than the life or potential life of the fetus.... The Court
simply fashions and announces a new constitutional right for pregnant mothers
and, with scarcely any reason or authority for its action, invests that right with
sufficient substance to override most existing state abortion statutes.... [I]n my
view, [the Court's] judgment is an improvident and extravagant exercise of the
power of judicial review that the Constitution extends to this Court" (221–22).

Furthermore, the dissenting justices argued that this was an issue more properly left to the political process, the people and their elected representatives.

The ideological lineup of the decision foreshadowed, to some degree, a liberal–conservative dimension to the issues of the right to privacy and the right to abortion. The most conservative justice on the court, William Rehnquist, opposed the decision when it was reargued, as did Justice White, who, although generally liberal on civil rights issues, became a consistent opponent to the expansion of the right to abortion and was conservative on social and criminal jurisprudence issues.

Chief Justice Burger, also conservative, later renounced his support for abortion rights in subsequent cases. There are also some indications that Burger attempted to control the assignment of the majority opinion in *Roe v. Wade*. The case was originally argued in December of 1971, when the Court possessed only seven justices due to the retirements of Justices Hugo Black and John Harlan; Lewis Powell and William Rehnquist had been confirmed to the Court, but had yet to be sworn in. The initial vote was confusing, and Chief Justice Burger capitalized on this confusion to assign the majority opinion to his friend, Justice Harry Blackmun. Justice Douglas objected, arguing that Burger voted with the minority and so he, as the senior associate justice, should have the power of opinion assignment in the case. In the end, Blackmun was assigned the opinion; the conventional wisdom is that Burger feared an opinion written by either Justices Douglas or Brennan, both of whom rank among the liberal justices in Court history. The draft opinion initially circulated by Blackmun was widely disliked. The Court thus decided to schedule the case for reargument, such that the two new justices could also participate. After a 6-3 vote, Blackmun retained authorship of the majority opinion. And, in a surprise twist, Burger later joined the majority, bringing the final vote to 7-2 (see e.g., Neubauer and Meinhold 2009, 449–50; Wrightsman 1999, 80–81). However, he would reject his support for *Roe* in the 1986 case of *Thornburgh v. American College of Obstetricians and Gynecologists*, a position Blackmun viewed as a "defection" (Greenhouse 2005, 183). And, by 1986, a number of justices had joined the Court who agreed that *Roe* should be limited, if not overturned.

3. The Response to *Roe v. Wade*

The outcry against the Court's decision in *Roe* was immediate. One of the most striking developments was the creation of numerous pro-life groups which sought to mobilize both the public and elected officials to either overturn *Roe* or, at the very least, circumscribe its reach. In many ways, pro-choice organizations assumed they had won a stable victory, the establishment of a constitutional right. However, these newly created pro-life groups were not about to declare defeat. And, the fight over abortion revealed the many cleavages that existed over the issue of motherhood itself. As Kristen Luker describes in her book *Abortion and the Politics of Motherhood* (1985), pro-life and pro-choice activists hold vastly different views on issues concerning motherhood, women's rights and the place of women in society. On one hand, the pro-life activists Luker interviewed were more likely to emphasize the importance of motherhood not just in raising children but also in shaping society, and to oppose suggestions to allow women in combat because they believe such changes will fundamentally reshape society by undermining the importance of motherhood. On the other hand, pro-choice women were more likely to stress the need for women to be viewed as equals who possess the ability to assume roles in society and the public sphere that they have long been denied. Thus, in many ways the debate over abortion is also a debate over the role of women in society and how women should view their role as the creators of life. Does the right to abortion free women from traditional constraints and allow them to freely participate in society, or does the right to abortion cruelly end life and undermine the vital role women play in bearing and raising the next generation?

These questions gripped the nation, and led numerous states to quickly make an effort to determine the limits of the Court's decision in *Roe*. While the trimester system on the face of it presented a fairly cut-and-dried determination of the right to abortion, it also left unanswered a number of practical questions. For example, did this right extend to minor females, who, as minors generally did not possess the same rights as their adult counterparts? What role was the father of the child to have in this decision? To what degree could the state try to ensure that the woman was making an informed and voluntary choice? And, what types of regulations concerning maternal health would be allowed during the second trimester?

The effect of *Roe* was to raise more questions than it answered, and to initiate a decades-long battle between legislatures and the federal courts over the boundaries of this newly established right. State legislatures passed laws during the mid-1970s which sought to prevent minors from obtaining abortions without parental consent, cut off public funding for abortions and through the imposition of waiting periods and mandated counseling or information sessions prior to obtaining an abortion attempted to ensure that the woman's ultimate decision was an "informed" one. Each law was subsequently challenged in court, and so the state and federal courts since 1973 have issued thousands of rulings concerning laws intended to limit the reach of the Supreme Court's decision in *Roe v. Wade*. And, as the opening paragraphs of this chapter attest, this battle is far from over as new technologies push back the date of viability as well as offer new methods for monitoring the growth of the fetus.

Changes in society and in the membership of the Supreme Court have also occurred. President Nixon did not publicly acknowledge the Court's decision in *Roe*, but under President Reagan, the Republican Party adopted a platform of opposition to the decision and abortion in general. Additionally, the justices who decided *Roe v. Wade* have all left the Court, and their successors have had to wrestle for themselves with the question of whether a right to abortion exists. To get some idea of what that direction might be, we examine the ideological trend of the Supreme Court since *Roe v. Wade*. Figure 5.1 shows the ideology of the Supreme Court since 1973.

Figure 5.1 Supreme Court Median Ideology, 1973–2007

In the aftermath of *Roe*, and aided by the domination of Supreme Court nominations by Republican presidents, the Supreme Court moved in a much more conservative ideological direction. The only Democratic president from 1968 through 1993, Jimmy Carter, did not make any appointments to the Supreme Court, resulting in a twenty-five-year period where every appointment was made by a Republican president. Thus, particularly in the aftermath of Ronald Reagan's election, the Court veered sharply to the right. It was only with the election of President Bill Clinton and the leftward shift of Sandra Day O'Connor that we began to see the Court shift back to the ideological middle.

The biggest doctrinal change occurred in 1992 in the case of *Planned Parenthood of Southeastern Pennsylvania v. Casey*. In *Casey*, the Court reaffirmed the "essential holding" of *Roe*, but also replaced the much maligned trimester system with Justice Sandra Day O'Connor's "undue burden" standard. Under the undue burden standard, a state was permitted to encourage childbirth over abortion, but was prohibited from enacting any regulation which placed a "substantial obstacle" in the way of a woman's right to choose to have an abortion and thus was "calculated [not] to inform the woman's free choice, [but to] hinder it" (877). Furthermore, the Court declared, "What is at stake is the woman's right to make the ultimate decision, not a right to be insulated from all others in doing so. Regulations which do no more than create a structural mechanism by which the State ... may express profound respect for the life of the unborn are permitted" (877). However, the Court also reiterated that women must be free to choose whether to bear a child: "The mother who carries a child to full term is subject to anxieties, to physical constraints, to pain that only she must bear.... Her suf-

fering is too intimate and personal for the State to insist, without more, upon its own vision of the woman's role, however dominant that vision has been in the course of our history and our culture. The destiny of woman must be shaped to a large extent on her own conception of her spiritual imperatives and her place in society..." (852).

The practical implication of *Casey* was to uphold provisions, such as mandating informed consent and waiting periods, which were previously found to be unconstitutional by the Supreme Court. As Table 5.1 documents, the major Supreme Court decisions since *Casey* have all upheld provisions which would likely have been declared unconstitutional under *Roe*'s trimester framework.

Table 5.1 Major Supreme Court Cases Concerning Reproductive Rights

Case	Year	Supreme Court Holding
Griswold v. Connecticut (381 U.S. 479)	1965	Struck down Connecticut law prohibiting the use of contraceptives by married couples. Established a Right to Privacy covering intimate decisions about reproduction
Eisenstadt v. Baird (405 U.S. 438)	1972	Struck down a Massachusetts law prohibiting the use of contraceptives by unmarried couples, extending the reach of the right to privacy
Roe v. Wade (410 U.S. 113)	1973	Struck down a Texas law prohibiting abortion except to save the life of the mother
Carey v. Population Services International (431 U.S. 678)	1977	Struck down a New York statute criminalizing the sale or distribution of contraceptives to minors under 16
Maher v. Roe (432 U.S. 464); *Beal v. Doe* (432 U.S. 438); *Poelker v. Doe* (432 U.S. 519)	1977 (decided same day)	In all three cases, the Supreme Court upheld federal and state statutes which restricted the use of public funds for abortions
Bellotti v. Baird (443 U.S. 622)	1979	Struck down a Massachusetts law requiring parental consent for abortions for minors under 18
Harris v. McRae (448 U.S. 297)	1980	Upheld the federal Hyde amendment which limited federal funding for abortions under Medicaid to those necessary to save a woman's life
City of Akron v. Akron Center for Reproductive Health (462 U.S. 416)	1983	Struck down a Ohio city ordinance requiring a 24-hour waiting period, informed consent, parental consent for minors, and all 2nd trimester abortions be performed in a hospital.
Thornburgh v. American College of Obstetricians & Gynecologists (476 U.S. 747)	1986	Struck down a Pennsylvania law in its entirety which required, among other things, that women given "informed consent" before abortions, as well as requirements concerning recordkeeping and use of certain medical techniques

(continued)

Table 5.1 Continued

Case	Year	Supreme Court Holding
Webster v. Reproductive Health Services (492 U.S. 490)	1989	Upheld a Missouri law banning the use of public employees and facilities for abortions, except where necessary to save a woman's life
Hodgson v. Minnesota (497 U.S. 417); *Ohio v. Akron Center for Reproductive Health* (497 U.S. 502)	1990 (decided same day)	In both cases, upheld state statutes requiring parental notification, but also allowing for a judicial bypass mechanism
Planned Parenthood of Southeastern Pennsylvania v. Casey (505 U.S. 833)	1992	Established a new standard for judging abortion restrictions: undue burden. Upheld a Pennsylvania statute requiring informed consent coupled with a 24-hour waiting period. Also struck down a provision requiring spousal notification
Stenberg v. Carhart (530 U.S. 914)	2000	Struck down a Nebraska law on "partial-birth abortions" which lacked an exception to preserve the health of the woman
Gonzales v. Carhart (550 U.S. 124)	2007	Upheld a federal ban on a particular late-term abortion method (i.e., "partial-birth" abortion) which does not include an exception for the health of the mother

More specifically, *Casey* allowed for a broader set of regulations to be imposed from the start of pregnancy, so long as they were intended to inform the woman's choice rather than impede it. The question, still being addressed today, is what types of provisions enable one's choice and what types of laws hinder this choice? Does viewing an ultrasound of one's fetus inform a woman's choice, or may it hinder it by subjecting her to a potentially traumatic event? Do waiting periods merely ensure women make an informed choice about a highly significant decision, or do they reinforce stereotypical notions that women are incapable of making such important decisions on their own, or do they potentially make obtaining an abortion more difficult by increasing the number of days women must take off work, travel or find alternative care for their children? These questions and more are still under debate. In fact, in 2010 alone, seventeen different states passed laws either regulating or restricting abortion, for a total of thirty-five different bills, many of which make significant changes in existing law (see Leland 2010).

Table 5.2 lists all of these bills, and Figure 5.2 charts, utilizing the Berry et al. (1998) scores described previously, how many of these state governments have shifted rightward, or remained very conservative in the intervening years.

Table 5.2 List of State Laws Related to Abortion Enacted in 2010

State	Summary of Provision Enacted
Alaska	Requires parental notification by physician for minors seeking abortions 48 hours prior to procedure; contains a judicial bypass procedure and exceptions for abuse and emergencies
Arkansas	Prohibits organizations from receiving state funds if they offer abortion counseling or refer women for abortion services
Arizona	Expanded existing reporting requirements to include information about minors seeking judicial bypasses
Arizona	Limits state Medicaid funding of abortions to life, endangerment, rape or incest
Arizona	Prohibits state funds being used for abortions for state employees except in cases of severe health endangerment or life
Arizona	Prohibits abortion coverage in state health-insurance exchanges (as required to be created under the Affordable Care Act)
Colorado	Restricts use of Medicaid funds for abortion
Colorado	Re-enacted a prohibition on the use of state family planning funds for organizations that provide abortion services using their own funds
Iowa	Re-enacted law that state will only pay for abortions under Medicaid in cases of life endangerment, rape, incest or severe fetal abnormality
Idaho	Permits health-care providers, including pharmacists, to refuse to provide services related to abortion or contraception based on moral, religious or ethical objections
Louisiana	Expanded requirements concerning ultrasound prior to receiving an abortion to require provider to give the woman the option to hear description or view ultrasound image; also added a two-hour waiting period between ultrasound and procedure
Louisiana	Permits the state to close abortion clinics for any violation of state or federal law
Louisiana	Excludes providers that perform "elective" post-viability abortions from medical malpractice protections
Maryland	Re-enacted law restricting the public funding of abortion except in cases of life endangerment, serious health impairment, rape, incest or fetal abnormality
Mississippi	Prohibits abortion coverage in state health-insurance exchanges (as required to be created under the Affordable Care Act)
Missouri	Requires abortion clinics to offer women opportunity to have an ultrasound and view images as well as hear fetal heartbeat prior to abortion. If woman agrees, must be done 24 hours prior to procedure.
Missouri	Expanded existing counseling law to mandate women receive a description about the "anatomical and physiological characteristics of the unborn child," as well as hear about the possibility of fetal pain after 22 weeks and that abortion involves ending the life of a "separate, unique, living human being"

(continued)

83

Table 5.2 Continued

State	Summary of Provision Enacted
Missouri	Prohibits abortion coverage in state health-insurance exchanges (as required to be created under the Affordable Care Act)
Nebraska	Prohibits all abortions after 20 weeks (based on arguments about fetal pain)
Nebraska	Requires pre-abortion counseling, including information about the risks associated with potential complications
Oklahoma	Requires women to have an ultrasound at least one hour before procedure and to listen to doctor describe the image
Oklahoma	Expands reporting requirements to include information about why seeking an abortion and information about requests for and grants of judicial bypasses for minors
Oklahoma	Prohibits lawsuits against doctors for failing, including knowingly, to provide women with information about the health and status of the fetus
Oklahoma	Prohibits all abortions based on the sex of the fetus
Oklahoma	Prohibits all medication abortions (i.e., use of mifepristone) from being performed by non-physicians
Oklahoma	Requires abortion clinics to post signs that women cannot be forced into abortions
Oklahoma	Amends existing abortion refusal law to include any health care provider in the state, except in cases of life endangerment
South Carolina	Expands waiting period from one hour between counseling and procedure to 24 hours
South Carolina	Re-enacted provision restricting abortion in state employee health plan to cases of life endangerment, severe health impairment, rape and incest
Tennessee	Requires abortion clinics to post signs that women cannot be forced into abortions
Tennessee	Prohibits abortion coverage in state health-insurance exchanges (as required to be created under the Affordable Care Act)
Utah	Establishes that miscarriages due to "intentional, knowing or reckless behavior" will be treated as criminal homicides
Utah	Requires that if an ultrasound is performed, the provider must offer to display images of the ultrasound
Virginia	Restricted use of state Medicaid funding for abortions to life endangerment, rape and incest (eliminating exceptions for health and fetal abnormalities)
West Virginia	Requires that if an ultrasound is performed prior to procedure, must offer to display the image and offer a description

In Figure 5.2, we use the solid line to delineate the midpoint of ideology. In this figure we compare the state ideologies of the seventeen states that passed restrictive abortion bills in 2010 over time. The white column represents the ideology of each state government in 1970 and the black column 2005. As we can see, of the seventeen states in the figure, twelve have become more conservative since 1970. In addition, only four of the states in 2005 have government ideologies above the midpoint, as compared to six previously. Finally, the degree of the observed conservative shift is quite dramatic in several of the states, most notably Alaska, Arizona, Arkansas, Colorado and Utah.

Not surprisingly, almost all of these laws will—or already have begun to—face legal challenges alleging that they unconstitutionally burden a woman's right to choose. The current state of affairs is that battles over access to abortion are continually being fought, both in the legislatures and in the courts. One successful line of attack has concerned the granting of legal exemptions for health-care providers who do not wish to provide abortion services. Thus, many states, as well as the federal government, have enacted so-called conscience clause laws which allow pharmacists and other health-care personnel to decline to perform certain acts, due to their personal beliefs, which otherwise fall under their job descriptions. The earliest conscience clause law was enacted by the U.S. Congress immediately following *Roe v. Wade*, and exempted private hospitals receiving federal funds from any requirement to provide abortions or sterilizations if they objected due to "religious beliefs or moral convictions." The so-called Church Amendment, named after its sponsor, Senator Frank Church, also prohibited any institution receiving federal money from discriminating against individuals who refused to participate in abortion procedures. Notably, however, the Second Circuit Court of Appeals ruled on November 23, 2010, that the Church Amendment does not provide a private cause of action for enforcement of the statute

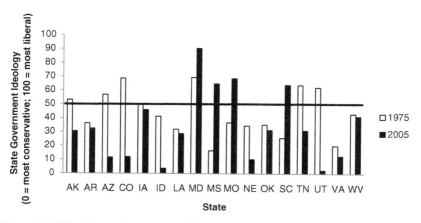

Figure 5.2 Shift of State Government Ideology, 1975–2005

with regards to individual claims; thus, in *Cenzon-DeCarlo v. Mount Sinai Hospital* (no. 10-556), the Court dismissed a nurse's claim that she was unlawfully forced to participate in performing a late-term abortion.

By the end of the 1970s, nearly every state had passed similar laws to protect the rights of institutions and health-care providers to refuse to perform abortions, which were used in particular to allow Catholic hospitals receiving Medicaid funds to maintain a pro-life policy. As of 2010, forty-six states allow some health-care providers to refuse to provide abortion services; forty-four states allow health-care institutions to refuse as well, with fifteen states limiting that exemption to private health-care institutions (Guttmacher Institute 2010). The question is how far such protections extend. For example, an emergency medical technician in Illinois is currently suing an ambulance company which fired her after she refused to transport a patient to an abortion clinic (*Adamson v. Superior Ambulance Service*, N.D. Ill.). In another case, *Moncivzaiz v. DeKalb County Health Department* (N.D. Ill.), settled in 2007, a county health department employee was denied a promotion for refusing to translate information on abortion options into Spanish.

However, the question of reproductive rights does not merely concern the question of abortion. Rather, a host of issues and legislative regulations affect the reproductive choices of women, and more fundamentally, our views of the role of women and mothers. For example, laws concerning contraceptives—including their availability, coverage by private and public health insurers—and laws aimed at criminalizing some actions of pregnant women as harmful to their fetuses all affect the broader issues which influence the ongoing legal and political debates over reproductive rights. We now turn to an examination of how the federal courts have significantly influenced policy on these issues and, in many ways, been the final arbiters of what types of statutes and regulations are permissible.

4. Birth Control

While *Griswold v. Connecticut* and *Eisenstadt v. Baird* seemed to definitively determine that states could not bar access to contraceptives, questions over the use and accessibility of birth control have continued to be raised over the years as states and the federal government have continually sought to determine the boundaries of these rights. Attempts to prevent a family planning center from providing contraception information and services to minors without parental consent were rejected in 1980 by the Sixth Circuit Court of Appeals in *Doe v. Irwin*. In 1983, in the case of *Bolger v. Youngs Drug Products*, the Supreme Court struck down a federal law prohibiting the mailing of unsolicited advertisements for contraceptives as a violation of the First Amendment. More directly, in *Charles v. Daley* (1984) the Seventh Circuit Court struck down an Illinois law that required physicians to notify patients when they prescribe any substance or device that can be classified as an abortifacient, defined as a substance or device which is known to cause fetal death. The Circuit Court held that the law violated a woman's right to privacy, by impermissibly intruding on the physician–patient relationship and imposing "the State's theory of when life begins upon the physician's patient" (462). Finally, recent issues concern whether employers, including state and local governments, must provide coverage for prescription contraception. The Eighth Circuit Court held in *Standridge v. Union Pacific Railroad Company* (2007) that employers have not engaged in unlawful sex discrimination when their health insurance plans do not cover prescription contraceptives, since the health plans did not cover any types of contraception, whether used by women or men. Alternatively, California passed the Women's Contraception Equity Act which required insurance carriers operating in California to cover birth control medications; this law was upheld by the California Supreme Court in *Catholic Charities of Sacramento v. California* (2004). Hawaii permits employees to request birth control coverage from their health insurer if their employer opposes such coverage.

Perhaps the most visible issue concerns whether pharmacists who are morally or religiously opposed to birth control can refuse to fill birth control prescriptions. As discussed above, the overwhelming majority of states, along with the federal government, have enacted "conscience clauses" which permit individual health-care workers to refrain from providing abortion services. A small number of states, thirteen as of 2010, have also passed laws which allow health-care providers to refuse to provide services related to contraception, with some state laws specifically pertaining to the right of pharmacists to refuse to fill legal prescriptions due to religious or moral objections; a number of other states have considered similar laws in recent years (see e.g., Feder 2005). For example, Georgia permits pharmacists to refuse to fill any prescriptions "based on his/her professional judgment or ethical or moral beliefs" (Ga. Comp. R. & Regs. R. 480-5-03), while South Dakota law stipulates that pharmacists are not required to dispense medication they believe will be used to destroy an "unborn child" (S.D. Codified Laws §36-11-70).

However, some states have also passed laws to protect a woman's right to gain access to prescription contraception. Eight states have laws as of 2010 requiring pharmacists or pharmacies to issue all lawfully prescribed medications, including Nevada and New Jersey. Other states allow pharmacist refusals but also prohibit pharmacists from restricting patient access to medication; for example, Texas and Oklahoma both stipulate that pharmacists must transfer prescriptions to another pharmacist at the request of the customer. Some state laws focus explicitly on access to prescription contraceptives: In 2005, Illinois put in place a regulation requiring pharmacists and pharmacies to fill all lawful prescriptions for contraceptives, including Plan B or "emergency contraception." It was challenged, however, on free exercise grounds by a group of seven pharmacists. A district court in Illinois acknowledged that a valid claim may exist that the regulation was intentionally targeted at religious objectors to Plan B, in part based on public statements by then-Governor Rod Blagojevich (*Menges v. Blagojevich*, N.D. Ill. 2006). As a result of that ruling, which would have allowed a full-scale trial to commence, the state agreed to a settlement stipulating that the regulation applied only to pharmacies, and not individual pharmacists. Washington enacted a similar law in 2007, in part due to concerns over the dispensing of Plan B, which required pharmacies to fill all lawfully prescribed medications and to stock Plan B for dispensing purposes. It did not require individual pharmacists, however, to dispense medication they find personally objectionable. This law was challenged under the free exercise clause of the First Amendment in 2009 (*Stormans, Inc. v. Selecky*). The Ninth Circuit Court upheld the law, which it viewed as being targeted at increasing access to lawfully prescribed medications, noting that free exercise rights do not "relieve an individual of the obligation to comply with a valid and neutral law of general applicability."

More recently, individual pharmacists have maintained that they should have the right to refuse to dispense prescriptions which conflict with their personal beliefs, and that attempts to force them to do so are in turn a violation of the First Amendment free exercise clause. In particular, some religions prohibit the use of all forms of contraception, and particularly prescription-only birth control, on the grounds that "the pill" stops not only fertilization (or conception), but also the implantation of a fertilized egg in a woman's uterus, a step that takes place approximately eight days after fertilization. Thus, by preventing implantation of a fertilized egg, prescription birth control is not only preventing conception but also in some cases actually acting as an early stage abortifacient. Similar arguments have also been made against emergency contraception pills, otherwise known as "morning after pills," which must be taken within seventy-two hours of having unprotected sex and are intended to prevent both ovulation and implantation of a fertilized egg. Pharmacists advocating for conscience clauses argue that they should not be forced to perform services, such as dispensing prescriptions viewed as abortifacients, which violate their personal and religious beliefs. As of 2010, fourteen states allow some health-care providers to refuse to provide contraception services, with five states explicitly permitting pharmacists to refuse to dispense contraceptives.

This issue highlights the delicate balance that exists between pharmacists' rights, including protection of their religious beliefs, and the right of women to receive prescribed medications without hindrance. The concern arises when the practical implications of conscience clauses are considered; for example, if a pharmacist refuses to dispense a birth control pill prescription, must he or she refer the patient to another pharmacist who will? What if only one pharmacist works at the pharmacy or if there is only one pharmacy in town? What obligations does the pharmacist have to aid the patient in getting her prescription filled? And, what rights do pharmacists have to refuse to perform services they find morally egregious?

Not surprisingly, conflicts over these conflicting rights have arisen in recent years. In 2007, in one of the few cases to advance through the courts, the Seventh Circuit Court of Appeals decided *Noesen v. Medical Staffing Network*, concerning a pharmacist who refused to interact with any person, no matter how brief, seeking birth control and wanted his employer, Wal-Mart, to insulate him from all such interactions. Neil Noesen, a Roman Catholic, is a licensed pharmacist who refused to fill birth control prescriptions. His manager agreed to relieve Noesen from filling birth control prescriptions, take orders for birth control prescriptions or handling birth control medications. However, Noesen subsequently refused to perform other customer-service duties: he would place on hold patients and physicians attempting to place orders for birth control and also not alert other pharmacy staff that someone was holding. He would also walk away if someone approached the counter with a birth control prescription and refuse to find another employee to assist the customer. The manager again proposed a solution whereby Noesen would only assist male customers or those not of child-bearing age. Noesen refused, arguing that the other pharmacy employees should first prescreen all customers in order to shield him from those seeking birth control. The manager agreed that other employees could first assist all walk-in customers, but due to the high volume of calls the pharmacy received, Noesen would need to answer the telephones, but could then refer calls pertaining to birth control to another employee. Noesen again refused, and was subsequently fired. Noesen filed suit, and the district court ruled in Wal-Mart's favor.

On appeal, the Seventh Circuit Court affirmed the trial court's judgment, arguing that Wal-Mart provided a "reasonable accommodation" for Noesen's religious beliefs as required under Title VII, but that Noesen's stated accommodation of relieving him of all counter and telephone duties would create an "undue hardship" on the employer. Thus, the Circuit Court argued that accommodating Noesen's religious beliefs did not mean his employer had to also exempt him from the regular duties of his job. However, at the time, Wisconsin did not have a separate "conscience clause" exception to its codified standards of pharmacist's professional conduct. In fact, current Wisconsin law actually requires pharmacies to fill valid contraceptive prescriptions. Noesen was later reprimanded by the state pharmacy board due to his refusal to refer patients to other pharmacies or even transfer their prescriptions to another pharmacy when asked.

To date few cases have addressed these clauses and their implications, but that is likely due to the relative infancy of many of these statutes. Opponents of such laws argue that they are merely another way to deny women their constitutionally guaranteed reproductive rights and, in some cases, deny necessary medical care (such as in the case of women who are prescribed birth control pills to treat conditions such as endometriosis and polycystic ovary syndrome). Thus, the debates that have taken place in the state legislatures and among the public have focused not just on the rights of the pharmacists, but also on the rights of women seeking access to birth control. A high-profile example concerned a proposed federal regulation called the "Provider Refusal Rule." It was proposed by the George W. Bush administration in August of 2008 and enacted on January 20, 2009, the day Barack Obama was sworn into office. The rule expanded the federal law, discussed earlier, that was passed in the wake of *Roe v. Wade* and allowed "health care professionals" to opt out of performing abortions for moral and religious reasons. This new rule allowed all workers in health-care settings, whether they were doctors or nurses or janitors, to refuse to provide any services, information or advice that they morally opposed, ranging from contraception to blood transfusions to vaccine counseling.

On one side, organizations such as the American Medical Association opposed the new rules, arguing that health-care providers are obligated to treat their patients and advise them of their options regardless of the providers' own beliefs. On the other side, organizations such as the Family Research Council argued in favor of "the right of all health-care providers to make professional judgments based on moral convictions and ethical standards ... chang[ing] the language of these protections would result in the government becoming the conscience and not the individual. It is a person's right to exercise their moral judgment, not the government's to decide it for them" (Young 2009). The Obama administration announced its opposition to the rule as written, citing concerns that it would limit women's access to necessary medical care.

5. Prosecution of Pregnant Women

Another issue related to the question of the boundaries of the right to privacy and reproductive rights concerns attempts by states and local governments to criminally prosecute pregnant women with regard to their actions during pregnancy. These situations tap into the question of whether women, when they choose to carry a child to term, should be then held responsible for how their actions potentially affect their unborn children. They also implicitly stretch the boundaries of the right to abortion by suggesting that women should be held liable for actions which harm their fetuses, including abortion itself. Pregnant women have been prosecuted in a number of instances based on the argument that their actions or inactions risked fetal harm. The one Supreme Court case even tangentially related to the criminal prosecution of pregnant women, *Ferguson v. City of Charleston* (2001), addressed the question of whether hospitals could conduct drug tests without a patient's consent in order to try and reduce the use of illegal drugs by women during pregnancy. The Supreme Court held that the Fourth Amendment protection against unreasonable searches and seizures prohibited such searches, especially since the test results were preserved in the case of eventual prosecution.

One particularly potent issue concerns the use of drugs by women during their pregnancy, and whether they can then be charged under existing drug and child abuse statutes. For example, G. experienced a stillbirth at sixteen in Mississippi. She was then charged with "depraved heart homicide," based on allegations that her drug use caused the stillbirth. Harris and Paltrow's (2003) examination of state-level appeals cases through 2001 revealed twenty-two cases in sixteen states where women were prosecuted based on allegations of fetal harm, generally in relation to illegal drug use during pregnancy. As Fentiman (2009) overviews, the first criminal indictment occurred in 1977 when a woman was charged with felony child endangerment in California due to heroin use during her pregnancy.

However, in this case (*Reyes v. Superior Court*, Cal. Ct. App.), the California Court of Appeals determined that this prosecution was not supported by the specific legislative text, arguing that the word "child" does not also refer to unborn children or fetuses (Fentiman 2009; see also Harris and Paltrow 2003). This determination was made in all similar state cases with the exceptions of South Carolina, Alabama and Kentucky. For example, the Arkansas Supreme Court held in *Arkansas Department of Human Services v. Collier* (2003) that the Arkansas law concerning "dependent-neglected juveniles" did not encompass unborn fetuses. Similarly, the Wisconsin Supreme Court held in *State ex rel. Angela M.W. v. Kruzicki* (1997) that Wisconsin child welfare laws used "child" in terms of "a human being born alive," in part because the statute assumes possible separation of the child from the parent, a separation that is impossible in the case of a pregnant woman and her fetus. In response to this decision, Wisconsin passed a law in 1998 which allows authorities to civilly detain pregnant women found to be abusing drugs or alcohol until the child is born; it does not, however, also charge them criminally (Pasternak 1998). South Dakota passed a similar set of laws in early 1998, becoming the first state to do so (Aamot 1998).

Conversely, the South Carolina high court held in *Whitner v. South Carolina* (1997) that the word "child" in its criminal child endangerment statute encompassed viable fetuses. The South Carolina Supreme Court therefore upheld Whitner's conviction for criminal child neglect based on her ingestion of crack cocaine during the third trimester of pregnancy. In part, the South Carolina Supreme Court reasoned that it "would be absurd to recognize the viable fetus as a person for purposes of homicide laws and wrongful death statutes [which the court held in *State v. Horne* 1984] but not for purposes of statutes proscribing child abuse" (780). Similarly, Regina McKnight was convicted in 2001 of homicide by child abuse in South Carolina on the grounds that her illegal drug use resulted in her pregnancy ending in a stillbirth. The state Supreme Court affirmed her conviction (*State v. McKnight* 2003), in part by holding that the statute was intended to apply to fetuses and that her drug use amounted to acting "with extreme indifference to her child's life" (646); the U.S. Supreme Court denied her petition for certiorari.

A number of states have proposed or enacted laws targeted at protecting pregnant women and their fetuses from violence, with some laws establishing the fetus as an independent "victim" for purposes of criminal prosecution (i.e., "feticide" laws). Thus, under these laws, if a person murders a pregnant woman, the accused may be charged with two separate counts of murder, one for the woman and one for the fetus. However, some of these laws have also been used against the pregnant women themselves. For example, in 1999, Utah amended its homicide law to include victims who are "unborn children." Under this law, prosecutors in Utah charged Melissa Rowland with murder and child endangerment in 2004 for waiting to have a cesarean section to deliver twins based on the allegation that her actions resulted in one of the twins being born stillborn; she eventually pled guilty to two counts of child endangerment (Reuters 2004).

Similarly, Jessica Clyburn of South Carolina was charged with homicide by child abuse in 2009 after her eight-month-old fetus was determined to have died when she attempted suicide.

Perhaps the most extreme case concerned a seventeen-year-old minor female who paid a man $150 to beat her in order to try and induce a miscarriage. In response, Utah passed a "Criminal Miscarriage" law (H.B. 12) in early 2010 which states that "the killing or attempted killing of a live unborn child in a manner that is not abortion shall be punished as ... criminal homicide." It further states that an "intentional, knowing or reckless act of the woman" can be punishable as criminal homicide. The concern is whether this law thus puts women at risk for having to prove that miscarriages they suffer were not caused by their own reckless behavior. For example, the ACLU questioned whether a woman failing to wear a seatbelt could be charged with reckless homicide if she miscarries as a result of a car accident (American Civil Liberties Union [ACLU] 2009). Similarly, the American Medical Association expressed concern that "[p]regnant women will be likely to avoid seeking prenatal or open medical care for fear that their physician's knowledge of substance abuse or other potentially harmful behavior could result in a jail sentence" (Sclamberg 2010). This law also raises the question of whether women will have to prove that their abortions were lawfully obtained, by blurring the line between miscarriages and abortion.

Similarly, the courts have had to deal with whether children born alive can bring negligence claims against their mothers for injuries sustained *in utero*. The Illinois Supreme Court, in *Stallman v. Youngquist* (1988), held that a cause of action cannot be brought by a fetus, subsequently born alive, against its mother for the unintentional infliction of prenatal injuries. Here, the child attempted to sue the mother for injuries caused *in utero* as a result of a car accident when the mother was five months pregnant. The court argued that

> [h]olding a mother liable for the unintentional infliction of prenatal injuries subjects to State scrutiny all the decisions a woman must make in attempting to carry a pregnancy to term, and infringes on her right to privacy and bodily autonomy ... it is the mother's every waking and sleeping moment which, for better or worse, shapes the prenatal environment which forms the world for the developing fetus. That this is so is not a pregnant woman's fault: it is a fact of life. (278–79)

While most other state courts have ruled similarly, the Supreme Court of New Hampshire determined in 1992 in *Bonte v. Bonte* that a child born alive can bring a tort action against his or her mother for injuries sustained *in utero* due to the mother's negligent conduct. The dissenting justices argued that extending such liability would have to necessarily "govern such details of a woman's life as her diet, sleep, exercise, sexual activity, work and living environment, and, of course, nearly every aspect of her health care," and questioned whether it is "possible to subject a woman's judgment, action, and behavior as they relate to the well-being of her fetus to a judicial determination of reasonableness in a manner that is consistent and free from arbitrary results" (292).

In all of these different situations, laws targeted at pregnant women serve two purposes. On the one hand, they strive to protect the state's interest in potential life, as stipulated by *Roe v. Wade*, and upheld in *Casey*. These laws suggest that women who choose to bear children implicitly accept responsibility for the well-being of their growing children and can be punished accordingly. On the other hand, these laws are also seen by many as a way to restrict a woman's right to choose. By seeking to define "unborn children" as "children," and to equate harm to a fetus with harm to a living child, these laws suggest that fetuses should be protected like children and, ultimately, protected from the practice of abortion. As a result, courts must contend with the question of whether these laws are a way of valuing life, or a mechanism for circumscribing the right to privacy as it extends to the right to obtain an abortion.

6. Conclusion

With its decision in *Roe v. Wade*, the Supreme Court determined that the right to privacy established in *Griswold v. Connecticut* encompassed a woman's right to choose whether to terminate a pregnancy. Not surprisingly, this decision sparked an ongoing legal battle which shows no signs of being resolved in the near future. On the one hand, pro-choice advocates argue women must retain the right to make decisions about something as fundamental as what happens to their own bodies. On the other hand, pro-life advocates maintain that the person growing inside the woman deserves protection as well, and so the practice of abortion should be limited, if not completely prohibited. Given the courts' central role in establishing the right to privacy, they also play a key role in shaping its limits and boundaries, and determining whether federal and state laws are permissible.

While fights are still being waged over abortion itself, the battle has also spread to other areas concerning women's reproductive rights. Simply put, whose rights should matter more—those of the mother or those of the unborn child? For example, Angela Carder was twenty-six weeks pregnant and critically ill from cancer. Over her objections, as well as those of her family and attending physicians, a hospital petitioned the court for permission to perform a cesarean to deliver the baby; the trial court granted the petition and both the baby and Carder died shortly after the surgery was performed. The District of Columbia Court of Appeals, in *In re AC* (1990), ruled against the hospital, arguing that the decision of appropriate medical treatment remains with the patient on behalf of herself and the fetus. The court noted that while it is possible the state's interests might swamp those of the pregnant patient in some circumstances, "it would be an extraordinary case indeed in which a court might ever be justified in over-riding the patient's wishes and authorizing a major surgical procedure such as a caesarean section" (1252).

Such a case did arise in Tallahassee, Florida: Laura Pemberton attempted to give birth at home, but sought medical care at a hospital when she became dehydrated. The hospital then sought a court order to force Pemberton to give birth via a cesarean section, arguing that her previous C-section scars pointed to the high likelihood of uterine rupture and fetal death. A state court granted the hospital's request, and a C-section was performed over her objections. Pemberton then sued the hospital in federal district court. In *Pemberton v. Tallahassee Memorial Regional Medical Center* (1999), the district court held that her personal constitutional rights did not outweigh the interests of the state in preserving the life of the unborn child, especially given that the fetus was well past the point of viability. A similar situation also arose in Florida in 2009: Samantha Burton started experiencing preterm labor around her twenty-fifth week of pregnancy and went to the hospital. When it was suggested she stay in the hospital for the remainder of her pregnancy, she objected, in part because she had two other children to care for at home. In response, hospital officials obtained a court order to force her to submit to anything deemed necessary to "preserve the life and health of the unborn child," and involuntarily confined her to the hospital (James 2010). Burton miscarried three days later, and then sued the hospital for infringing on her rights of privacy and liberty. In a decision handed down on August 12, 2010, a Florida appeals court ruled in Burton's favor, arguing that if viability is shown, courts must still weigh the state's interest to protect the fetus against the mother's constitutional right of privacy to refuse medical treatment. In this instance, the state's method for achieving its aims was more intrusive than necessary to achieve the state's goals and protect the mother's constitutional rights (*Burton v. Florida*).

As these three cases demonstrate, these situations are neither easy nor clear cut, and disputes over the correct course of action will likely continue to dominate both public debates and the courts' dockets. At the end of the day, the courts' role in establishing the right to privacy also means the courts must play a central role in resolving disputes over its parameters. While *Roe* established a fairly broad right to privacy, subsequent cases have limited the reach of this right. States can now require that women give informed consent before obtaining an abortion and wait some period of time before having the procedure. Certain abortion procedures can also be prohibited, especially with respect to late-term abortions. The emerging question is the degree to which the rights of others— such as the rights of the fetus or the rights of pharmacists—can be elevated over the rights of the woman. Since the right to privacy is a judicially created constitutional right, these questions in the end can only be resolved by the courts.

6

FEDERAL COURT POLICYMAKING
Discrimination and Educational Affirmative Action

1. Introduction: Racial Discrimination and the Courts

In this chapter, we explore our final issue area with regard to federal court policymaking: educational affirmative action. The issue of affirmative action raises a complex set of considerations which all serve to illuminate the central role of the courts in this issue arena. First, affirmative action programs stem from the courts' equity power. When a party alleges that he or she has been harmed, if the court finds a violation has occurred, the court has the power to issue a remedy. The court's remedy will focus on making the injured party "whole" again; thus, if a driver is found responsible for an accident, the court will likely order that driver to pay the other driver(s) whatever amount is necessary for their cars to be properly fixed. Remedies can also be issued when discriminatory treatment occurs. In such cases, the court can order the responsible party to take some action to right the alleged harm.

Second, affirmative action programs raise the question of what is the proper remedy for discriminatory actions. In particular, what if the discriminatory action is not directed merely at one individual, but an entire group of people? What is the proper response if, for example, as occurred in the case of *United States v. Paradise* (1987), the state of Alabama refused for many decades to hire African Americans to serve as state troopers? Should the court order the state to stop such discriminatory treatment? Or should it go further and require the state to take affirmative steps to correct these past injustices by ensuring that African Americans will be hired going forward?

Third, affirmative action programs tap into the constitutional question of equal protection on two different levels. On the one hand, affirmative action programs are generally remedies for discriminatory treatment which violates the guarantee of equal protection. On the other hand, since affirmative action programs are many times forward looking, they also potentially raise concerns about "reverse discrimination," or the notion that by favoring one group—even if that favoritism is to correct a past wrong—another group is by necessity being disfavored. Claims of reverse discrimination similarly raise equal protection concerns. As a result, the courts are asked not only to determine if discrimination has occurred and, if yes, what is the proper remedy, but also whether the remedy itself is potentially unconstitutional. Thus, questions concerning affirmative action—while also a hotly debated political topic—are many times ultimately answered by the federal courts.

In this chapter we focus on federal court policymaking in the area of discrimination and remedies for discrimination with an emphasis on racial discrimination and remedies for it. We particularly examine the controversial remedy of affirmative action with regard to education. We first provide a brief review of the history of racial discrimination and the political system's response to this discrimination. We then examine the gradual elimination of discriminatory barriers through both litigation and legislative action. We end with a focus on affirmative action rulings and the aftermath of these rulings.

2. Race, Racial Discrimination and Equal Protection

Prior to the Civil War, the prevailing view of African Americans by white society was expressed in the infamous *Dred Scott* (1857) decision—an "inferior order, to be bought and sold." The Supreme Court's interpretation in this case solidified the institution of slavery and many believe paved the way for the Civil War. Not only were African Americans held as slaves throughout the South, but even freed blacks enjoyed few of the rights of citizenship. However, in the aftermath of the Civil War and the defeat of the Confederacy, the post-Civil War Congress passed and subsequently saw ratified the Thirteenth, Fourteenth and Fifteenth Amendments to the U.S. Constitution. The Thirteenth Amendment outlawed slavery and involuntary servitude, while the Fifteenth Amendment guaranteed the right of all citizens to vote.[1] The Fourteenth Amendment was of particular importance for providing subsequent remedies for discrimination, with its now famous phrase stating that "Nor shall any state ... deny to any person within its jurisdiction the equal protection of the laws." The use of the word "state" means the amendment specifically applies to state governments and their political subdivisions, while the word "person" means it protects all people, not just former slaves, not just citizens and not just those suffering racial discrimination. Finally, the equal protection clause specifically prohibited discrimination in the treatment of the individual.

Of course, what does discrimination mean? As discussed in Chapter 4, all legislation and many governmental actions treat groups or individuals differently. For example, changes in tax legislation usually result in some groups paying more or less taxes depending on their income or status. Homeowners get to deduct their mortgage interest, but renters are not allowed to deduct their rental payments. Similarly, many social welfare programs provide benefits to individuals based upon their incomes. As a result, aid in the form of rental assistance, food subsidies or free or reduced health care is many times reserved for those who cannot otherwise afford them. The courts have thus had to recognize that "equal protection" does not literally mean "equal treatment." Rather, the courts have determined that rational legislative distinctions among groups in the achievement of legitimate governmental aims are constitutional. Problems arise, however, when the distinctions can be viewed not as rational differentiations but rather as mechanisms for invidious discrimination against particular groups.

Despite the Thirteenth, Fourteenth and Fifteenth Amendments, the former Confederacy moved swiftly to reinstitute the racial status quo that had existed before the Civil War, by first adopting laws that disadvantaged blacks, and then adopting laws which segregated them. And these efforts were ultimately successful: for more than a century after the Civil War, the Fourteenth Amendment was not viewed as prohibiting racial segregation in public and private facilities. In the 1896 case *Plessy v. Ferguson*, the Supreme Court established a standard known as "separate but equal." Under the notion of separate but equal, the equal protection clause did not outlaw state-mandated segregation whereby blacks and whites were kept segregated and apart; rather, it required only that each group be given equal benefits and facilities. Throughout the Southern states, segregation laws applied to everything from drinking fountains and education, to transportation facilities and public restaurants and hotels.

The evident fact that these facilities were anything but "equal" was not taken seriously for most of this period, and equal protection was often viewed as an inadequate legal claim. For example, Justice Oliver Wendell Holmes referred to equal protection as the "usual last resort of constitutional arguments" (*Buck v. Bell* 1927). The late constitutional scholar Gerald Gunther similarly argued that the equal protection clause for most of U.S. constitutional history simply meant that the government only may not *impose* differential treatment (1986, 253).

3. The Evolution of Attempts to End Racial Discrimination

Initially, it was the U.S. Congress and not the federal courts that attempted to upend these patterns of racial discrimination.

Attempts Prior to 1930

Almost immediately after the end of the Civil War, the U.S. Congress enacted the Civil Rights Act of 1866 and the Civil Rights Act of 1875 under Section 5 of the Fourteenth Amendment, which gave Congress power to enforce the Fourteenth Amendment through appropriate legislation. Both acts sought to bar racial discrimination in public accommodations. The law made it a federal crime to prohibit any person from denying a citizen "full and equal enjoyment of the accommodations, advantages, facilitates, and privileges of Inns, Public conveyances on land or water, theaters and other places of amusement." However, the Supreme Court struck down these laws in the *Civil Rights Cases* (1883). In these cases, the United States had charged four establishments and two individuals with violating the Civil Rights Act, but the Court refused to enforce the mandates of the statutes. Instead, in a 7-1 ruling, Justice Bradley, writing for the Court, determined that the Fourteenth Amendment's guarantees against unequal treatment were limited to state action. Here, there were only allegations of private and not state/governmental violations. In other words, the Supreme Court held that unless private discrimination was in some way supported by state authority, there is nothing that Congress can do to prevent it.

The result of this case was to undercut congressional power and constitutionally legitimate private racial discrimination. This case also demonstrates the limits of political and legal action and the notion of how courts operate within the legal set. By the time of the decision, the Reconstruction period in American political life was over. The congressional electoral defeat suffered by the Republican Party in 1874, combined with the behind-the-scenes machinations of the presidential election of 1876, ended the nation's commitment to eradicate racial discrimination. As a result of a bargain made by Republican officials in return for Southern Electoral College votes, Rutherford B. Hayes assumed the office of the presidency despite losing the popular vote to Samuel J. Tilden. In return, federal troops were removed from South Carolina and two other Southern states. Thus, arguably the ruling in the *Civil Rights Cases* was consistent with the dominant preferences of the electorate and the elected political officials as of 1883.

It should be noted that in at least one instance, the Supreme Court did strike down a clear instance of state-mandated segregation. In *Strauder v. West Virginia* (1879), the Court struck down a state law that declared only whites could serve on juries. However, despite this ruling, less than two decades later the Court went even further and gave legitimacy to state-sanctioned segregation by upholding the idea of "separate but equal" governmental treatment. *Plessy v. Ferguson* (1896) upheld an 1890 Louisiana law that required railroad companies to provide separate but equal facilities for whites and blacks. The law made it a crime for a person of one race to insist on taking the seat of a person of another race. In upholding the law with a 7-1 vote, the Court gave a very narrow meaning to equal protection, finding that it meant to abolish distinctions based on race before the law, but was not meant to abolish social distinctions or enforce social, as opposed to legal or political, equality. Separation, the opinion went on to note, does not and is not meant to signal the inferiority of either race, even if black Americans chose to view it that way.

As in the *Civil Rights Cases* decision, the Court was operating within the accepted range of political beliefs. The legal set enforced by the Court was well within the options mandated by the political system. The *Plessy* decision went largely unnoticed at the time and for many years afterward: the *New York Times*, for example, gave the decision only passing notice in its column on railway news. Charles Warren's *History of the Supreme Court*, published in 1922, ignored the decision, and only referred to it in a footnote in a 1926 update. Even the prominent historian Henry Steel Commager omitted it in his constitutional history texts.

Attempts After 1930

As suggested above, among other problems with the *Plessy* decision was the idea that any of these separate facilities were remotely equal, and the degree of segregation throughout society was truly stunning. For example, only about 12% of all black school children attended racially mixed schools in the late nineteenth century. The country—and the Court—did not really begin to change until well into the twentieth century. A long, slow process of change began with the advent of the New Deal and World War II. Congress remained unwilling to act as Southern Democrats, in positions of great power due in large part to the seniority system, formed alliances with conservative Republicans and blocked the advance of most civil rights legislation. However, change did occur because of executive action. President Franklin D. Roosevelt created a Civil Liberties Unit within the Department of Justice in 1939. In 1948, President Harry S. Truman issued an executive order desegregating the military. Roosevelt and Truman's judicial appointments also contributed to an ideological shift on the Supreme Court toward a more progressive attitude concerning equal protection and civil rights.

As a result of these changes in the executive and their subsequent appointments to the federal bench, a formidable, legally oriented assault on segregation was launched. Blocked in Congress by a coalition of Southern Democrats and Northern conservative Republicans, the National Association for the Advancement of Colored People (NAACP) conceived a strategy for using the Fourteenth and Fifth Amendments to the U.S. Constitution to alter *de jure* (i.e., legally mandated) segregation in education. Their first efforts concerned the need to show that the *Plessy* doctrine of separate but equal was vulnerable in the field of graduate education before moving on to public primary education.

The first decision came in 1938 in *Missouri ex rel. Gaines v. Canada* (1938). Gaines was a black applicant who was refused admission to the University of Missouri Law School because of his race. The state argued it would pay for his tuition to an out-of-state law school, pending construction of a law school in the state for black students. The Court held, by a 7-2 vote, that Missouri was obligated to build within its borders a school substantially similar to that offered to the whites, or, in the absence of such facilities, the state must allow Gaines to attend the existing school.

This decision was followed by *Sweatt v. Painter* (1950). Homer Sweatt was an African American denied admission to the University of Texas Law School. The state sought time to create a separate but equal law school for blacks, but Sweatt refused to attend the newly created law school. In a sharp rebuke to Texas, the Court found the attempt to create a separate school lacking and ordered Sweatt admitted to the law school. Most notably, the opinion appeared to question the ability of a state to ever construct a truly separate but equal law school because of the intangible factors associated with both attending and graduating from an elite law school.

These decisions were the forerunners to the famous case of *Brown v. Board of Education* I (1954) where the Court, now led by Chief Justice Earl Warren, held unanimously that separate but unequal schools violated the equal protection clause of the Fourteenth Amendment. The opinion determined that "separate education facilities are inherently unequal," and led to a detrimental effect on school children (495). Separation, the Court held, particularly of young children, "solely because of their race generates a feeling of inferiority as to their status in the community that may affect their hearts and minds in a way unlikely ever to be undone" (494).

Brown was not the end of the Court's rulings breaking down segregation. Over the next several years, the Court overturned public segregation in almost all areas of American public life. The Court extended the *Brown* principle to places such as beaches, buses, golf courses, parks and municipal restaurants, and also struck down legislative restrictions on interracial marriage (*Loving v. Virginia* 1967). By 1963, the Court stated, "it is no longer open to question that a state may not constitutionally require segregation of public facilities" (*Johnson v. Virginia* 1963), disallowing a judge's sectioning off a section of a courtroom for blacks. The Court also began to chip away at private discrimination through a concept known as the "nexus" approach by finding a connection between state authority and some private enterprises in cases such as *Shelley v. Kramer* (1948; disallowing a state court from legally enforcing a racially restrictive housing covenant), and *Burton v. Wilmington Parking Authority* (1961; holding that prohibitions on segregation in public places extended to a privately owned restaurant located in a building owned, operated and maintained by the city).

The process of educational desegregation, however, and despite these rulings, was long, often violent, and could not be achieved simply by judicial decree. The opposition to the Court's ruling in *Brown* led to bitter and violent confrontations. In 1956, nineteen Senators and eighty-two House members denounced *Brown* as unconstitutional in a "Southern Manifesto," and President Eisenhower did little in the late 1950s to force compliance. One civil rights attorney estimated that from 1954 to 1964, only 2% of black children began attending white schools.

The Court recognized the potential for enforcement difficulties by delaying for one year a decision on the mechanism for implementation of its order, which came with the decision known as *Brown II* (1955). In *Brown II*, the Court determined that, given the variations in local conditions, as well as the complexity of school rezoning efforts, local school boards would have the "primary responsibility for elucidating, assessing and solving these problems," while the district courts would be charged with determining "whether the action of school authorities constitutes good faith implementation of the governing constitutional principles" (299). The Court also determined that the implementation of desegregation in public primary and secondary schools was to occur, based on a phrase adopted from the Solicitor General's amicus brief, with "all deliberate speed."

The problem with the term was its vagueness. The Court itself had to revisit its *Brown II* ruling in *Cooper v. Aaron* (1958). In this case, the Arkansas governor and legislature were attempting to frustrate implementation of *Brown* in the City of Little Rock, Arkansas. Desegregation was to start with the admission of nine black school children in 1957 and eventually the system was to be fully integrated by 1963. However, the governor sent National Guard troops to block the nine students from attending, leading the school board to request that the students not attend and that the board be allowed to delay implementation. The Court, in another unanimous opinion, rejected any delay in the plan and eventually President Eisenhower ordered in federal troops to implement the decision.

A still hotly debated question is the reach and impact of the Supreme Court's decision in *Brown*. Put simply, did the decision in *Brown* act as a catalyst for rather massive social changes, or did the Court's decision have relatively little impact on the social changes that eventually occurred? In many ways, *Brown* provides significant evidence of the courts' lack of ability to influence widespread policy change. Gerald Rosenberg argues in *The Hollow Hope* (2008) that the pace of desegregation showed little change in the aftermath of *Brown*, and instead, it was the eventual commitment of the president and Congress, the elected branches of government that truly led to desegregation. While the president and Congress were initially hesitant to act, they ultimately enacted the Civil Rights Acts of 1964 and 1968 as well as the Elementary and Secondary Education Act in 1965. With the passage of these laws, the Department of Justice and other federal administrative agencies assumed a greater role in fighting discrimination, which included using the Department of Justice to sue recalcitrant school districts. Rosenberg (2008, 50–51) specifically notes that while only 2.3% of African American students in the South attended schools which also enrolled white students in the 1964–65 school year—one decade after the Court's decision in *Brown*—this number jumped to 32.0% for the 1968–1969 school year (or four years after congressional and presidential action, and to 91.3% for the 1972–73 school year (or eight years after congressional and presidential action). Thus, Rosenberg argues that these data on school integration suggest that in the decade during which only the Court was speaking out forcefully against segregation, little progress toward desegregation actually occurred. It was only after the legislative and executive branches began contributing substantially to the implementation and enforcement process that desegregation efforts succeeded.

However, this simple accounting of the aftermath of *Brown* fails to tell the entire story. First, as other scholars have shown (Flemming, Bohte and Wood 1997; Hoekstra 2000; Johnson and Martin 1998), Supreme Court rulings can increase public awareness and attention to an issue area and this can in turn lead to increased electoral attention. Second, it fails to account for the idea of the Court fitting into the American legal system and the legal set. As we have done for other areas, we charted the mean ideology of the Court, the two branches of Congress and the president from 1938 through 2008. To this figure, we also add the major Supreme Court cases on discrimination and the major pieces of legislation that occurred during this time period. We report the results in Figure 6.1 below.

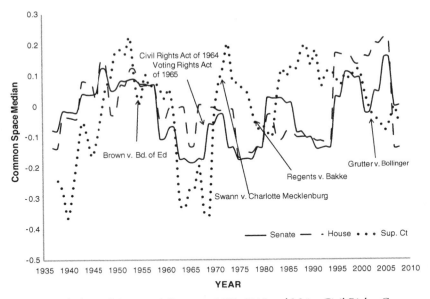

Figure 6.1 Ideology of Court and Congress, 1938–2010 and Major Civil Rights Cases

As one can see from Figure 6.1, the Court and the Congress were not that much out of ideological alignment during this period. For example, the *Swann* decision of 1971 mandating busing as a remedy for school desegregation was issued by a Supreme Court whose median ideology was actually more conservative than that of the Congress, ensuring that the Congress would not seek to overturn the decision. The Court therefore had some freedom to operate during this time frame and was generally pursuing policy supported by—or at least not out of sync with—the elected branches of government.

4. Remedial Efforts to Achieve Equal Educational Opportunity

However, while the country was generally in line with the Court and agreed that racial discrimination should be outlawed, the remedies available to ban or change previous patterns of discrimination remained in dispute. For example, the Burger Court grew increasingly impatient with the slow pace of school desegregation, and placed increasing emphasis not on *de jure* law, but on *de facto* (i.e., in reality or fact) segregation. The continuing resistance to desegregation efforts, and the search for adequate remedies, led to the decision in *Swann v. Charlotte Mecklenburg Board of Education* (1971). In *Swann*, the Court addressed what remedies could be imposed on school districts in order to achieve the goal of creating unified school systems. The local district court judge—who, under *Brown II* was given the power to create and enforce desegregation schemes—proposed a plan involving forced busing, as well as widespread changes in administration, teachers, funding and other areas. The Supreme Court, in a unanimous decision, held that the use of mandated busing of school children to achieve racial balance, along with numerous other broad-scale remedies, was constitutional. In particular, the Court noted that "[o]nce a right and a violation have been shown, the scope of a district court's equitable powers to remedy past wrongs is broad, for breadth and flexibility are inherent in equitable remedies" (15). In other words, the Court's decision stipulated that when a constitutional violation such as discrimination is found, courts then have the power to fashion remedies to correct the legal wrong. And when, as here, the scope of the violation is large, the scope of the remedy may be necessarily large as well.

Affirmative Action as a Viable Remedy for Educational Inequality

The *Swann* decision, as well as many of *Brown's* progeny, was important because the Supreme Court reiterated that the judicial power of equity allows courts to remedy constitutional violations. However, the notion of courts intruding into local school board decision making provoked significant defiance and disapproval. Even today, so-called affirmative action programs—whereby the government takes affirmative steps to remedy a constitutional violation—remain perhaps the most controversial aspect of equal protection analysis. Simply put, can the state take positive measures to remedy past *de jure* discrimination, such as requiring the admission or hiring of minorities previously discriminated against? In the words of President John F. Kennedy in Executive Order 10925, "discrimination because of race, creed, color, or national origin is contrary to the Constitutional principles and policies of the United States … it is the plain and positive obligation of the United States Government to promote and ensure equal opportunity for all qualified persons, without regard to race, creed, color, or national origin."

The central notion of affirmative action plans is to ensure that all are given an equal place at the starting line. With education, affirmative action plans focus on overcoming the vestiges of *de jure* discrimination, such as inequalities in school resources. The most important initial case in the area of educational affirmative action was the case of *Regents of University of California v. Bakke* (1978). An earlier case, *DeFunis v. Odegaard* (1974), involving a denial of admission to law school because of affirmative action, was ruled moot because the petitioner was later admitted to the law school and was near graduation.[2] *Bakke* concerned the admissions program for the University of California at Davis's medical school. The medical school used a two-tier admission process for determining the one hundred students who would be admitted. Students could either apply to the "regular" admissions program or to the "special admissions" program for minorities who were economically or educationally disadvantaged; 16% of the seats in the class were reserved for those admitted through the special admissions program. The result was the admission of some minority students through the special admissions program with lower qualifications than those rejected from the regular admissions program, one of whom was Alan Bakke, a white applicant. Bakke sued, arguing that the two-tier admissions process discriminated on the basis of race by favoring minority applicants over white applicants solely because of their race. He alleged that affirmative action programs such as the one at UC Davis violated the Fourteenth Amendment equal protection clause.

In a classic "split decision," the Supreme Court ruled in favor of the notion of affirmative action programs, but declared the University's affirmative action program improper. Justice Powell authored the majority opinion and was the key vote in both rulings. Four justices voted to admit Bakke and strike down affirmative action programs altogether, while four other justices voted to sustain the University's position and find affirmative action programs a constitutionally permissible remedy for past discrimination. Finally Powell, who provided the essential fifth vote, held that affirmative action programs were constitutionally permissible within limited and careful guidelines and procedures.

Powell used "exacting scrutiny," and under this approach he found that programs that discriminate on the basis of race, however worthwhile their intention, violate the Fourteenth Amendment. However, he also maintained that "educational diversity" is a laudable and constitutionally permissible goal; thus, affirmative action programs that promote diversity and are not solely premised on race will survive exacting scrutiny. Here, the University's approach focused solely on ethnicity, rendering it unconstitutional. Rather, true diversity includes other factors such as geography, and programs which seek true diversity would be viewed as constitutionally permissible.

5. The Backlash Against Affirmative Action in Education

In the aftermath of the *Bakke* decision, almost all schools rewrote their admissions policies to incorporate the concept of diversity. However, the concept and application remained problematic, and opposition continued to such programs. Opponents claimed that affirmative action programs resulted in reverse discrimination and violated the Fourteenth Amendment's sanction against preferences of any sort based on race. Perhaps most interestingly, the backlash to the Supreme Court's decision in *Bakke* has been seen both through legislative and public reactions as well as some recent court decisions which signal an increasing willingness to question the efficacy and propriety of affirmative action plans.

First, several states, including California and Washington, have over the years enacted legislation and state constitutional mandates against any type of affirmative action programs in college admissions. A list of all proposed ballot initiatives related to educational affirmative action appears in Table 6.1. Perhaps the most widely known incident concerns the successful passage of Proposition 209 in California. In 1996, 54% of California voters approved a ballot initiative amending the California Constitution to prohibit "preferential treatment to any individual or group on the basis of race, sex, color, ethnicity, or national origin in the operation of public employment, public education, or public contracting."

Table 6.1 Proposed State-Level Ballot Initiatives Concerning Educational Affirmative Action

State	Initiative Name	Amend Constitutional or Statutory Law	Year Initiative Appeared on Ballot	Enacted or Defeated
Arizona	Proposition 107	Constitution	2010	Enacted
California	Proposition 209	Constitution	1996	Enacted
Colorado	Amendment 46	Constitution	2008	Defeated
Michigan	Proposal 2	Constitution	2006	Enacted
Nebraska	Initiative 424	Constitution	2008	Enacted
Washington	Initiative 200	Statute	1998	Enacted

Much of the focus of the implications of Proposition 209 involved its effect on higher education. In 1995, the University of California regents passed a measure eliminating preferential admissions for graduate students (Golden 1997). The passage of Proposition 209 enshrined that action in the state constitution, and also extended its reach to undergraduate admissions. The initial results of Proposition 209, which went into effect for the 1997–1998 school year were striking: the number of minorities admitted to the freshman class at the UC system's premier school, the University of California at Berkeley, was cut in half, and the numbers were exceedingly low at Berkeley's law school, Boalt Hall. However, the following year saw a roughly 30% increase in the number of minority admits for both the undergraduate program and the law school (Traub 1999). And, one intriguing and unexpected side effect, as detailed by Traub, was the increase in state-funded outreach programs targeted at raising the academic performance of minority students. However, even though many people supported Proposition 209 and the abolishment of educational affirmative action, many of these same individuals were concerned about the decrease in minority enrollment. Thus, the regents—who initially banned affirmative action for graduate admissions in 1995—passed a measure as of 2001 that all students graduating in the top 4% of their class must be accepted to some University of California school.

A similar story occurred in the state of Washington. In the 1998 elections, Washington voters approved, with 58% support, a ballot initiative which amended state law concerning the use of affirmative action. Using almost the same language as Proposition 209, the initiative banned the use of preferential treatment in public education, along with public employment and public contracting. The major difference between the two state-level actions was that the Washington initiative did not also alter the state's constitution, thus allowing the possibility for a (more simple) legislative reversal in the future.

Since 1998, other ballot initiatives have also been successfully passed in Michigan (2006), Nebraska (2008) and Arizona (2010), while, to date, only one attempt has been defeated, that of Amendment 46 in Colorado in 2008. The initiatives in Michigan, Arizona and Colorado all mirrored the language utilized by both Texas and Washington. However, Nebraska's Initiative 424, specifically eliminates the use of affirmative action in admissions at the state's public colleges and universities. Thus, as will be discussed in more detail below, three of the five successful ballot initiatives were all proposed after the U.S. Supreme Court once again upheld the use of affirmative action programs in higher education.

The first successful legal challenges to *Bakke* occurred in 1996. In the case of *Hopwood v. Texas* (1996), the Fifth Circuit Court of Appeals struck down an affirmative action program utilized by the University of Texas Law School which was targeted at African American and Mexican American students. The Fifth Circuit determined that *Bakke* was no long applicable, and that past discrimination and diversity did not justify admissions-based affirmative action programs; thus, the use of race as a factor was prohibited. However, as a result of the initial case filing, the law school had changed its policy in 1994 to one that treated race as one of many factors. Consequently, the U.S. Supreme Court denied certiorari on appeal, stating that the case had been rendered moot by the law school's subsequent admissions policy changes (*Texas v. Hopwood* 1996). The effect of the Supreme Court's denial, however, was to leave the Fifth Circuit's opinion in effect in Louisiana, Mississippi and Texas, thus potentially complicating the use of any admissions procedures which utilized race—even if the program followed *Bakke*'s edict that race can only be used in conjunction with a multitude of other factors in the achievement of diversity. The State of Texas responded in part by passing H.B. 588 in 1997 which required the Texas university system to admit all students who graduated in the top 10% of their high school class to the public institution of their choice. The program was somewhat revised in 2009 to cap the number of students admitted each year under the program to no more than 75% of the entering class, as many universities were facing the possibility of 100% of their entering class being comprised of students admitted under the "10 Percent Plan."

Eventually the U.S. Supreme Court reentered the issue arena in a set of companion cases from the state of Michigan: Gratz v. Bollinger (2003), and *Grutter v. Bollinger* (2003). In *Gratz*, the Court struck down the University of Michigan's point-based undergraduate admissions policy, deeming it a race-based quota system. However, in *Grutter*, which concerned the Law School's admission policy, the Court reached the opposite result. And, the effect of this case was to abrogate the Fifth Circuit's decision in *Hopwood v. Texas*.

The *Grutter* case resulted from the University of Michigan Law School's attempt to draft its admissions policy to comply with *Bakke* in 1992. The policy states that the Law School's "goal is to admit a group of students who individually and collectively are among the most capable" and provides that the Law School "seeks a mix of students with varying backgrounds and experiences who will respect and learn from each other." According to the opinion, admissions officials read each application and factor all of the accompanying information into their decision. Officials must look beyond grades and scores to "soft variables," such as recommenders' enthusiasm, the quality of the applicant's undergraduate institution and written essay, and the areas and difficulty of undergraduate course selection. The policy does not define diversity solely in terms of racial and ethnic status and does not restrict the types of diversity contributions eligible for "substantial weight," but it does reaffirm the Law School's commitment to diversity with special reference to the inclusion of African American, Hispanic, and Native American students who otherwise might not be represented in the student body in meaningful numbers. The Law School argued that by enrolling a "critical mass" of underrepresented minority students, the admissions policy seeks to ensure their ability to contribute to the Law School's character and to the legal profession. Barbara Grutter, a white female Michigan resident with a 3.8 GPA and 161 LSAT score was denied admission and sued, claiming the policy violated the equal protection clause.

The Court, with a narrow 5-4 majority and Justice O'Connor writing the majority opinion, upheld the Law School's narrowly tailored use of race in admissions decisions to further its compelling interest in obtaining the educational benefits that flow from a diverse student body. O'Connor wrote that all governmental racial classifications must be analyzed under strict scrutiny, expanding the exacting scrutiny standard offered by Powell in *Bakke*. However, the Court made clear that not all uses of race-based classifications are invalidated by strict scrutiny. Race-based actions which are necessary to further a compelling governmental interest do not violate the equal protection clause so long as they are narrowly tailored to further that interest. O'Connor notes that Justice Powell's opinion constitutes *Bakke's* holding and provides the standard in *Grutter*—namely, that educational diversity is a compelling state interest that can justify using race in university admissions. O' Connor writes that

> The Law School's educational judgment that diversity is essential to its educational mission is one to which we defer.... Our scrutiny of the interest asserted by the Law School is no less strict for taking into account complex educational judgments in an area that lies primarily within the expertise of the university ... attaining a diverse student body is at the heart of the Law School's proper institutional mission ... the Law School seeks to "enroll a 'critical mass' of minority students." The Law School's interest is not simply "to assure some specified percentage of a particular group merely because of its race or ethnic origin." That would amount to outright racial balancing, which is patently unconstitutional. Rather, the Law School's concept of critical mass is defined by reference to the educational benefits that diversity is designed to produce. These benefits are substantial ... [including] promot[ing] "cross-racial understanding," help[ing] to break down racial stereotypes, and "enabl[ing] students to better understand persons of different races." (328–30)

Ginsburg's concurrence notes that many minority students continue to encounter inadequate and unequal educational opportunities. She argues that as primary and secondary education in minority communities improves, so too will the academic ability of students graduating from the schools in these communities. Thus, "from today's vantage point, progress toward nondiscrimination and genuinely equal opportunity will make it safe to sunset affirmative action" (346).

It should also be noted that the Court's majority has not responded as favorably toward affirmative action in general. While current precedent supports the notion of educational affirmative action programs targeted at ensuring educational diversity, the Court has at the same time moved to strike down similar programs in the area of employment. Table 6.2 lists the major affirmative action cases the Supreme Court has decided, including those in fields beyond educa-

Table 6.2 Major Supreme Court Affirmative Action Cases, 1978–2003

Case Name (Year)	Supreme Court Holding
Regents of the University of California v. Bakke (1978)	Struck down race-based admissions program, but also noted that admissions policies which sought "educational diversity" with race as one factor out of many would likely be found constitutional
Fullilove v. Klutznick (1980)	Upheld a federal law requiring 15% of funds for public works programs be awarded to minority contractors
Wygant v. Jackson Board of Education (1986)	Struck down a school board policy which protected minority employees over non-minority employees with greater seniority. The Court drew a distinction between the relatively small burden imposed by hiring plans as opposed to the larger burdens felt with layoff plans.
United States v. Paradise (1987)	Upheld remedial plan that forced the state of Alabama to both hire and promote African American state troopers according to strict quotas in response to continued, overt racial discrimination in hiring and promotion
City of Richmond v. Croson (1989)	Struck down a local-level minority set-aside program involving city construction funds. Held that affirmative action programs must be subject to "strict scrutiny" and suggested that the only potential justification for affirmative action programs in public contracting was remedying *de jure*, as opposed to *de facto*, discrimination.
Adarand Constructors, Inc. v. Pena (1995)	Struck down a federal minority set-aside program. The Court extended its holding in *Croson*, holding that only remedial programs would be able to withstand constitutional scrutiny
Gratz v. Bollinger (2003)	Struck down undergraduate admissions program at University of Michigan. The Court based its decision on the program's use of a rigid point system which resulted in a type of racial quota.
Grutter v. Bollinger (2003)	Upheld the admissions program at the University of Michigan Law School. The Court reaffirmed its decision in Bakke, holding that admissions programs targeted at achieving educational diversity were constitutionally permissible.

tion. Beginning in 1989 with its decision in *City of Richmond v. Croson* (1989), the Supreme Court has consistently struck down state and federal level affirmative action programs which are not strictly remedial in nature (see also *Adarand Constructors, Inc. v. Pena* 1995). In other words, while educational diversity can justify admissions programs which look to factors such as race, the Court has continually held that the only compelling reason for affirmative action programs in employment or contracting is to remedy clear *de jure* discrimination by the government, as opposed to seeking to ameliorate more societal-based harms. Education is given special status, as the Court has continually held that diversity in education has numerous benefits, including increased academic performance, better preparation for the workforce and society and increased potential to train national civic and military leaders (*Grutter v. Bollinger* at 330–33).

The response to the Supreme Court's decisions in *Gratz* and *Grutter* has for the most part been positive. In fact, amicus participation on the side of the University of Michigan included more than twenty-two states, over eighty different colleges, universities and law schools, along with a group of retired military leaders and a number of Fortune 500 corporations. The result was for most colleges and universities to continue using their respective admissions programs, or to revise them in accordance with the Court's holdings in the two cases. On the other hand, the backlash has been rather minimal: since 2003, voters in only four states have considered ballot initiatives restricting the use of affirmative action, and these measures were successfully enacted in three states. Thus, it appears that the Court's decisions in the realm of educational affirmative action have been viewed as well within the legislative–executive core, even by state-level elected officials and the public.

6. Equal Protection and Equal Educational Opportunity in the New Century

As we continue into the twenty-first century, the question raised by Justice Ginsburg's concurrence in *Grutter* continues to be asked: when will we have moved far enough away from the vestiges of *de jure* discrimination that affirmative action programs to remedy or help overcome such discrimination are no longer necessary? One of the most persistent and troubling issues in education policy is the finding of a very real achievement gap between white and minority students (Sirin 2005; U.S. Department of Education 2000), in part because of the link between minority status and lower socioeconomic status or neighborhood status (see e.g., Clune 1994; Dornbusch, Ritter and Steinberg 1991; Gonzales, Cauce, Friedman and Mason 1996). The question thus becomes whether affirmative action programs need to remain in place until a time when these clear achievement gaps have been eliminated or at least substantially minimized.

Additionally, the debate over affirmative action raises the question of whether student grades and standardized tests are, in fact, unbiased and accurate predictive measures of future success in school and beyond. Data and analyses, however, suggest these assumptions may be flawed. For example, in an article entitled "Nothing Personal," Bruce Headlam (2002) notes that since the *Bakke* decision in 1978, the debate has revolved more around the displacement of deserving white candidates by minority applicants—and less around their outcomes. A counterexample was provided by an unintended situation at the University of Texas Medical School. In 1979, the school initially selected one hundred and fifty first-year students from a pool of eight hundred interviewees. The state legislature then mandated that the class size be increased by fifty students, who had to be pulled from the bottom of the original pool. These fifty initially rejected students came in with inferior marks, poorer test scores and lower personal evaluations than the originally admitted students. However, at almost every measurable step during their medical education, their performance as a group was indistinguishable not just from the rest of their peers but also from the top 50 students in the class. A 1998 study provides similar evidence about the effects of educational affirmative action programs. In *The Shape of the River*, William Bowen and Derek Bok find that students admitted with the benefit of affirmative action performed only slightly below class averages, and, after graduation, outgained many of their peers.

The effect of educational affirmative action plans is to increase minority enrollments at premier universities and colleges. As shown in California and Texas, when racial preferences were prohibited from use altogether, minority enrollments fell. Thus, the Supreme Court's continuing support for such programs also means that these benefits will continue to be felt at institutions of higher learning across the country. The story, however, is not so simple: in both California and Texas, affirmative state-level efforts were made to try and address the problems noted above by working to improve the education received by minority students prior to high school education. An important question is whether affirmative action programs create a type of perverse incentive, whereby the use of affirmative action allows states and localities to ignore very real and troubling inequalities in primary and secondary education. In fact, such a critique—as well as a criticism of the idea of "unbiased" standardized tests—was raised by Justice Clarence Thomas in his dissent in *Grutter*. Justice Thomas noted in his dissent that most studies find that the Law School Admissions Test (LSAT) is systematically biased against minority students. Justice Thomas then questions why the response to this known inequality is affirmative action programs, rather than a move by schools to stop relying on a known biased source of information. In other words, Justice Thomas suggests that schools are justifying their affirmative action programs by refusing to address the source of the actual problem. And, until courts start disallowing such programs, schools will likely continue to rely on affirmative action programs rather than spending the time and effort to eradicate the real inequalities and discrimination.

The end result is that educational affirmative action programs have continued to be found constitutionally permissible by the Supreme Court, and these programs have ensured that minority students are able to attend colleges and universities and reap the benefits of higher education. The Court has also consistently recognized the tangible and intangible benefits of a diverse student population, especially in a country long-described as a melting pot. And, with the Court's support, the vast majority of colleges and universities follow the rules stipulated by the Court in *Bakke* and *Grutter*. The debate over affirmative action will continue to be argued in the courts for many years to come because of increasing resistance by the Court to affirmative action more broadly, as well as suggestions even by supporters of affirmative action that at some point such remedial efforts will no longer be necessary.

Part 2

STATE COURT POLICYMAKING

7

STATE COURT POLICYMAKING
School Finance Reform

1. Introduction

Up to this point, we have examined the ways in which the federal courts influence and in many cases make public and social policy when they hand down their rulings. In the United States, each state also has its own separate and distinct court system. These state courts can also substantially influence policy with their decisions; however, their decisions are binding only on the particular state. Thus, state courts, much like state legislatures (see e.g., Karch 2007; Volden 2006), often serve as minilaboratories for policy change. As Supreme Court Justice Louis Brandeis noted in a dissent, "It is one of the happy incidents of the federal system that a state may, if its citizens choose, serve as a laboratory; and try novel social and economic experiments without risk to the rest of the country" (*New State Ice Co. v. Liebmann* 1932). States, aided by state courts, can therefore craft policies which apply only to their states as well as serve as a type of laboratory where other states and outside actors can gauge the success of such policies or political strategies. State courts, like all courts, play an essential role in this laboratory function, and they are particularly powerful when they address issues that are constitutionally reserved to the states or can be addressed solely by examining state law.

Education policy provides an excellent counterpoint to the other court-influenced policy domains that we have explored so far because it is an area primarily dominated by state and not federal courts. This is particularly true in the area of education financing. There are several reasons for this development. First, education policy has traditionally been left to the states and principally local control. The U.S. Constitution does not contain any actual reference to education. However, almost all state constitutions contain specific educational clauses. Forty-nine state constitutions contain a clause or passage guaranteeing some type of free public education. This has not gone unnoticed by the U.S. Supreme Court. Chief Justice Warren stated in *Brown* that "education is perhaps the most important function of state and local governments…" (*Brown v. Board of Education I* 1954, at 493).

Second, public education is financed chiefly through local revenue, and most of that revenue derives from taxes on commercial and residential property. Although local districts do receive state and federal dollars for local education, almost one-half (46%) of primary and secondary public education funding throughout the United States comes from local funding (U.S. Department of Education 1990–2010). This means that the funding that is available throughout most states varies considerably from state to state and from district to district within each state. There is significant expenditure variation between states and districts and not all of it can be attributed to cost differentials between the states. For example, in the school year 1993–94, the state of New Jersey spent over $9,400 per pupil, while Utah spent one-third of that amount. New Jersey, on average, paid $17,000 in salary more per teacher than did Utah.

Third, significant variation exists not only between states, but within states. With property taxes providing around 50% of public school revenue for school expenditures it means that areas with better, more expensive homes and more businesses will have a larger property tax base to spend on education. Presumably a greater tax base means more spending on public schools, and more spending on public schools usually translates to better opportunities and better teachers at those schools.

This emphasis on local funding sources and the resultant inequality of resources creates the classical problem of circularity. The single biggest determinant of housing values in a particular area is the quality of public schools in the area (Kane, Riegg and Staiger 2006). The better the school, the higher are the property values, and the higher the property values, the greater the property tax base and thus the larger the amount of money to spend on public education.

Fourth and perhaps most importantly, the U.S. Supreme Court declined to take an active role in the area of education financing in the seminal case of *San Antonio Independent School District v Rodriguez* (1973). Because of this important decision, those opposed to the educational financing schemes which place a heavy emphasis on local revenues to fund public education had little recourse but to seek out state court relief. In some instances, state legislators reviewed and changed the school financing schemes, but in many others, litigants sought relief from the state courts in order to force state legislative relief. In this way, state courts have played a prominent role (Wilhelm 2007).

Education financing has received not only public, political and institutional attention, but also significant scholarly consideration. Economists, policy analysts, legal scholars and political scientists have all examined the issue from perspectives appropriate to each discipline. Legal scholars have examined the normative justifications for equal financing in education (see e.g., Coons, Clune and Sugarman 1970), and fashioned arguments based on equal protection, the creation of a suspect classification based on income disparity, and the use of state equal protection and guarantee of education clauses as justification. Economists and policy scholars (e.g. Evans, Murray and Schwab 1997; Wood and Theobald 2003) generally examine the issue of school finance from the perspective of impact (Evans et al. 1997) or revenue allocation (Wood and Theobald 2000). Thus, court or legislative action becomes a determination of citizens' tax burden and the issue becomes the potential trade-off of equity and efficiency. Finally, political scientists have examined school finance by examining judicial decision making (Bosworth 2001) and the impact of litigation on promoting changes in school financing, even if such litigation is unsuccessful (Gambitta 1981). They have also investigated whether policy change is more likely to occur through court or legislative action (Cann and Wilhelm 2011; Roch and Howard 2008).

In this chapter we examine this important area of policy and, specifically, the role of courts in changing school finance policies within states. We first examine the importance of public education and analyze efforts at the federal level to change local school financing and the U.S. Supreme Court's response, and then we turn to subsequent state-level efforts. We assess both initial litigation attempts and court responses to these efforts as well as the ensuing legislative responses to these court challenges. Finally, we offer our analysis of the efficacy of the use of state courts and state constitutions to effect change in this area.

2. The Importance of Education and the Supreme Court

Brown v. Board of Education I (1954) represented a significant milestone in the understanding of the importance of education in modern society. While concerned with whether school desegregation violated the equal protection clause of the U.S. Constitution, the opinion went much further than merely declaring segregation in public education unconstitutional. Chief Justice Earl Warren, the author of the Court's unanimous opinion, noted the key role public education plays in American life. Furthermore, the Court argued that it could not turn the clock back to 1868, the year of the adoption of the Fourteenth Amendment, nor even to 1896, the year the Supreme Court issued its decision in *Plessy v. Ferguson* upholding state-mandated segregation, when assessing the effects of segregation. Instead, to Warren and his brethren it was only relevant to consider public education in light of its present place in American life. The *Brown* opinion stated that "education is ... required in the performance of our most basic public responsibilities, even service in the armed forces. It is the very foundation of good citizenship.... In these days, it is doubtful that any child may reasonably be expected to succeed in life if he is denied the opportunity of an education" (493). Segregation, the opinion went on to hold, engendered a feeling of inferiority in black school children, impeding their educational and mental development.

Brown v. Board of Education fostered the idea that education helps create the shared experiences that are critical for opening and sustaining a dialogue between the sometimes seemingly disparate groups that reside in the United States. Perhaps more importantly, education also acts as an agent of social mobility, and equal access to education helps sustain a sense of possibility—of someday attaining the "American dream." However, the Supreme Court's decision in *San*

Antonio Independent School District v. Rodriguez (1973) appeared to alter the position of the Court on education.

3. *San Antonio Independent School District v. Rodriguez* (1973)

Even with the Court's decision in *Brown v. Board of Education* and the subsequent commitment of the national government to educational equality, funding disparities made the goal of equal education seem distant and unobtainable for those students who attended schools in poor districts. These funding disparities created a form of unequal educational opportunity that *Brown* and its progeny could not solve.

In an attempt to remedy these disparities, a lawsuit was brought in the federal district court for the Western District of Texas in 1968 by members of the Edgewood Concerned Parent Association. The Edgewood school district was part of the greater San Antonio, Texas school system. The parents represented their children and similarly situated students. In the initial complaint, the parents sued five other wealthier school districts, including Alamo Heights. Eventually the school districts were dropped from the case and the state of Texas became the sole defendant.

The parents argued that the "Texas method of school financing violated the equal protection clause of the Fourteenth Amendment to the U. S. Constitution." The lawsuit alleged, following the dictates of *Brown*, that education was a fundamental right and that wealth-based discrimination in the provision of education created in the poor, or those of lesser wealth, a constitutionally suspect class. To support their argument, the plaintiffs offered data demonstrating the disparity between the Edgewood and Alamo school districts. The funding each received on average per pupil is listed in Table 7.1 below.

Although Edgewood received more federal aid than Alamo, this greater amount of federal aid could not compensate for the more than ten times disparity in local funding available to spend per pupil. Based on subsequent agreed upon data, this difference was enormous. For example, in the 1968–69 school year

all of the Alamo Heights teachers had college degrees, while 80% of the Edgewood teachers had them; 37.17% of the Alamo Heights teachers had advanced degrees, while 14.98% of the Edgewood teachers had

Table 7.1 Comparison of Financing of San Antonio School Districts

Aid Source:	Edgewood	Alamo Heights
Local	$26.00/pupil	$333.00/pupil
State	$222.00/pupil	$225.00/pupil
Federal	$108.00/pupil	$36.00/pupil
Total	$356.00/pupil	$594.00/pupil

them; 11% of the Alamo Heights teachers depended on emergency teaching permits, while 47% of the Edgewood teachers depended on them; Alamo Heights' maximum teaching salary was 25% greater than Edgewood's maximum salary; Alamo Heights' teacher-student ratio was 1 to 20.5, while Edgewood's was 1 to 26.5; and Alamo Heights provided one counselor for every 645 students, while Edgewood provided one counselor for every 3,098 students. (Sutton 2008 citing brief of petitioner)

These disparities existed despite the fact that Edgewood property owners actually paid higher property tax rates. The property values in Edgewood were simply insufficient to cover the disparity with the wealthier districts. After the plaintiffs won in a decision issued by a three-judge district court panel, the state appealed to the Supreme Court. The Court did not hear arguments in the case until the fall of 1972 and the decision was not released until 1973.

The state of Texas was represented by Charles Alan Wright, a University of Texas law professor. Wright, who would later represent President Richard Nixon during the Watergate investigation, was a famed scholar of constitutional law and civil procedure and had extensive experience arguing before the Supreme Court. For Wright, the argument was simple: while acknowledging the disparity and admitting that the state should do a better job, there was simply no federal constitutional right to equal education. The equal protection clause did not apply to wealth and income, and thus wealth and income did not constitute any sort of protected class demanding greater Supreme Court scrutiny.

The 1973 Burger court consisted of four justices appointed by President Richard Nixon—Chief Justice Warren Burger, and Associate Justices Lewis Powell, Harry Blackmun and William Rehnquist. They replaced Chief Justice Earl Warren, and Associate Justices Black, Fortas and Harlan. The Segal-Cover scores, which, as discussed in detail in Chapter 1, measure each justice's ideology through content analysis of newspaper editorials at the time of his or her confirmation, and run from 0 (most conservative) to 1 (most liberal), for the four retired justices were as follows:

1. Earl Warren: .75
2. Abe Fortas: 1.00
3. Hugo Black: .875
4. John Harlan: .875

The replacement ideology scores were as follows:

1. Warren Burger: .115
2. Harry Blackmun: .115
3. Lewis Powell, Jr.: .165
4. William Rehnquist: .045

The average ideology score for the four retired justices is .88, extremely liberal. The average ideology score for the four replacement justices is .11, very conservative. That is an average drop of more than .75, moving from liberal to conservative. Thus, some of the most liberal justices in the history of the U.S. Supreme Court, and some of the most important members of the Warren Court, were replaced by much more conservative justices. It is true that justice ideology is not constant (Epstein et al. 1998) and that Harry Blackmun, whose voting record so matched his friend and fellow Minnesotan Warren Burger that the two were referred to as the "Minnesota Twins" (Yarbrough 2008, ch. 6), did significantly deviate from his early conservative voting record the longer he sat on the bench (Greenhouse 2005). However, at the time of the *Rodriguez* decision, Blackmun still had a more conservative voting record, matching that of his sponsor, Warren Burger.

These four relatively new justices, along with Justice Potter Stewart, a Republican Eisenhower appointee, constituted the Supreme Court majority in *Rodriguez* and voted in favor of the state of Texas, rejecting the argument of the parents; Justice Stewart also filed a concurring opinion. Four justices, William O. Douglas, William Brennan, Thurgood Marshall and Byron White, supported the school district.

Justice Lewis Powell was both the swing vote and the majority opinion author. Powell, who had served on the Richmond Virginia Board of Education, wrote that education was "neither 'explicitly nor implicitly' protected in the Constitution," nor was there a suspect class related to poverty. This opinion allowed the state to continue its school financing plan so long as it was "rationally related to a legitimate state interest."

Thus, the effect of the Supreme Court's ruling was to clarify that "the Constitution did not prohibit the government from providing different services to children in poor school districts than it did to children in wealthy school districts" (Van Slyke, Tan and Orland 1994, 8). This decision effectively precluded any further court action at the federal level.

4. Adequate and Independent State Grounds and State Court Response

This result, however, did not preclude further court action at the state level. If a state court ruling relies solely on interpretations of state constitutional law, then its decisions are unreviewable by the federal courts; as Justice William Brennan explained: "We are utterly without jurisdiction to review such state decisions" (1977, 501). The supremacy clause of the U.S. Constitution, which makes the federal constitution and congressional law controlling over contrary state law, requires that state courts make decisions based on their understanding of applicable federal law, as well as the laws of their state. The historic case of *Martin v. Hunter's Lessee* (1816) confirmed that the U.S. Supreme Court has the final authority to review state court interpretations of federal law.

In *Martin*, a dispute arose over whether the state of Virginia could confiscate land held by a British Loyalist, when a treaty between England and the United States prevented confiscations. The U.S. Supreme Court held that the treaty superseded state law. The Virginia Supreme Court than argued that the U.S. Supreme Court did not have the power to review judgments issued by state courts of appeals. The U.S. Supreme Court held in *Martin* that it does not have appellate jurisdiction over state court rulings when those rulings concern questions of federal law.

However, the same principal does not exist for state court interpretations of state law. State high courts of last resort are the supreme arbiters of state law. The principle laid down by the U.S. Supreme Court in *Murdock v. City of Memphis* (1875) held that the U.S. Supreme Court could not review a decision of a state high court unless it involved an application of federal law—this is the principle known as adequate and independent state grounds. Put more simply, under the doctrine of adequate and independent state grounds, state high court decisions that are based on state law and independent of federal interpretation are outside the jurisdiction of the federal courts and, thus, nonreviewable by the U.S. Supreme Court (see *Michigan v. Long* 1983).

As a result, states can provide more expansive protections for their citizens through their constitutions, and decisions pertaining to the U.S. Constitution do not trump decisions which are based solely on interpretations of these state laws (see e.g., Tarr 1994). In particular, Justice William Brennan advocated that persons seeking individual rights and protections should look to their state constitutions, a concept known as "new judicial federalism." In a seminal 1977 article, Justice Brennan argued that "state courts cannot rest when they have afforded their citizens the full protections of the federal Constitution. State constitutions, too, are a font of individual liberties, their protections often extending beyond those required by the Supreme Court's interpretation of federal law" (491). And, it appears state courts were amenable to Justice Brennan's suggestion to do so: between 1970 and 1986, a study found over three hundred cases in which state judges utilized state constitutional provisions to provide greater individual rights than would be available through the U.S. Constitution (Collins and Galie 1986); in contrast, in a separate study they found only ten such cases between 1950 and 1969 (Collins, Galie and Kincaid 1986). In addition, states have at times interpreted provisions of state constitutions quite liberally, even when those provisions are similar or even identical to the U.S. Constitution. In a 1974 case concerning criminal due process rights, the Supreme Court of Hawaii explained that "while [our interpretation] results in a divergence of meaning between words which are the same in both federal and state constitutions, the system of federalism envisaged by the United States Constitution tolerates such divergence where the result is greater protection of individual rights under state law than under federal law" (*State v. Kaluna* 1974, 58, note 6).

In terms of educational financing, the doctrine of adequate and independent state grounds means that the U.S. Constitution and the U.S. Supreme Court do not necessarily have the final say in how a state chooses to finance public education. Instead if the state legislature fails to find an acceptable solution to school funding, litigants can turn to state constitutions and state courts for remedies. And, this doctrine then precludes the U.S. Supreme Court from even reviewing the state high court's decision if that decision is premised solely on its own laws and own state constitution.

Premised on the concept of adequate and independent state grounds, even before *Rodriguez*, state courts were pressed to use their state constitutions to alter state educational finance schemes. Every state has its own state constitution. Many contain language or clauses very similar to those found in the U.S. Constitution; however, the content of state constitutions varies considerably, often incorporating different language to articulate the legal rights of their citizens or extending overt protections that the U.S. Constitution does not.

One prominent example is that of constitutional provisions concerning education. Most state constitutions have provisions guaranteeing free public education. The very first state court case came out of California. In *Serrano v. Priest* (1971), the California Supreme Court demonstrated the potential effectiveness of the state courts as tools for education finance reform by overturning the California school finance system. One month after *Rodriguez*, the New Jersey Supreme Court in *Robinson v. Cahill* (1973) overturned the New Jersey educational finance system. These were the first in a series of state education finance cases that continues on until today, and the use of state courts gathered momentum following the *Rodriguez* decision. As of December 2009, forty-four states have experienced some form of state education finance litigation.[1] We list the states and their litigation efforts from 1971 through 2009 in Table 7.2.

In all there have been ninety-eight state court cases filed to remedy some aspect of school funding. Several of these cases have reached the highest courts in the applicable state and several are still pending even today. Some of the newer cases represent new legal actions, while a number of the cases either seek enforcement of previous court opinions or orders or additional legislative enactment of court rulings, or represent attempts to overturn previous court orders mandating finance reform. While six states have seen no litigation, other states have seen multiple court cases.

In the decade that followed *Rodriguez* cases originated in the West (California, Washington, Wyoming), East (New Jersey, Connecticut and Pennsylvania), Midwest (Ohio) and the South (Georgia, West Virginia). These states range from states with large concentrations of Democratic voters to states dominated by the Republican Party. Some of the states are urban and industrial with a high per capita income, while others are much more rural with a dominance of agriculture and much poorer. There thus seems to be no particular geographic, state wealth or state ideological pattern to the litigation.

Despite the early success of cases in California and New Jersey, much of the early phases of the litigation were often unsuccessful. These unsuccessful attempts relied on state constitution equal protections clauses. However, as

Table 7.2 List of State Cases on Education Finance

State	Case(s)	Year
Alabama	*Siegelman v. Alabama Association of School Boards,*	2001
Alaska	*Kasayulie v.State,*	2005
	Moore v. State	2007
Arizona	*Crane Elementary School District v. State of Arizona*	2003
	Roosevelt Elementary School Dist. No. 66 v. Bishop	1994
	Espinoza v. Arizona	2006
Arkansas	*DuPree v. Alma School District*	1983
	Lake View School District v. Huckabee	2007
California	*Serrano v. Priest*	1971
	Serrano v. Priest (Serrano II)	1977
Colorado	*Lujan v. Colorado State Board of Education*	1982
	Lobato v. State	2008
Connecticut	*Horton v. Meskill*	1977
	Sheff v. O'Neill	1996
Delaware	No Case	
Florida	*Coalition for Adequacy And Fairness in School Funding v. Chiles*	1996
	School Board of Miami-Dade County v. King	2006
Georgia	*McDaniel v. Thomas*	1981
Hawaii	No Case	
Idaho	*Idaho Schools for Equal Educational Opportunity v. State*	2005
Illinois	*Committee for Educational Rights v. Edgar*	1996
	Lewis E. v. Spagnolo	1999
Indiana	*Bonner v. Daniels*	2009
Iowa	No Case	
Kansas	*Unified School District No. 229 v. State*	1994
	Montoy v. Kansas	2003
	Caldwell v. State	1972
Kentucky	*Rose v. The Council for Better Education*	1989
	Young v. Williams	2007
Louisiana	*Charlet v. Legislature of the State of Louisiana*	1998
Maine	*School Administrative District No. 1 v. Commissioner*	1994
Maryland	*Bradford v. Maryland State Board of Education*	2005
	Hornbeck v. Somerset County Board of Education	1983
Massachusetts	*McDuffy v. Secretary*	1993
	Hancock v. Driscoll	2005
Michigan	*Durant v. State*	1997
	Milliken v. Green	1973
Minnesota	*Skeen v. State*	1993

(continued)

Table 7.2 Continued

State	Case(s)	Year
Mississippi	No Case	
Missouri	*Committee for Educational Equality v. State of Missouri*	2007
Montana	*Helena Elementary School District No. 1 v. State*	1989
	Columbia Falls Elementary School District No. 6 v. Montana	2005
New Hampshire	*Claremont School District v. Governor*	1993
	Claremont v. Governor (Claremont II)	1997
	Claremont v. Governor (Claremont III)	1999
	Londonderry School District v. State of New Hampshire	1993
Nebraska	*Gould v. Orr*	1993
	Neb. Coal. for Educational Equity and Adequacy v. Heineman	2007
Nevada	No Case	
New Jersey	*Robinson v. Cahill*	1973
	Abbott v. Burke	2009
	Abbott v. Burke (Abbott IV)	1997
	Abbott v. Burke (Abbott V)	1998
	Abbott v. Burke, (Abbott VI)	2000
New Mexico	*Zuni School District v. State*	1999
New York	*Campaign for Fiscal Equity, Inc. v. State*	2003
	Levittown v. Nyquist	1982
North Carolina	*Leandro v. State*	1997
	Britt v. North Carolina State Board of Education	1987
	Hoke County Board of Education v. State,	2000
North Dakota	*Bismarck Public School District No. 1 v. State*	1994
Ohio	*Board of Education of Cincinnati v. Walter*	1976
	DeRolph v. State (DeRolph I)	1997
	DeRolph II	2000
	De Rolph III	2001
Oklahoma	*Fair School Finance Council of Oklahoma v. State*	1987
	Oklahoma Education Association v. State	2007
Oregon	*Pendleton School District v. State of Oregon*	2009
	Coalition for Equitable School Funding v. State	1991
	Olsen v. State	1976
	Withers v. State	1995
	Withers v. State (Withers II)	1999
Pennsylvania	*Danson v. Casey*	1979
	Marrero v. Commonwealth	1998
	Pennsylvania Association of Rural and Small Schools v. Ridge	1998
Rhode Island	*City of Pawtucket v. Sundlun*	1995
South Carolina	*Richland County v. Campbell*	1988
South Dakota	*Bezdicheck v. State*	1995

State	Case(s)	Year
Tennessee	*Tennessee Small School Systems v. McWherter (Small Schools I)*	1993
	Tennessee Small School Systems v. McWherter (Small Schools II)	1995
	Tennessee Small School Systems v. McWherter (Small Schools III)	2002
Texas	*Edgewood Independent School District v. Kirby (Edgewood I)*	1989
	Edgewood II	1991
	Edgewood III	1992
	Edgewood IV	1995
	West Orange-Cove Consolidated ISD v. Neeley	2005
Utah	No Case	
Vermont	*Brigham v. State*	1997
Virginia	*Scott v. Commonwealth*	1994
Washington	*Seattle School District No. 1 v. State*	1978
	Federal Way School District v. State of Washington	2006
West Virginia	*Pauley v. Kelly*	1979
	Pauley v. Bailey	1984
	Tomblin v. Gainer	1995
Wisconsin	*Kukor v. Grover*	1989
	Vincent v. Voight	2000
Wyoming	*Washakie County School District v. Herschler*	1980
	Campbell County School District v. State (Campbell I)	1995
	Campbell County School District v. State (Campbell II)	2001

previously noted, almost all states have some form of constitutional provision that guarantees a free public education. Some of these constitutional clauses are very short, vague and imprecise while others are quite specific and lengthy. For example, the Kansas Constitution (Article 6, Section 1) speaks only of "establishing and maintaining public schools," while the Colorado Constitution merely guarantees the "maintenance of a thorough and uniform system of free public schools throughout the state" (Article 9, Section 2). In contrast, the Idaho Constitution (Article 9, Section 1) calls for a "general, uniform and thorough system of public, free, common schools," while the Minnesota Constitution calls for a "uniform system of public schools." The Minnesota Constitution goes on to note, "[T]he stability of a republican form of government depending mainly upon the intelligence of the people, it is the duty of the legislature to establish a general and uniform system of public schools. The legislature shall make such provisions by taxation or otherwise as will secure a thorough and efficient system of public schools throughout the state" (Article 13).

These education provisions act as a lens through which litigants and judges can assess the degree of inequality within a state and decide whether the inequalities are in fact great enough to justify reform through the courts. All else being equal, the stronger the educational provisions in the state constitutions, the more likely that finance reform litigation will be successful.

In addition, given our discussions of the legal set and electoral preferences, strong constitutional provisions might make legislative action less likely and court action more likely. Legislatures also make strategic calculations. Political scientist James Rogers (2001, 88) argues that legislatures will prefer to have the courts repeal laws due to the high transaction costs associated with legislative repeal and the information asymmetry between courts and legislatures. Of course, if the legislature believes that the policy preferences of the court differ from their own, then they must consider that potential action through the courts may restrict their future ability to achieve their preferred policy goals. In this case, a prospective legislature may act to circumvent action by the court.

Thus, legislatures in states with strong constitutional provisions might want the court to take action so as to avoid voting on unpopular legislation. No matter how a legislator votes on school finance reform, some constituency is going to be upset and the calculations often go beyond mere politics or partisanship. For example, normally one would expect Democrats to favor school finance reform. However, teachers' unions are often opposed to such measures. Some scholars have noted that teachers' unions are often seen as opposing any and all types of education reform (Boyd, Plank and Sykes 1998), while other scholars have commented that large public school bureaucracies, which are generally dominated by teachers' unions, often have interests in conflict with the reform aspirations of parents (Nechyba and Heise 2000). Reform is seen as a threat to the income and livelihood of the union membership and is therefore opposed by the union. Wealthy suburban districts, which are often a core base for Republican elected officials, usually oppose school finance reform, but rural constituencies, another part of the Republican electoral base, often have underfunded schools and seek education finance reform.

This process seems to have occurred in the realm of school financing as those seeking to remove or lessen funding disparities found little recourse in the state legislatures. After the initial lack of success using state constitution equal protection clauses, litigants began to use the state constitution education clauses with much more success. In fact, most of the later cases used the state education clauses to challenge the finance systems.

Of course, as we have noted, not all of the educational clauses are equally as strong. Several scholars have examined these provisions and have classified the educational clauses by the strength of the language used to support education. Ratner (1985) created a four tiered system ranking these provisions, while Roch and Howard (2008) created a three part ranking system. While some (Tractenberg n.d.) have noted that some states with weak constitutional provisions have ordered education finance reform, Roch and Howard (2008) found strong support for courts relying on specific constitutional language to order court reform. A review of outcomes in the states shows some support for this finding. Table 7.3 below lists states and the outcomes of court cases, the constitutional strength of the education clauses, whether the courts that ruled on the issue were either liberal, moderate or conservative, and finally in the last

Table 7.3 List of State Education Related Cases: Outcomes by Constitutional Provision, State Ideology and Selection System

State	Outcome	Constitutional Provision	Ideology	Appointed/ Merit
Alabama	System upheld	Strong	moderate	No
Alaska	Plaintiff Victory	Weak	Conservative	Yes
Arizona	Mixed results	Strong	Conservative	Yes
Arkansas	Plaintiff Victory	Strong	moderate	No
California	Plaintiff Victory	Strong	Liberal	Yes
Colorado	Mixed Results	Weak	Conservative	Yes
Connecticut	Plaintiff Victory	Strong	Liberal	Yes
Delaware	No Case	Strong	moderate	Yes
Florida	System Upheld	Strong	Conservative	Yes
Georgia	System Upheld	Weak	Conservative	No
Hawaii	No Case	N/A	Liberal	Yes
Idaho	Plaintiff Victory	Strong	Conservative	No
Illinois	System Upheld	Strong	moderate	No
Indiana	System Upheld	Strong	moderate	Yes
Iowa	No Case	Very weak	Conservative	Yes
Kansas	Plaintiff Victory	Weak	Conservative	Yes
Kentucky	Plaintiff Victory	Strong	moderate	No
Louisiana	System Upheld	Weak	moderate	No
Maine	System Upheld	Weak	moderate	Yes
Maryland	Plaintiff Victory	Strong	Liberal	Yes
Massachusetts	Plaintiff Victory	Weak	Liberal	Yes
Michigan	System Upheld	Weak	moderate	No
Minnesota	System Upheld	Strong	moderate	No
Mississippi	No Case	Very Weak	Conservative	No
Missouri	Plaintiff Victory	Weak	Conservative	Yes
Montana	Plaintiff Victory	Strong	Liberal	No
New Hampshire	Plaintiff Victory	Strong	moderate	Yes
Nebraska	System Upheld	Weak	Conservative	No
Nevada	No Case	Weak	Conservative	Yes
New Jersey	Plaintiff Victory	Strong	Liberal	Yes
New Mexico	Plaintiff Victory	Strong	Conservative	No
New York	Plaintiff Victory	Weak	Liberal	Yes

(continued)

Table 7.3 Continued

State	Outcome	Constitutional Provision	Ideology	Appointed/ Merit
North Carolina	Plaintiff Victory	Strong	moderate	No
North Dakota	Plaintiff Victory	Strong	moderate	No
Ohio	Plaintiff Victory	Strong	moderate	No
Oklahoma	System Upheld	Weak	moderate	Yes
Oregon	System Upheld	Strong	Conservative	No
Pennsylvania	System Upheld	Strong	moderate	No
Rhode Island	System Upheld	Weak	Liberal	Yes
South Carolina	Plaintiff Victory	Weak	moderate	Yes
South Dakota	System Upheld	Weak	Conservative	Yes
Tennessee	Plaintiff Victory	Weak	Liberal	Yes
Texas	Plaintiff Victory	Strong	moderate	No
Utah	No Case	Weak	Conservative	Yes
Vermont	Plaintiff Victory	Weak	Liberal	Yes
Virginia	System Upheld	Strong	moderate	Yes
Washington	Plaintiff Victory	Strong	moderate	No
West Virginia	Plaintiff Victory	Strong	moderate	No
Wisconsin	System Upheld	Strong	moderate	No
Wyoming	Plaintiff Victory	Strong	moderate	Yes

*Source for Outcomes: National Access Network, Teachers College, Columbia University

column, lists the selection method by which high court justices are seated on the bench—specifically, whether the judges are appointed in some fashion or elected in some manner.

Please note a caveat in using this table. Courts have ruled on educational finance reform over almost a thirty-year period, and state constitutions, including education provisions, change over time. State constitutions change at a much higher rate than the U.S. Constitution. The table does not match the exact year or years of the rulings with the exact year of the constitutional language. Nonetheless it is in large part correct and provides some interesting information. We see from Table 7.3 quite a mixture of success and failure for those who have used the courts to seek educational finance reform.

First we note that in seventeen states, the finance/taxing scheme has been upheld by the courts. In contrast, in twenty-five states plaintiffs have won a legal victory calling for the dismantling of the existing finance/taxing scheme. Two states have had mixed results, while six have not had any legal action or result. If we assume no legal action means that there has not been any change, an assumption strengthened by the fact that most of the states that have no legal outcomes are states with weak constitutional provisions, then the results are remarkably even. Half the states have seen court ordered change, and half have not.

Examining the constitutional provisions provides some evidence to support the idea of the linkage between strong constitutional provisions and litigation success. Of the twenty-two states with weak state educational constitutional provisions, plaintiffs won only eight of the cases or 37%, slightly more than one-third. Of the twenty-eight states with strong constitutional provisions, plaintiffs won fourteen of those cases, or 50%. Thus, again all else being equal, a strong constitutional provision seems more likely to lead to a favorable result for those challenging the current educational financing scheme.

In our introduction and our earlier chapters we have emphasized judicial ideology in our examination of courts and policy and in our discussion of the myth of the neutral judge. We have promoted the idea that judges' choices are a result of conscious decisions to influence and change policy in accordance with their policy preferences. We also use Table 7.3 to provide some analysis of the extent of ideological influence on rulings in this area.

As we discussed in Chapter 1, the dominant gauge of state court ideology is a measure developed by political scientists Paul Brace, Laura Langer and Melinda Gann Hall (2000). They refer to the measure as party adjusted judicial ideology (PAJID). For ease of presentation and discussion we reclassified these scores in our table into either liberal, moderate or conservative. We simply divided the actual scores into three categories with under 25 classified as conservative, 25 to 50 as moderate and over 50 as liberal. We used the average PAJID score at the time of the appropriate ruling for the analysis. That information is presented in the last column of Table 7.3.

At the time of the decisions, and based on their average PAJID score, we classified eleven courts as liberal, twenty-three as moderate and sixteen as conservative. Examining the rulings, we find that in the eleven liberal courts, plaintiffs won nine times or 82% of the time. Plaintiffs won eleven out of twenty-three times in the courts that are classified as moderate, for a 48% success rate. Plaintiffs won on only five out of sixteen occasions, or 31% of the time, when the courts were conservative. Again, the evidence shows ideology has some influence on this issue area.

Finally state courts have many different and varied institutional structures and constraints. Some are elected, some are appointed and some are appointed through a merit plan; some are appointed and then subject to retention elections. Some sit on courts of five judges, while others sit on courts with many more judges. Some states have intermediate appellate courts, while others do not. As we have already noted, state constitutional language can vary significantly from state to state. Because of these differences, there is a shifting dynamic in the policy arena depending upon the state. State courts have policymaking power but the extent of their ability to impose a legal set on policy outcomes will vary depending on the political and structural environment within which the courts exist. For our final examination, we assess whether the judges in each state serve on appointed or elected courts to see which type of court is more likely to order educational finance reform.

Twenty-eight states have some form of appointed or merit-based appointed state high court selection system. Of these twenty-eight states, seventeen found for the plaintiff and ordered finance reform for a plaintiff winning percentage of 61%. Twenty-two states have some form of electoral selection mechanism for high court judges and here eleven plaintiffs won, for a 50% victory rate. Thus it appears that all else being equal, appointed courts are more likely to order finance reform.

5. Courts and Legislatures

As we have argued throughout this book, courts do not exist in a vacuum. Courts can alter policy through the imposition of a legal set within the framework of policy options left them by the legislative and executive branches of government. While we have focused on federal policymaking in earlier chapters, this same dynamic exists within the state framework. However, there can be and usually are significant differences between federal court and federal elected official interactions and state court and state elected official interactions. State courts have policymaking power but the extent of each court's ability to impose a legal set on policy outcomes will vary depending on the political and structural environment within which the court exists. In Table 7.4 below, we list states that have attempted to reform education finance subsequent to a court ruling.

As we can see, many states responded to court orders, either through legislation or state constitutional amendments. Several states had multiple legislative changes in response to court rulings over time. However, Table 7.4 does not tell us why these states and not others changed their state laws in response to the court orders, or why states needed courts, and not the legislature, to initiate the process. To better understand this process, we now discuss some of the dynamics unique to state court–legislative interactions and how that dynamic influences state policymaking.

Many social, demographic, political, institutional and structural circumstances help determine legislative responses to education finance inequality or court-ordered education finance reform. State courts and state legislatures are both embedded in the same larger political environment, but their decision context is likely to differ. Electoral constraints cause legislatures to act as prospective decision makers—they are likely to be concerned with assessing the probabilities of the effect of potential legislation (Krehbiel 1991; Mayhew 1974). Thus, information in the policy environment that increases the legislature's certainty about the relationship between a bill and a set of preferred policy outcomes usually increases the likelihood of legislative action.

Table 7.4 State Legislative Responses to State Court Ordered Education Finance Reform

State	Amendment Statute/Constitution	Cases Prompting Amendment
Arizona	Ariz. Rev. Stat. § 15-2031 (Supp. 2002)	Roosevelt Elementary School Dist. No. 66 v. Bishop (1994)
Arkansas	Ark. Code Ann. § 6-20-301 - 319 (Repealed 1993)	Dupree v. Alma School Dist. No. 30 (1983)
	Acts 916 and 917 of 1995	Lakeview v. State (trial court decision)
	Act 57 & 109 of the 2nd Extraordinary Session 2003	Lakeview School District No. 25 v. Huckabee (2002)
	Amended Act 59 by Act 2283, 2007 Ark. Acts 272	Lakeview School District No. 25 v. Huckabee (2005)
California	Stats. 1972, ch. 1406; Stats. 1973, ch. 208	Serrano v. Priest, 487 P.2d 1241 (1971)
Colorado	§§ 22-53-101 to -208, 9 C.R.S. (1988),	In response to a trial court case that was later dismissed
Connecticut	C.R.S. 22-54-101 et seq.	Horton v. Meskill (1977)
	Conn. Gen. Stat. § 10 et seq.	Sheff v. O'Neill (1995)
Idaho	I.C. § 33-1017(7)-(12) and I.C. § 39-8001 et seq	ISEEO v. State (1998)
Kansas	Sch. Dist. Equal. (SDEA) in 1973, L. 1973, ch. 292	Caldwell v. State (Aug. 30 1972)
	K.S.A. 72-6405 et seq.	Unified School District No. 229 v. State (1994)
	H.B. 2247, S.B. 3 S.B. 549 (Kan. 2005)	Montoy v. State (2005)
Kentucky	Ky Education Reform Act of 1990, Ky. Acts Ch. 476.	Rose v. Council for Better Education (1989)
Maryland	Senate Bill 856 of the 2002 Legislative Session	Bradford v. Maryland State Board of Education (2000)
Massachusetts	Mass. Gen. Laws ch. 71, § 1 et seq. (Act)	Town of Holden v. Wachusett Reg'l Sch. Dist. Comm. (2005)
Missouri	§ 160.500 R.S.Mo. et seq.	Educational Equality v. State (1993)
Montana	Mont. Code Anno., § 20-9-101 et seq.	Helena Elementary School District v. State, 784 P.2d 412 (1990)

(continued)

Table 7.4 Continued

State	Amendment Statute/Constitution	Cases Prompting Amendment
New Hampshire	RSA 193-E:2	*Claremont v. Governor, 744 A.2d 1107 (1999)*
New Jersey	N.J. Stat. Ann. § 18A:7F-1 - 7F-33,	*Abbott v. Burke, 575 A.2d 359 (1990 & 1997)*
New York	NY CLS Educ § 211-d (2007)	*Campaign for Fiscal Equity v. State (828 N.Y.S. 2d 235)*
Ohio	Am. Sub. H.B. 94 (Ohio 2001)	*DeRolph v. State (2001)*
Tennessee	Tenn. Code Ann. §§ 49-3-351 to -360	*Tennessee Small School Sys. v. McWherter (1993)*
Texas	Senate Bill 1 (1990), 351 (1992)	*Edgewood Indep. Sch. Dist. v. Kirby (1989 & 1991)*
	Tex. S.J. Res. 7, 73rd Leg.1993 Tex. Gen. Laws 5560	*Carrollton-Farmers Sch. Dist. v. Edgewood. Sch. Dist. (1992)*
Vermont	Equal Ed. Opportunity Act (Act 60); 1997 Vt. ALS 60	*Brigham v. State (1997)*
Washington	Rev. Code Wash. (ARCW) § 28A.150.200 (1977)	*Northshore School Dist. v. Kinnear (1977)*
	Rev. Code Wash. (ARCW) § 28A.150.250 (1983)	*Seattle School District No. 1 v. State (1982)*
	Rev. Code Wash. (ARCW) § 84.52.0531	*Fed. Way Sch. Dist. No. 210 v. State, 219 (2009)*
West Virginia	West Virginia Code § 18-2E-5 (1998)	Trial Court order of April, 2, 1997 (unknown citation)
Wyoming	1983 WY Session Laws, Ch. 136, p. 399-400	*Washakie County Sch. Dist. v. Herschler (1980)*
Wyoming	WY Stat. § 21-9-101 (2002)	*State v. Campbell County Sch. Dist., 19 P.3d 518 (2001)*

Courts, on the other hand, are ill suited to act as prospective decision makers. They usually possess neither the electoral authority nor the information to realize the impact of their decisions on future allocations of resources (see Fuller 1960). Moreover, their agenda is reactive as opposed to proactive (Baumgartner 2001). Adjudication and lawmaking are very different, with the relevant actors focusing on very different factors. Courts must wait until a lawsuit appears on their docket before they can take any action.[2] Because of this, courts are more likely to act as retrospective decision makers—they are interested in the realized impact of existing laws (see Rogers 2001, 84), and in ensuring that the prospective decision makers follow established constitutional rules and boundaries.

For example, state culture might lead to different responses by the legislatures and the courts. Elazar (1966) characterizes the American political culture as having three distinct subcultures and the American states as having predominantly one of these three different subculture orientations: traditional, individual and moral. Culture represents what people believe and think about their government. An individual culture emphasizes markets and smaller government, while a moral culture emphasizes the common good and the importance of government in advancing the common good. A traditional culture falls in the middle; it is more resistant to change with mixed attitudes toward government and the marketplace.

According to this characterization, traditional states are less likely to adopt policy innovations and their general orientation is largely conservative; for example, Fisher and Pratt (2006) find that more traditional states are more likely to use the death penalty. In individual states, limited government involvement is favored and policy change is more likely to be driven by particular interests. In contrast, in moral states a strong public interest orientation should support broad-based reform for the public good. Koven and Mausolff (2002) find that more moral states have higher expenditures on education when compared to more traditional states, and Mead (2004) finds that moral states are most likely to have successful welfare reform. Thus, a moral orientation should similarly support a greater likelihood of educational finance reform.

However, we should also expect moral states to have a greater likelihood of reform through the legislature as opposed to the courts. A more moral state should have a legislature that reflects such values, and thus should be more sympathetic to government achieving the common good including equity in education financing. This should lead to a greater likelihood of legislative educational finance reform. However, this in turn means that a more moral state should be less likely to see reform through the courts. Given that traditional states are the least likely to seek reform, this means that litigants in individual states should be most likely to use the courts to achieve educational finance reform.

The voting public in a state also has preferences and public preferences can influence policy change. As Kingdon notes, "[I]t is likely that the constituency imposes some meaningful constraints on Congressmen's voting behavior" (1989, 68; see also McClosky and Zaller 1984; Verba and Nie 1972). The influence of public preferences also has been demonstrated in a range of studies that examine policy change in the states. For instance, Hill and Leighly (1992) demonstrate a link between the cultural conservatism of a state's citizens and state welfare payments while Wood and Theobald (2003) find a correlation between the conservatism of a state's citizens and state revenue allocations to school districts.

Not all state high courts have the same freedom to impose personal policy preferences. Many state court judges are elected or subject to retention elections. Scholarship shows that the selection and retention processes are important determinants of outcomes (Brace and Hall 1990; Hall 1992), and that elected judges often act as representatives of the electorate. For instance, research has shown the responsiveness of state courts to public opinion in the area of sentencing (Kuklinski and Stanga 1979), as well as retaliation by the public in the form of recall voting when judicial votes were inconsistent with public attitudes on the death penalty (Culver and Wold 1986). Other research demonstrates that competitive judicial elections are just as contested as elections in the House of Representatives (Hall 2001). Most importantly, elected judges do appear to alter their behavior in response to a perceived risk of electoral reprisal (Hall 2001; Huber and Gordon 2004). In addition, recent research by Langer (2002) has demonstrated how the relative autonomy of state high courts affects their ability to pursue policy objectives—more autonomous courts were more likely to premise rulings on personal preferences while elected courts are more likely to follow the wishes of the electorate. Thus, while law and legal issues matter far more to judges than to elected legislative office holders, elected judges should show a greater deference and more sensitivity to political factors than appointed judges.

Public preferences are not alone in driving institutions to change policy. The extent of the existing problem may also influence the likelihood of policy change. For instance, Berry and Berry (1994) report that states are more likely to adopt a tax increase when a fiscal crisis exists within the state. Wood and Theobald (2003) demonstrate that state courts are more likely to mandate educational finance reform when there is greater inequality in the financing of a state's schools. Alternatively, the degree of partisan conflict (e.g., gridlock), between chambers in the state legislature may limit the likelihood of change even if there exists significant inequality in education financing across schools. While gridlock many not stop policy change, it can have an inhibiting impact (Krehbiel 1996). Where there is partisan compatibility one is most likely to see consensus on the need for policy change. Bicameralism requires a level of consensus to pass new legislation. Enacting coalitions are quite often required to be bipartisan (Krehbiel 1998). The converse is that partisan conflict will reduce the likelihood of policy change.

Policy adoption by the states may also vary as a function of the resources available to the individual state. Hill and Leighly (1992) demonstrate that states with higher per capita incomes also have higher welfare expenditures per capita. In the case of education financing, the income capacity of a particular state should help determine the availability of state funds to aid less well-off districts.

Thus, wealth should influence prospective decision making since the availability of such funds may increase the certainty of the future success of such reform.

Neighboring state reform should also help assess the impact of a proposed policy by providing an existing laboratory to study the effect of policy change (Berry and Berry 1990; Gray 1973; Walker 1969). According to Walker (1969), by learning about the impact of policies in other states, policymakers may increase their ability to predict the potential impact of policies in their own state. Mooney (2001) further suggests that such diffusion is most likely during the early stages of a policy's implementation and in cases when policies are likely to have geographically based impacts.

Of course, particularly for educational finance reform, other state characteristics also influence the political environment. For example, much of the debate on educational finance reform often pits well-to-do school districts against poorer districts. This often means that poor urban districts are in alignment with rural districts in seeking educational finance reform in opposition to wealthier suburban school districts. As the number of poorer districts increases, the demand for education finance reform should increase and so should the probability of educational finance reform.

6. The Strategic Calculations of State Level Actors

In the last decade, scholars have increasingly relied on standard operating procedure (SOP) models to study the relationship between a changing policy environment, institutional structures and the actions of courts and legislatures (see e.g., Ferejohn and Shipan 1990). These positive political theorists argue that courts frequently must move policy toward legislative preferences in order to prevent overrides that would lead to less desirable policy outcomes. In other words, state court justices must be mindful of political constraints (Epstein and Knight 1998). Although SOP models at the federal level examine potential constraints imposed by the legislature, in the case of state courts, institutional structure creates political constraints that may influence how courts are likely to perceive subsequent strategic interactions. For example, while liberal state high courts may prefer to equalize educational finance spending, depending upon their institutional structures, there is the potential for retaliation. This threat would be the most pronounced when the judges are elected and least likely when judges are appointed. Courts will be the most willing to adjudicate when the court is appointed and thus free from retaliation and the most reluctant to adjudicate when there is divergence from public preferences and the court is elected. Premised on this notion, states with moral cultures, states with a more politically liberal citizenry and government and states with greater inequality should be more likely to propose educational finance reform both initially and in response to court ordered reform.

To demonstrate these factors and their relationship to legislative education finance reform, we introduce Table 7.5.

Table 7.5 State Characteristics and State Legislative Responses

State	Legis. Response	Culture	State Ideology	Court Selection	Severity
Alabama	Status Quo	Traditional	Moderate	Elect/Ret	Mild
Alaska	No		Conservative	App/merit	Severe
Arizona	Yes	Traditional	Moderate	App/merit	Severe
Arkansas	Yes	Traditional	Moderate	Elect/Ret	Mild
California	Yes	Individual	Moderate	App/merit	Severe
Colorado	Yes	Moral	Conservative	App/merit	Moderate
Connecticut	Yes	Individual	Liberal	App/merit	Mild
Delaware	System	Individual	Liberal	App/merit	Mild
Florida	Status Quo	Traditional	Conservative	App/merit	Moderate
Georgia	Status Quo	Traditional	Conservative	Elect/Ret	Mild
Hawaii	Status Quo		Liberal	App/merit	Mild
Idaho	Yes	Individual	Conservative	Elect/Ret	Severe
Illinois	Status Quo	Individual	Liberal	Elect/Ret	Moderate
Indiana	Status Quo	Individual	Conservative	App/merit	Mild
Iowa	Status Quo	Individual	Liberal	App/merit	Moderate
Kansas	Yes	Individual	Moderate	App/merit	Mild
Kentucky	Yes	Traditional	Conservative	Elect/Ret	Mild
Louisiana	Status Quo	Traditional	Liberal	Elect/Ret	Mild
Maine	Status Quo	Moral	Liberal	App/merit	Moderate
Maryland	Yes	Individual	Moderate	App/merit	Severe
Massachusetts	Yes	Individual	Liberal	App/merit	Moderate
Michigan	Status Quo	Moral	Liberal	Elect/Ret	Moderate
Minnesota	Status Quo	Moral	Conservative	Elect/Ret	Severe
Mississippi	Status Quo	Traditional	Conservative	Elect/Ret	Mild
Missouri	Yes	Individual	Conservative	App/merit	Mild
Montana	Yes	Individual	Liberal	Elect/Ret	Mild
New Hampshire	Yes	Moral	Conservative	App/merit	Severe
Nebraska	Status Quo	Individual	Conservative	Elect/Ret	Moderate
Nevada	Status Quo	Individual	Moderate	App/merit	Severe
New Jersey	Yes	Individual	Liberal	App/merit	Severe
New Mexico	No	Traditional	Liberal	Elect/Ret	Moderate
New York	No	Individual	Moderate	App/merit	Moderate
North Carolina	No	Traditional	Liberal	Elect/Ret	Severe

State	Legis. Response	Culture	State Ideology	Court Selection	Severity
North Dakota	No	Individual	Conservative	Elect/Ret	Severe
Ohio	Yes	Individual	Conservative	Elect/Ret	Severe
Oklahoma	Status Quo	Traditional	Moderate	App/merit	Severe
Oregon	Status Quo	Individual	Liberal	Elect/Ret	Severe
Pennsylvania	Status Quo	Individual	Liberal	Elect/Ret	Moderate
Rhode Island	Status Quo	Individual	Liberal	App/merit	Mild
South Carolina	No	Traditional	Conservative	App/merit	Mild
South Dakota	Status Quo	Individual	Conservative	App/merit	Moderate
Tennessee	Yes	Traditional	Liberal	App/merit	Moderate
Texas	Yes	Traditional	Conservative	Elect/Ret	Mild
Utah	Status Quo	Moral	Conservative	App/merit	Moderate
Vermont	Yes	Moral	Liberal	App/merit	Moderate
Virginia	Status Quo	Traditional	Moderate	App/merit	Moderate
Washington	Yes	Individual	Liberal	Elect/Ret	Severe
West Virginia	Yes	Traditional	Liberal	Elect/Ret	Moderate
Wisconsin	Status Quo	Moral	Moderate	Elect/Ret	Mild
Wyoming	Yes	Individual	Moderate	App/merit	Mild

Table 7.5 is similar to our Table 7.3, which listed various factors that might lead a state court to order educational finance reform. Here we list various factors which might lead to a state legislature enacting court-ordered reform following a court ruling in this area. The first column lists each state in alphabetical order and then lists the response of the state and various state characteristics. The state characteristics listed in columns three, four, five, and six are, respectively, culture, state ideology, high court selection method and the severity of the school finance inequality problem throughout the state. We classify the legislative response as either "yes," meaning the legislature amended statutory law or the state constitution in response to the court ruling, or "no," meaning the legislature failed to respond to the court ruling, or status quo, meaning that either there was no law suit, or the court did not order any type of finance reform.

Our culture measure is the classification of the states into one of three possible categories—moral, traditional or individual as developed by Elazar (1966) and classified by Mead (2004). We omit the dual characteristics of some states and rely on the initial and dominant classification. Our measure of state government ideology uses the Berry et al. (1998) state ideology measures which reflect the level of liberalism in each state government. This measure is premised on scores that have been revised using data provided by Klarner (2003) and theoretically run from 0 (most conservative) to 100 (most liberal). These measures take into account changes in ideology over time and thus may have an advantage over other measures—including those developed by Wright, Erikson and McIver (1995, see also Erikson, Wright and McIver 1989; McIver, Erikson and Wright 1993). The state governmental liberalisms score is based on the aggregated scores of the estimated ideology of the two chambers of the state legislature and the ideology of the governor. In addition, the benefit of using these state ideology scores is that they are strictly comparable to measures of state level judicial ideology developed by Brace et al. (2000), and which we previously used in Table 7.3. As we did in Table 7.3, we classify state governments as liberal (60 and above), moderate (30 to 60) and conservative (below 30), which roughly corresponds to dividing the states into thirds. In order to examine the effect of state court selection mechanisms, we explicitly classify state courts into two categories: appointed/ merit or elected/retention-elected.

Finally, the last column of Table 7.5 measures the severity of the educational financing disparities within each state. To measure the severity of the problem, we use the variation in instructional expenditures per district per state to measure the extent of education financing inequality in a given state (Roch and Howard 2008, 2010). The measure runs from 0 to 1. Hawaii, which has a unified school district, has a coefficient of 0, meaning absolutely no variation, while California has a coefficient of over .8, meaning significant variation. We classified the variation as mild, moderate or severe by dividing the states into thirds. Below 0.3 we classified as mild, 0.3 to 0.5 was classified as moderate and above 0.5 was classified as severe.

In our dataset we have twenty-seven instances over time of a state court ordering some form of education finance reform. In six states the legislature has failed to act, while the legislatures of the other twenty-one states enacted some type of reform. As Table 7.5 reveals, of the six times where the legislature did not respond, no state with a moral culture was involved. Three legislatures in traditional states and three legislatures in individual states failed to act. The dominant belief system in a moral culture is that government is a positive force, so perhaps these legislatures knew that the public would support their follow-up reforms. Thus in the three moral states with court-ordered reform, the legislatures in all three followed the court ruling with changes to the law. Following along with this column, twelve state legislatures with individual political cultures did enact new laws while failing to do so only three times; in other words, 80% of the time they did obey the court.

Turning to our state government ideology measure, ten states are classified as having liberal governments. In these states, eight out of the ten state legislatures responded to the court order with legislation or constitutional change. The two states that failed to respond to the courts both had traditional political cultures which are classified as states seeking government to maintain the existing order. Seven states were classified as having moderate state governments and six times the legislature responded, while ten states were classified as conservative with a response in seven of them, or 70%.

Turning to the selection mechanism, sixteen courts are either appointed or the judges obtain their positions through some sort of merit system. Of those sixteen courts with this type of selection mechanism, the legislature responded thirteen times with legislative action, or almost 82% of the time. Eleven courts are elected and of these the legislature responded eight times for a response rate of 73%. The differences appear minor, and therefore it does not appear that the selection mechanism is a reason for differences in response rates. The relative independence of a court appears to have little impact on the legislature.

The severity of the existing problem also appears to have had little influence. Where the expenditure variation is mild, the legislature responded to a court order on eight out of nine occasions. For moderate variation, the legislature responded five out of seven times. Finally when the expenditure variation is severe, the legislature responded eight out of eleven times. It is the lowest of the response rates for this particular state characteristic.

7. Conclusion

State courts played a dominant and important role in the educational finance reform movement. The 1973 Supreme Court decision in *San Antonio Independent School District v. Rodriguez* eliminated federal court involvement, but not state court participation. Using state education clauses has led to significant changes in the pattern of education expenditures in many states. As our examination shows, however, state court patterns mimic federal court patterns. Ideological preferences highly influence court decisions but ultimately the courts must rely on the elected branches of government to enact legislative or constitutional change in order to amend the education financing system throughout the state. Ultimately, more liberal legislatures in states that have a positive view of government are more likely to follow court orders. The courts' ability to influence state education reform policy works best when their decisions lie within the legal set of the policy domain of the other branches of government.

This conclusion does not, however, minimize the importance of the state courts of last resort. Obviously the courts are a prime mover in this particular policy process. State legislatures were not acting, nor was the federal court system offering any relief. The courts, by utilizing their state constitutions, were able to move state educational finance policy and help minimize the level of inequality in educational opportunity for children.

8

STATE COURT POLICYMAKING
Same-Sex Marriage

1. Introduction

In Chapter 7, we turned our attention from the role of federal courts in influencing policy to the role of state courts. Chapter 7 explored state education financing, a crucial public policy issue. In this chapter, we examine one of the best examples of the use of state courts to influence social policy: same-sex marriage. Same-sex marriage is an important, and highly contentious, sociomoral issue, and the regulation of marriage is a power generally reserved to the states.[1] Until late 2010, only state courts had been asked to rule on whether laws could restrict marriage to heterosexual couples. Same-sex marriage litigation attempts also present a particularly stark example of how courts may face significant backlash when their rulings fall outside the policy preferences held by the other branches of government and the people.

Consider, for example, the attempt to establish same-sex marriage in Iowa: On April 3, 2009, the Iowa Supreme Court unanimously struck down an Iowa statute limiting marriage to couples composed of one man and one woman. In *Varnum v. Brien*, the Iowa Supreme Court determined that the Iowa marriage statute violated the Iowa Constitution's equal protection clause, and instructed the state to begin issuing marriage certificates to both opposite sex and same-sex couples. Since the Iowa Supreme Court's decision was predicated on state law grounds, and the Supreme Court is the highest court in the state, this decision is final. The decision is also not reviewable by the federal courts as it lacks any federal question; instead, the decision rested solely on what are known as "adequate and independent state grounds." As the U.S. Supreme Court stated in *Hortonville Joint School District No. 1 v. Hortonville Education Association* (1976), "We are, of course, bound to accept the interpretation of [state] law by the highest court of the State" (488). On April 24, 2009, Iowa began recognizing same-sex marriages.

However, while the Iowa Supreme Court's decision is final and nonreviewable, other ways exist to try to overrule the decision. One way is to remove from office those justices who voted to strike down the same-sex marriage prohibition law, with the hope that newly appointed justices will support reversing the decision. Such a campaign was launched in 2010, and spearheaded by former

Republican gubernatorial candidate Bob Vander Plaats. Interest groups such as the National Organization for Marriage and the American Family Association also helped waged the high-profile campaign to defeat the three Iowa Supreme Court justices facing election. In Iowa, justices of the high court sit for retention elections whereby the public is asked simply whether or not the justice should keep his or her seat; retention elections do not include challengers. If the justice fails to receive a majority of "yes" votes, he or she is removed from office. The governor is then given the power to appoint a new justice to fill the vacancy from a slate of candidates nominated by the State Judicial Nominating Commission.

The three justices facing retention elections announced that they would not campaign to keep their seats, even in the face of organized opposition, because they were concerned about the increasing politicization of the judiciary. In particular, the three justices expressed concerns that future lawyers and litigants might fear that future rulings could be affected by campaign donations. As explained by Chief Justice Marsha Ternus, "We [do] not want to contribute to the politicization of the judiciary here in Iowa, and so we have not formed campaign committees and we have not engaged in fundraising" (*Omaha World-Herald* 2010; see also Russell 2010). Alternatively, opponents spent a considerable amount of money to defeat these three justices, arguing that judges who issue unpopular decisions should be held accountable to the people. As Vander Plaats explained, "I think it will send a message across the country that the power resides with the people. It's we the people, not we the courts" (Sulzberger 2010, A1).

On November 3, 2010, all three justices were defeated, the first time since the merit system was established in 1962 that an Iowa Supreme Court justice has failed to win a retention election. This defeat was either a call for judges to pay more attention to the wishes of the people when issuing their decisions, or a harbinger of the risks judges face when they issue potentially unpopular decisions such as *Varnum* where the Iowa Supreme Court protected the rights of a minority group against the wishes of the majority. As 2011 began, others were pushing for the remaining four justices who joined the *Varnum* opinion to be impeached. Three Republican representatives are drafting a bill to begin impeachment proceedings against the four justices; however, questions have arisen as to whether it can be shown that the justices engaged in a "misdemeanor or [were] malfeasant in office," as required by the Iowa Constitution (Schulte 2010).

This story of the battle over same-sex marriage in Iowa—and the central role played by the state judiciary—highlights the tensions that arise when courts are forced to decide key questions that have implications for social and public policy. It also underscores the issues highlighted in Chapter 1 about the interaction between legal sets and the preferences of external actors. Gay marriage presents an area where the rulings of state courts have not been easily accepted, thus suggesting they lie outside either the preferences of the electorate or of the legislative–executive core. Such rulings present risks for courts and the judges who sit on them—risks such as having their rulings reversed through statutory or constitutional means or removal from the court itself in states with elected judges—but also suggests that these courts may in part view their role as one of protecting minority interests and fostering social change. This chapter therefore traces attempts by gay rights advocates in a number of states to try to legalize gay marriage through the courts, and the subsequent responses from state legislatures and the public, while exploring the broad themes addressed throughout the book.

2. Strategies for Gaining Recognition of Gay Marriage

Attempts to gain recognition for same-sex marriages began in the 1970s. Couples attempted to obtain marriage licenses at their local courthouses, and individual couples filed lawsuits in Minnesota, Washington and Kentucky (Leonard 1997). However, most attempts by gay couples to legally marry were thwarted, and appeals to the courts for help were generally unsuccessful (Gash 2010; Pierceson 2005). In the late 1970s, states began to pass laws which limited marriage to opposite sex couples: in 1977, Florida passed a law prohibiting homosexual marriage, while California passed a law preventing clerks from issuing marriage licenses to gay couples. Through the 1980s, individual gay couples attempted to obtain marriage licenses, but most national gay rights groups focused on other issues, such as HIV awareness and securing broad protections for gays and lesbians (Pierceson 2005). In fact, according to one scholar, the numerous losses in state courts in the early and mid-1970s "convinced public-interest lawyers working on lesbian and gay issues (who had not represented petitions in these cases) that further attempts to seek same-sex marriage were futile" (Leonard 1997, ix–x).

The debate over gay marriage gained national prominence in the 1990s. On the one hand, gay marriage opponents successfully passed a number of statutes and state constitutional amendments to prevent or overrule court rulings that were favorable to gay marriage. As is discussed in detail below, in 1993 the Hawaii Supreme Court handed down a decision favoring gay marriage. By the end of 1993, nine states had responded by passing laws limiting marriage to heterosexual couples. Haider-Markel and Lake (1998) examine the introduction of state-level bills concerning the regulation or prohibition of same-sex unions between 1993 and 1998, and found 209 different bills were considered by state legislatures.

On the other hand, some gay rights advocates began seeking to legalize same-sex marriage in a number of states, with a particular focus on court-based strategies. Most notably, these attempts to secure favorable protections through the courts—much like the litigation strategies undertaken by the civil rights movement and the women's movement—have generally focused on utilizing state laws and state constitutions, rather than the U.S. Constitution. While the federal Constitution provides for the "equal protection" of all persons, as discussed in Chapter 4, the Supreme Court has also recognized that to one degree or another all laws treat people differently. Thus, the Court has asked whether the distinction made between groups is legitimate, or is it one reflecting invidi-ous discrimination against a "suspect" class. With regard to sexual orientation, the Supreme Court has declined to date to consider whether sexual orientation should be considered a suspect class. Arguments that suggest prohibitions on gay marriage violate the equal protection clause are therefore unlikely to succeed in the federal courts, unless gay marriage advocates can successfully argue that treating opposite sex and same-sex couples differently lacks even a "legitimate" government purpose and is merely a mechanism to discriminate against gay and lesbian people. The Supreme Court reached a similar conclusion in the 1996 case of *Romer v. Evans*. In a 6-3 decision, the Court struck down an amendment to the Colorado Constitution which removed the category of sexual orientation from all existing antidiscrimination statutes and prohibited any Colorado legisla-tive body from passing an antidiscrimination law in the future which included sexual orientation. The Supreme Court held that this law blatantly discriminated against homosexuals, in part because it denied them protections open to all other persons and essentially created a new class of unprotected citizens.

However, most gay marriage advocates feared challenging statutes prohibit-ing same-sex marriage under the equal protection clause because of concerns that preserving the "traditional" definition of marriage would not be viewed as a mechanism of discrimination by the Supreme Court. There is also the ques-tion of whether the current Court will be amenable to the argument that the equal protection clause was intended to offer protections on the basis of sexual orientation. A number of legal scholars have argued that the Fourteenth Amend-ment was not intended to apply to anything but race discrimination, especially in terms of the intent of those ratifying the amendment in the late 1860s (see e.g., Bork 2003; Graglia 2005; see also Strauss 2010; Taylor 1993). This view was also articulated by Justice Antonin Scalia in a recent interview: "Certainly the Constitution does not require discrimination on the basis of sex. The only issue is whether it prohibits it. It doesn't. Nobody ever thought that that's what it meant. Nobody ever voted for that. If the current society wants to outlaw discrimination by sex, hey we have things called legislatures, and they enact things called laws. You don't need a constitution to keep things up-to-date" (cited in Massey 2011). Finally, and more fundamentally, a negative decision by the U.S. Supreme Court would apply to the entire nation, and mean that a ruling stating that the prohibi-tion of gay marriage is *not* a violation of equal protection would give every state in the nation the power, if it so choose, to ban same-sex marriage.

3. Adequate and Independent State Grounds

This concern did not mean, however, that gay marriage advocates were without options. Instead, they strategically turned to state-level campaigns based on state constitutional provisions. As discussed in Chapter 7, the doctrine of adequate and independent state grounds states that if a state high court ruling is premised solely on an interpretation of state law and the state constitution, the decision is subsequently unreviewable by the federal courts. In other words, the final decision on the matter rests with the state high court. This doctrine, as with school financing, is particularly applicable to the issue of same-sex marriage. Specifically, many state constitutions provide more and more explicit protections than the U.S. Constitution. Under the U.S. Constitution, the Fourteenth Amendment provides that "no State shall ... deny to any person within its jurisdiction the equal protection of the laws." As highlighted in Chapter 4, the U.S. Supreme Court has determined that certain classifications—primarily race and sex—will be afforded greater scrutiny under the equal protection clause, while laws pertaining to all other classifications will be accorded great deference by the Court. Comparatively, many state constitutions explicitly extend the idea of heightened protections against discrimination to a wide variety of groups. For example, Article I, Section 3 of the Louisiana Constitution provides, "No person shall be denied the equal protection of the laws. No law shall discriminate against a person because of race or religious ideas, beliefs or affiliations. No law shall arbitrarily, capriciously or unreasonably discriminate against a person because of birth, age, sex, culture, physical condition, or political ideas or affiliations." Such constitutional provisions both offer more protections to citizens of that state, as well as offer state courts more leeway to strike down state statutes as unconstitutional under the state's constitution. And, since such a decision would be based solely on interpretations of state law, such decisions are final.

In addition, some of those arguing against federal court lawsuits argued that a state-by-state strategy would also work over the long-term to, with a series of victories, entrench the idea of gay marriage and provide state-level support, rather than relying on a U.S. Supreme Court decision to act as a catalyst for major changes (see e.g., Dolan 2008; Rosenberg 2008). The hope is that such a buildup of state-level support would eventually make a U.S. Supreme Court ruling on same-sex marriage a *fait accompli*, thereby making the decision itself much more in line with current social norms and more likely to be implemented nationally without the risk of significant backlash (see e.g., Rosenberg 2008).

4. State Courts and Lawsuits Seeking Recognition of Gay Marriages

Focusing on state constitutional provisions, advocates began filing suits in selected states in the 1990s to challenge those states' statutory prohibitions on same-sex marriage. Table 8.1 lists the major state court cases that have been decided concerning same-sex marriage and their eventual outcomes. To date, eighteen lawsuits have been filed, and in eight of these cases, the state high court issued a decision favoring same-sex marriage.

In May of 1993, the Hawaii Supreme Court handed down the first pro-gay marriage ruling in *Baehr v. Lewin*. The court did not, however, legalize same-sex marriage. Rather it remanded the case, which challenged a Hawaii statute

Table 8.1 State Court Rulings on Same-Sex Marriage

Case Name	Holding	Legislative or Public Response to Decision
Baehr v. Lewin/Baehr v. Miike (Hawaii, 1993/1996)	Determined that statute prohibiting same-sex marriage may violate the Hawaii Constitution; remanded case to lower court for consideration	In response, Hawaii voters approved in 1998 an amendment to the Hawaii Constitution which gave lawmakers, and not the courts, the power to define marriage. The Hawaiian legislature then voted to prohibit gay marriage.
Brause v. Bureau of Vital Statistics (Alaska, 1998)	Declared same-sex marriage a fundamental right and instructed the state to provide a compelling interest for prohibiting same-sex marriage	Decision reversed by a successful voter-driven ballot initiative which amended the Alaska Constitution to prohibit same-sex marriages
Baker v. State of Vermont (Vermont, 1999)	Struck down law barring same-sex marriage. Ordered state to either extend marriage to same-sex couples or to create a legally equivalent status for them	Vermont legislature enacted a bill authorizing civil unions in 2000. In 2009, the Vermont Legislature extended marriage to include same-sex couples
Goodridge v. Department of Public Health (Massachusetts, 2004)	Struck down law barring same-sex marriage. Ordered state to grant same-sex couples right to marry	The legislature complied, and Massachusetts became the first state to legalize gay marriage
Lewis v. Harris (New Jersey, 2006)	Struck down law barring same-sex marriage. Ordered the state to either extend marriage to same-sex couples or to create a legally equivalent status	New Jersey legislature enacted a bill authorizing civil unions in December of 2006
Anderson v. King County (Washington, 2006)	Upheld law limiting marriage to heterosexual couples	n/a
In re Marriage Cases (California, 2008)	Struck down law limiting marriages to heterosexual couples	The legislature enacted a law allowing gay marriage. That law, and the high court's decision were then reversed by Proposition 8, a ballot initiative which amended the California Constitution to prohibit same-sex marriages

(continued)

145

Table 8.1 Continued

Case Name	Holding	Legislative or Public Response to Decision
Kerrigan v. Commissioner of Public Health (Connecticut, 2008)	Held that the statutory scheme providing "marriage" to heterosexual couples and "civil unions" to same-sex couples was unconstitutional. Ordered state to extend marriage to same-sex couples	The Connecticut legislature complied, and the marriage law was formally amended to include same-sex couples in April 2009
Varnum v. Brien (Iowa, 2009)	Held the state's prohibition of same-sex marriage violated the Iowa Constitution's equal protection clause. Ordered state to grant marriage licenses to same-sex couples.	The state complied quickly, issuing the first gay marriage licenses less than a month later. However, three justices who joined the ruling were defeated in the November 2010 elections and there is currently a move to impeach the remaining four justices

prohibiting same-sex marriage, to the lower court, with instructions for the court to assess at trial whether the state possessed a compelling interest to justify the prohibition on same-sex marriage. However, the reaction to this decision was both swift and negative: the Hawaii legislature responded by explicating the state's compelling interest for prohibiting gay marriage. And, in 1998, Hawaii voters amended the state Constitution to restrict marriage to heterosexual couples (Reid 1995).

In 1998, a superior court judge in Alaska handed down a similar ruling in *Brause v. Bureau of Vital Statistics*, declaring that same-sex marriage was a fundamental right under the Alaska Constitution and ordering the state to again provide a compelling interest for justifying its prohibition on same-sex marriages. The voters again responded quickly by amending the Alaska Constitution to ban gay marriage in the November 1998 elections.

The third successful attempt to gain state-level recognition for same-sex marriage is notable in that court's decision both favored same-sex unions and was ultimately accepted by the state legislature and the state's citizens. In December of 1999, the Vermont Supreme Court struck down the state's prohibition on same-sex marriage in *Baker v. State of Vermont*. However, rather than requiring that "marriage" be extended to all couples, the high court tasked the state legislature with creating a system whereby same-sex couples could enter into a legal partnership conferring the same benefits enjoyed by their married heterosexual counterparts. Thus, the legislature was given the choice to either extend marriage to same-sex couples or to create a legally equivalent status for same-sex couples, such as "domestic partnerships." The Vermont legislature complied and chose the latter option, establishing what it termed "civil unions" in 2000.

The fourth successful attempt to secure state-level marriage benefits occurred in Massachusetts in 2003. In *Goodridge v. Department of Public Health*, the Massachusetts Supreme Judicial Court struck down a law limiting marriage to heterosexual couples, arguing that "[t]he Massachusetts Constitution affirms the dignity and quality of all individuals. It forbids the creation of second-class citizens" (948). The legislature responded by asking whether legally equivalent "civil unions," such as those established in Vermont, would be constitutionally acceptable. The court, in an advisory opinion, ruled that the legislature must enact a law extending marriage to all eligible couples, regardless of sexual orientation (*Opinions of the Justices to the Senate*, 2004); the legislature did so in 2004.

In 2006, the New Jersey Supreme Court similarly struck down a state law prohibiting same-sex marriage in *Lewis v. Harris* as a violation of the New Jersey Constitution's equal protection guarantee. The high court determined that "the unequal dispensation of rights and benefits to committed same-sex partners can no longer be tolerated under our State Constitution" (200). The New Jersey Supreme Court did not, however, require that the legislature extend marriage to include same-sex couples; rather, much like the high court in Vermont, the court stipulated that gay couples must be given the same legal rights and benefits as heterosexual couples, but that this status did not have to be called "marriage." The high court argued that "[t]he name to be given to the statutory scheme that provides full rights and benefits to same-sex couples, whether marriage or some other term, is a matter left to the democratic process" (200). In response, New Jersey enacted a bill providing civil unions for gay couples in December of 2006 (Graham 2006). Advocates of gay marriage have continued to push the state legislature to extend marriage to cover same-sex couples, but this push has yet to be successful.

However, in 2006 a setback also occurred. In July of 2006, the Washington Supreme Court ruled that the state statute limiting marriage to heterosexual couples was permissible under the state constitution. The decision in *Andersen v. King County* split the state high court justices 5-4, with the majority ruling that, since sexual orientation has not been deemed a suspect class, the state provided a legitimate reason for limiting marriage to heterosexual couples. The high court also determined that the state constitution's equal rights provision pertains to sex, and not sexual orientation; thus, under the law, there is no unconstitutional discrimination because both sexes are treated the same.

In May of 2008, the California Supreme Court struck down a law restricting marriage to heterosexual couples (*In re Marriage Cases*). This case was notable for the history of gay marriage advocacy in California: In 1999, California began enacting a series of "domestic partnership" provisions which granted many of the rights and benefits granted to heterosexual couples to same-sex couples. Partially in response to these domestic partnership laws, a voter-initiated ballot proposition (Proposition 22) successfully amended California law to restrict marriage to one man and one woman in 2000. In 2004, the City and County of San Francisco unilaterally began issuing marriage licenses to same-sex couples. The

California Supreme Court, in *Lockyer v. City & County of San Francisco* (2004) ruled that these actions by the local governments were unlawful. However, the court also stated clearly that the question before them did not concern the constitutionality of California's marriage statutes, but rather simply whether the local governments could take actions which contravened current state law. Between 2004 and 2008, California did establish what it termed legal "domestic partnerships," which accorded "virtually all" of the rights and benefits accorded to married couples (*In re Marriage Cases*, note 2). The 2008 case raised the question, however, whether the "right to marry" found in the California Constitution, as well as the equal protection clause of the California Constitution, rendered unconstitutional the separate, but legally equivalent, statutory schemes. The court held that the existing laws did violate the California Constitution, explaining that "the constitutionally based right to marry properly must be understood to encompass the core set of basic *substantive* legal rights and attributes traditionally associated with marriage that are so integral to an individual's liberty and personal autonomy that they may not be eliminated or abrogated by the Legislature or by the electorate through the statutory initiative process" (399). However, as will be discussed more fully below, this decision was eventually reversed by a successful voter-driven ballot initiative which amended the California constitution to prohibit same-sex marriage.

In Connecticut, the Connecticut Supreme Court ruled 4-3 in favor of gay marriage in October of 2008 (*Kerrigan v. Commissioner of Public Health*). This case was similar to that addressed by the California Supreme Court in that Connecticut actually passed a state law in 2005 which established civil unions for same-sex couples, with the same rights and privileges as marriage, becoming the first state to do so without a court order (McFadden 2008). The state marriage law was then amended to stipulate that "marriage" was reserved for heterosexual couples; this action secured the support of the state's then Governor, Republican M. Jodi Rell (Haigh 2005). The civil union law was challenged, however, with opponents arguing that the creation of a separate status for gay couples violated the Connecticut constitution's equal protection clause. The Connecticut Supreme Court agreed, arguing that "[i]interpreting our state constitutional provisions in accordance with firmly established equal protection principles leads inevitably to the conclusion that gay persons are entitled to marry the otherwise qualified same sex partner of their choice. To decide otherwise would require us to apply one set of constitutional principles to gay persons and another to all others" (482). After the ruling, the governor and attorney general of Connecticut both stated that the ruling would be implemented, and no attempts to date have been made to reverse the Supreme Court's decision (McFadden 2008). In April of 2009, the state legislature formally amended the state's marriage law to include same-sex couples, with the law passing by wide margins in both chambers, and the law was signed by the governor less than twenty-four hours later (Dixon 2009).

Finally, as discussed in the introduction to this chapter, the Iowa Supreme Court struck down a state law prohibiting same-sex marriages as a violation of equal protection under the Iowa Constitution in 2009 in the case of *Varnum v. Brien*. The high court ordered the state to extend marriage to same-sex couples, and the state complied quickly, recognizing gay marriages less than a month later. While gay marriage is still legal in Iowa, ongoing attempts to replace the justices who supported the ruling, along with attempts to amend the Iowa Constitution, continue.

It is also notable that supporters of gay marriage have *not* filed lawsuits in many states, including those that either at the time lacked constitutional prohibitions against same-sex marriage or contained constitutional provisions which were broader than those in the U.S. Constitution. Similarly, while the earliest cases were filed by individuals in Kentucky and Minnesota, attempts have not been made during the more recent wave of litigation. One explanation for this reality may be the ideology of the courts themselves.

As we did in Chapter 7, we again utilize the PAJID scores to examine the ideology of state high court judges in relation to the probability of citizens both filing a lawsuit concerning same-sex marriage as well as winning such a lawsuit. As a reminder, these scores range from 0, most conservative to 100, most liberal. For ease of presentation and discussion, we again reclassified these scores in our table into either liberal, moderate or conservative. We simply divided the actual scores into three categories with under 25 classified as conservative, 25 to 50 as moderate and over 50 as liberal. For states in which lawsuits have been filed, we utilize the average PAJID score as of the date of the final court decision. For states in which lawsuits have not been filed, we use the average PAJID score for each high court as of 2004 in order to investigate whether the ideology of the state high court judges provides any hints as to why cases have been filed in some states, but not others. The results are reported in Table 8.2.

Table 8.2 reveals that five state high courts are ideologically conservative, twenty-eight are ideologically moderate and the remaining seventeen are ideologically liberal. In eighteen of these states, lawsuits seeking to extend marriage to same-sex couples have been filed; eight of these attempts, or approximately 44%, have been successful. Only one lawsuit has been filed in a state with an ideologically conservative high court, and, not surprisingly, this lawsuit was unsuccessful. At the other end of the spectrum, seven cases have been filed in states with liberal high courts, and four (57%) of these attempts were ultimately successful. The remaining ten cases were filed in states with moderate high courts, and four of these lawsuits were also successful. While tentative, these results suggest that gay marriage advocates are both more likely to file lawsuits seeking legal recognition of same-sex marriage in states with liberal high courts and more likely to win. Legal activity in moderate states is less likely as well as more trepidatious. Finally, gay marriage advocates have generally avoided filing lawsuits in states with conservative high courts.

Table 8.2 Examination of State High Court Ideology and Likelihood of Advocates Pursuing Same-Sex Marriage Litigation

State	State High Court Ideology	Same-Sex Marriage Lawsuit Filed in State Court	Ultimate Outcome of Lawsuit (court listed if not state high court)
Alabama	Moderate	No	
Alaska	Moderate	Yes, 1998	Suggested gay marriage ban unconstitutional (AK Superior Court)
Arizona	Conservative	Yes, 2003	Upheld ban (AZ Court of Appeals)
Arkansas	Moderate	No	
California	Moderate?	Yes, 2008	Struck down ban
Colorado	Moderate	No	
Connecticut	Liberal	Yes, 2008	Struck down ban
Delaware	Liberal	No	
Florida	Moderate	Yes, 2002	Upheld ban
Georgia	Moderate	Yes, 2002	Upheld ban (GA Court of Appeals)
Hawaii	Liberal	Yes, 1993	Suggested ban unconstitutional
Idaho	Conservative	No	
Illinois	Liberal	No	
Indiana	Moderate	Yes, 2003	Upheld ban (Indiana Superior Court)
Iowa	Moderate	Yes, 2009	Struck down ban
Kansas	Conservative	No	
Kentucky	Moderate	Yes, 1973	Upheld ban
Louisiana	Moderate	No	
Maine	Liberal	No	
Maryland	Liberal	Yes, 2007	Upheld ban
Massachusetts	Liberal	Yes, 2004	Struck down ban
Michigan	Liberal	No	
Minnesota	Liberal	Yes, 1971	Upheld ban
Mississippi	Moderate	No	
Missouri	Moderate	No	
Montana	Moderate	No	
New Hampshire	Moderate	No	

State	State High Court Ideology	Same-Sex Marriage Lawsuit Filed in State Court	Ultimate Outcome of Lawsuit (court listed if not state high court)
Nebraska	Moderate	No	
Nevada	Moderate	No	
New Jersey	Moderate	Yes, 2005	Struck down ban
New Mexico	Moderate	No	
New York	Liberal	Yes, 2006	Upheld ban
North Carolina	Moderate	No	
North Dakota	Liberal	No	
Ohio	Moderate	No	
Oklahoma	Moderate	No	
Oregon	Liberal	No	
Pennsylvania	Liberal	No	
Rhode Island	Liberal	No	
South Carolina	Moderate	No	
South Dakota	Moderate	No	
Tennessee	Moderate	No	
Texas	Moderate	Yes, 2010	Upheld ban (TX Court of Appeals)
Utah	Conservative	No	
Vermont	Liberal	Yes, 1998	Struck down ban
Virginia	Moderate	No	
Washington	Moderate	Yes, 2006	Upheld ban
West Virginia	Liberal	No	
Wisconsin	Liberal	No	
Wyoming	Conservative	No	

As noted in Chapter 7, states have also adopted a wide variety of institutional structures and designs when creating their state courts. State courts differ as to their modes of selecting judges, the number of judges who serve on each court and whether an intermediate appeals court exists. As a result, these various structural features serve to potentially constrain the ability of courts to issue decisions which greatly influence public and social policy. In particular, state court selection and retention mechanisms may directly influence how state court judges rule. Since elected judges are accountable to the electorate, they are more likely to look not only to the relevant laws and precedents when deciding cases, but also to weigh how their decisions might affect their reelection chances. Alternatively, appointed judges are much more like federal court judges in that they are relatively insulated from the possibility of direct public backlash, and so are less likely to base their decisions on current citizen attitudes. Numerous studies find that elected, as opposed to appointed, judges may be constrained in their decision-making options or may even alter their decisions completely in the face of reelection concerns (see e.g., Brace and Hall 1990; M. Hall 1992, 2001; Huber and Gordon 2004; Langer 2002). Table 8.3 thus investigates whether appointed or elected courts are more likely to support gay marriage as well as whether advocates are more or less likely to even file lawsuits when facing elected, as opposed to appointed, judges.

Table 8.3 reveals that twenty-two states use some sort of election to select judges, while the other twenty-eight states either appoint judges or utilize a merit selection system. Of the eighteen states in which lawsuits concerning gay

Table 8.3 Examination of State Court Selection Mechanism and Likelihood of Advocates Pursuing Same-Sex Marriage Litigation

State	State High Court Selection Mechanism	Same-Sex Marriage Lawsuit Filed in State Court	Decision Supported Gay Marriage?
Alabama	Elect/Ret	No	
Alaska	App/merit	Yes, 1998	Yes (AK Superior Court)
Arizona	App/merit	Yes, 2003	No (AZ Court of Appeals)
Arkansas	Elect/Ret	No	
California	App/merit	Yes, 2008	Yes
Colorado	App/merit	No	
Connecticut	App/merit	Yes, 2008	Yes
Delaware	App/merit	No	
Florida	App/merit	Yes, 2002	No
Georgia	Elect/Ret	Yes, 2002	No (GA Court of Appeals)
Hawaii	App/merit	Yes, 1993	Yes
Idaho	Elect/Ret	No	
Illinois	Elect/Ret	No	
Indiana	App/merit	Yes, 2003	No (Indiana Superior Court)
Iowa	App/merit	Yes, 2009	Yes
Kansas	App/merit	No	
Kentucky	Elect/Ret	Yes, 1973	No
Louisiana	Elect/Ret	No	

State	State High Court Selection Mechanism	Same-Sex Marriage Lawsuit Filed in State Court	Decision Supported Gay Marriage?
Maine	App/merit	No	
Maryland	App/merit	Yes, 2007	No
Massachusetts	App/merit	Yes, 2004	Yes
Michigan	Elect/Ret	No	
Minnesota	Elect/Ret	Yes, 1971	No
Mississippi	Elect/Ret	No	
Missouri	App/merit	No	
Montana	Elect/Ret	No	
New Hampshire	App/merit	No	
Nebraska	Elect/Ret	No	
Nevada	App/merit	No	
New Jersey	App/merit	Yes, 2005	Yes
New Mexico	Elect/Ret	No	
New York	App/merit	Yes, 2006	No
North Carolina	Elect/Ret	No	
North Dakota	Elect/Ret	No	
Ohio	Elect/Ret	No	
Oklahoma	App/merit	No	
Oregon	Elect/Ret	No	
Pennsylvania	Elect/Ret	No	
Rhode Island	App/merit	No	
South Carolina	App/merit	No	
South Dakota	App/merit	No	
Tennessee	App/merit	No	
Texas	Elect/Ret	Yes, 2010	No (TX Court of Appeals)
Utah	App/merit	No	
Vermont	App/merit	Yes, 1998	Yes
Virginia	App/merit	No	
Washington	Elect/Ret	Yes, 2006	No
West Virginia	Elect/Ret	No	
Wisconsin	Elect/Ret	No	
Wyoming	App/merit	No	

marriage have been filed, the majority (13 of 18, or 72.2%) have been filed in states which either appoint judges to the bench or utilize a merit selection system. This finding suggests that gay marriage advocates have not only selected more states with more liberal high courts to file their suits, but also overwhelmingly chosen states where the high courts are relatively removed from the possibility of public backlash. Even more strikingly, none of the five cases filed in states with elective judicial selection systems were successful, suggesting that gay marriage advocates were right to be strategic in choosing the targets of their litigation attempts. Comparatively, 61.5% (8 out of 13) of the cases brought in states utilizing appointive or merit selection systems were successful; notably, these cases constitute all of the successful cases which were brought. Thus, these findings suggest that those seeking recognition of same-sex marriage have, more so than high court ideology, taken into account how the high court judges attain their seats. And, these calculations have paid off: judges in these states, who are more insulated from political pressures and electoral considerations than their elected counterparts, have been much more willing to strike down majoritarian-supported laws prohibiting gay marriage and to uphold the rights of the minority.

The end result is that eight state high courts have handed down rulings in favor of legalizing same-sex unions, whether through marriage or some other legally equivalent procedure. Yet, as has also been briefly noted above, the story in many of these states does not end with these court rulings. Instead, in many of these states where gay marriage bans were struck down, attempts—some successful—have been made to repudiate these court decisions. We thus now turn to an examination of the backlash generated by these decisions both in state legislatures and by the public, in both these states as well as across the nation.

5. The Backlash: Legislative and Public Responses to Pro-Gay Marriage Court Rulings

While court decisions have led to numerous policy changes across the nation and within states, the judiciary is merely one branch of the government. And, when it comes to state governments, the relationship between the courts and the other branches can vary tremendously. Consequently, when state courts issue rulings on important public policy issues, they must consider the potential responses from other actors and, in particular, whether the state legislature will follow their commands. Furthermore, given the highly contentious sociomoral debate surrounding same-sex marriage, the possibility also exists that state high court rulings in one state will prompt state legislatures in *other* states to act preemptively to forestall such rulings.

This last prediction is exactly what happened in many states. In response to attempts in other states to legalize gay marriage in the early 1990s, numerous states proposed laws which stipulated that marriage would be defined as a union between one man and one woman. Aiding this legislative retrenchment in favor of "traditional" marriage, the U.S. Congress enacted the Defense of Marriage

Act in 1996 (DOMA; Public Law 104-199). This law stated that same-sex marriages would not be recognized by the federal government and allowed the states to determine whether they would recognize same-sex marriages. More fundamentally, it also allowed states the power to *not* recognize same-sex marriages performed in other states. Normally, the full faith and credit clause of the U.S. Constitution requires states to recognize laws and legal designations conferred by other states. Thus, if a couple is married in Georgia, under full faith and credit, other states are required to recognize the couple as married; this issue particularly arises when people move residences. However, under DOMA, even if same-sex couples are able to legally marry in one state, other states do not have to recognize this marriage, such as in the case of the couple moving to a new state. As a result, in 1996 alone, thirteen states enacted laws prohibiting same-sex marriage, and by 2000, the majority of states possessed such laws (see Gash 2010). Table 8.4 lists, as of 2010, the status of state laws pertaining to same-sex marriage, and breaks them down by the specific policy advanced in the law. The date indicates the date the law or constitutional amendment was enacted; a blank entry indicates that no such provision exists. Overall, the overwhelming majority of laws possess, as of 2010, some prohibition on gay marriage.

However, it must be noted that not all state legislatures joined this growing backlash. As shown in Table 8.4, some states have moved to pass laws which either allow same-sex marriage or recognize same-sex marriages performed in other states. While Vermont was one of the first states to have its statute prohibiting same-sex marriage struck down, the legislature dutifully created legally equivalent civil unions the following year in compliance with the state high court's ruling. Perhaps more notably, in 2009, and without legal coercion, the state legislature enacted Vermont Senate Bill No. 115 which extended marriage to all couples, heterosexual or homosexual.

Similarly, in June of 2009, the state of New Hampshire became the first state to legislatively extend marriage to gay couples without being ordered to by its state courts. Gay couples could legally wed as of January 1, 2010, and, as of January 2011, more than one thousand couples had married (Hogan 2011). New questions are being raised, however, about whether the newly elected Republican legislature will reverse course. At least two bills have been introduced to revise the marriage laws to pertain only to opposite-sex couples, while a movement pushed by Let New Hampshire Vote seeks to place on the ballot in 2012 a constitutional amendment aimed at prohibiting gay marriage (Hogan 2011). Supporters of New Hampshire's law fear a similar fate as occurred in Maine: a same-sex marriage law, again enacted without court order, was passed in the summer of 2009. Maine was technically the first state to legislatively enact such a law without court intervention, but no gay couple was ever legally wed. Then, in November of 2009, Maine residents voted 53–47% to repeal the law (Sacchetti 2009). However, Maine does still recognize domestic partnerships. In December of 2009, the District of Columbia passed a law legalizing same-sex marriage; the U.S. Congress declined to block the law in March of 2010. Finally, a bill to

Table 8.4 List of State Statutes and Constitutional Provisions Relating to Same-Sex Marriage

State	Statute Defining Marriage as between One Man & One Woman	Constitutional Amendment Defining Marriage as Between One Man & One Woman	Statute Stipulating that Anti-Discrimination Law Not to be Construed as Authorizing Same-Sex Marriage	Statute Providing for Gay Marriage, Civil Unions, or Domestic Partnership Benefits	Statute Recognizing Out of State or Foreign Same-Sex Marriages
Alabama	1998	2006			
Alaska	1996	1998			
Arkansas	2007	2004			
Arizona	1996	2008			
California	1993	2008		1999, 2001	2009*
Colorado	1989	2006			
Connecticut			1991	2005, 2008	
Delaware	1996				
District of Columbia				1992, 2010	2009
Florida	1997	2008			
Georgia	1996	2004			
Hawaii	1997	1998		1997	
Idaho	1996	2006			
Illinois	1996				
Indiana	1986				
Iowa	1998		2007		
Kansas	1996	2005			

State					
Kentucky	1998	2004			
Louisiana	1987	2004			
Maine	1997			2003, 2009	
Maryland	1984				
Massachusetts	1996	2004			2008
Michigan	1996	2004			
Minnesota	1977		1993	1993	
Mississippi	1997	2004			
Missouri	1996	2004			
Montana	1975	2004			
Nebraska		2000			
Nevada		2002		2009	
New Hampshire	1987			2009	2008
New Jersey				2004, 2006	
New Mexico					
New York				2004	
North Carolina	1996				
North Dakota	1997	2004			
Ohio	2004	2004			
Oklahoma	1996	2004			

(continued)

Table 8.4 Continued

State	Statute Defining Marriage as between One Man & One Woman	Constitutional Amendment Defining Marriage as Between One Man & One Woman	Statute Stipulating that Anti-Discrimination Law Not to be Construed as Authorizing Same-Sex Marriage	Statute Providing for Gay Marriage, Civil Unions, or Domestic Partnership Benefits	Statute Recognizing Out of State or Foreign Same-Sex Marriages
Oregon	1965	2004		2007	
Pennsylvania	1996				
Rhode Island				2001	
South Carolina	1996	2006			
South Dakota	1996	2006			
Tennessee	1996	2006			
Texas	1973	2005			
Utah	1993	2004			
Vermont	2000			2000, 2009	
Virginia	1975	2006			
Washington	1998			2007, 2009	
West Virginia	2001				
Wisconsin	1979	2006		2009	
Wyoming	1957				

*Only applies to same-sex couples who were married prior to November 5, 2008.

legalize gay marriage was introduced in the Rhode Island legislature on January 6, 2011 (Gregg 2011). This bill is still currently pending as of March 2011.

A number of states have also, without court prompting, extended many of the legal benefits of marriage to same-sex couples, while still prohibiting them from being legally "married." Most of these states have therefore created a new legal category for legally recognized relationships, usually called either "civil unions" or "domestic partnerships." These laws provide increased legal recognition and protections to same-sex couples, but also vary widely by state as to the extent of the protections offered. For example, even though the state high court upheld a ban on same-sex marriage, the legislature in the state of Washington established domestic partnerships in 2007, and expanded the benefits granted in 2008 and 2009. Similarly, Oregon established domestic partnerships in 2007, as did Maryland in 2008 and Wisconsin in 2009; these laws provide certain legal protections to domestic partners, including hospital visitation rights and the right to make funeral decisions, but do not extend all the rights available to married spouses. Nevada, as of October 2009, also recognized domestic partnerships, and permitted both same-sex couples and opposite-sex couples to register as domestic partners.

The public's response to gay marriage lawsuits has similarly been quite mixed. On the one hand, the succession of successful state-level litigation campaigns in favor of gay marriage prompted gay marriage opponents in many states to revisit their own laws. Since the state high court decisions in places such as Vermont and Massachusetts suggested statutes prohibiting gay marriage were open to attack, a number of constitutional amendments banning same-sex marriage were proposed between 2004 and 2008. As Gash (2010) shows, the end result is that few states currently recognize same-sex marriage, and many have prohibited it through constitutional amendments.

In all of these states, the constitutional amendments were the result of voter-driven ballot propositions. Thus, another distinct feature of state politics, as opposed to national politics, is that many states allow for voter-driven ballot initiatives. If organized groups of voters are able to gain enough public support (acquired through signatures of registered voters in the state), they can place on state-wide ballots initiatives which either amend current state law or even amend the current state constitution. Following the *Goodridge* decision in Massachusetts, numerous voter-driven ballot initiatives were placed on ballots around the country, and many of them were successful. Organized interest groups opposed to gay marriage also joined the battle in favor of such ballot initiatives, and these groups are generally well-funded. For example, Cahill (2004, 20–22) compared the resources of national gay rights groups to those leading the charge against gay marriage and found that the thirteen largest national gay rights groups have a combined annual income of $54 million as compared to $217 million for thirteen opposition groups (see also Rosenberg 2008). Many of these groups, such as Focus on the Family and Concerned Women for America, which advocate in general for conservative, morally based issues, have continually played a role in antigay marriage battles across the country since the early 1990s, and continue to do so today. And, these groups are many times quite successful. As Donovan, Mooney and Smith (2008) argue, ballot initiatives restricting gay marriage were in part highly successful because "[o]pponents of same-sex marriage were able to explain their arguments simply and convincingly: traditional marriage is important and same-sex marriage threatens it—just see your Bible" (441).

California presents a particularly good example of successful voter backlash: as discussed above, California voters originally passed Proposition 22 which amended California law to restrict marriage to opposite-sex couples. In 2008, this law was found to be unconstitutional under the state's constitution. However, California voters successfully overturned this high court ruling in November of 2008 through the use of another voter-initiated ballot initiative, Proposition 8, which amended the California Constitution to reserve marriage to one man and one woman. The fight over Proposition 8 resulted in the most expensive state ballot campaign in history. A number of lawsuits immediately followed, including lawsuits that challenged the proposition's legal validity and impact on same-sex marriages performed prior to the proposition's enactment. In *Strauss v. Horton* (2009), the California Supreme Court upheld Proposition 8, but also determined that same-sex marriages performed prior to November 5, 2008, were still legally valid.

Similarly, the recent 2010 judicial election results in Iowa highlight a potential risk for the judges themselves who vote to strike down statutes restricting marriage to heterosexual couples. Due to intense public outrage and organized opposition from leading gay marriage opponents, all three of the Iowa Supreme Court justices who had retention elections in 2010 were defeated. The campaigns against their judgeships were almost solely based on hostility to the high court's decision in *Varnum*. And, as we saw earlier in Table 8.3, the situation in Iowa both foretells the risks to elected judges, but also to those who are appointed and face retention elections.

The question thus becomes, why do we see such differing responses from state legislatures and the citizens of different states? First, as previously discussed, one of the biggest issues is the relative policy preferences of the legislature as compared to the courts. Courts are more likely to act, and to act in strong ways, when the legal set is within the policy set. And, proponents of gay marriage are strategic actors who consider whether a state and its leaders and culture are likely to be amenable to such changes. In some states, a litigation strategy is not necessary. In others, litigation may be necessary, as altering the status quo is generally the least preferred option. Alternatively, if the proposed legal change—here, the removal of prohibitions on gay marriage—is well outside the policy views held by the legislature, then proponents of the proposed change are less likely to even try for such changes, even through litigation. Hence, it is perhaps not surprising that we have yet to see pushes for gay marriage in traditionally conservative (and highly religious) states such as Mississippi and Utah. Furthermore, it is these states where we also expect to see legislative responses to movements in *other* states and, specifically, legislative backlashes.

Second, gay marriage presents an interesting opportunity to separately examine how the *public* plays a role in influencing the degree to which courts can influence public policy. In particular, the negative reactions in many states to court decisions about gay marriage have involved voter-driven ballot initiatives to amend a particular state's constitution. Constitutional amendments, rather than statutory changes have been necessary because all of the state high court decisions concerning gay marriage have struck down the offending statutes on constitutional grounds. As a result, the only way to reverse the court's decision is to amend the constitution itself, and this action can be achieved in many states through public, rather than legislative, action. Thus, to truly understand the role of the courts, and the potential for public backlash, we also need to understand how the courts compare to the public writ large.

Table 8.5 thus assesses the relationship between the ideology of each state's high court as compared to the ideology of the state government and the state's citizenry. It also reports whether the legislature or public in each state acted to respond to a court ruling, whether the ruling occurred in that state or in another state. Column 2 reports each state high court's ideology score, as utilized previously in Table 8.2; Column 3 lists whether a state court ruling supporting gay marriage was handed down in each state, as well as the date of any relevant decision. In order to examine the ideology of the other state government actors, we utilize the Berry et al. (1998) state ideology measure, discussed in detail in Chapter 7, which reflects the level of liberalism in each state government. Similarly to Table 8.2, Column 4 classify state governments and state courts as liberal (60 and above), moderate (30 to 60), and conservative (below 30). For this table, we use the state government ideology score for the year in which a legislative response was enacted; if no legislative response was enacted, we use the state's score from 2004. We then compare these estimates to the state high court ideology rankings we utilized previously in Table 8.2. Column 5 denotes any legislative response enacted by the state, regardless of whether a lawsuit was filed in the case. Column 6 again utilizes the state-level ideology scores created by Berry et al. (1998), but this time uses the second dimension scores which reflect the ideology of the citizenry. Berry et al. (1998, 330–31) estimate the ideology of a state's citizens at a given moment in time by assessing the ideological positions of a state's Members of Congress and their challengers in the previous election. We classify state citizenries as liberal (60 and above), moderate (30 to 60) or conservative (below 30); we use the citizenry score from the year of any voter activity and the score from 2004 if no such activity was attempted. Finally, Column 7 lists whether the citizens of each state attempted through a ballot measure to alter either state law or the state constitution concerning gay marriage as well as whether these attempts were successful.

The results of Table 8.5 highlight the extent to which both state legislatures and the public responded negatively to state high court rulings in favor of gay marriage, even when—and perhaps especially when—the decision concerned the laws of another state. If we first look to eight states where the high courts

Table 8.5 Influence of State Government and Citizenry Ideology on Responses to Same-Sex Marriage Court Rulings

State	State High Court Ideology	Court Decision Supporting Gay Marriage?	State Government Ideology	State Legislative Response	State Citizen Ideology	Voter-Initiated Response (generally by constitutional amendment)
Alabama	Moderate	No	Moderate	Passed law prohibiting same-sex marriage (1998)	Moderate	None
Alaska	Moderate	Yes (1998 decision)	Moderate	Law passed in response to new constitutional amendment prohibiting same-sex marriage (1999)	Conservative	Constitutional amendment prohibiting same-sex marriage passed (1998)
Arizona	Conservative	No (2003 decision)	Conservative	Passed law prohibiting same-sex marriage (1996)	Conservative	Adopted constitutional amendment banning same-sex marriage (2008); Failed to approve amendment banning same-sex marriage (2006)
Arkansas	Moderate	No	Moderate	Passed law prohibiting same-sex marriage (1997)	Moderate	Constitutional amendment prohibiting same-sex marriage passed (2004)
California	Moderate?	Yes (2008 decision)	Moderate	Amended law in accordance with court ruling	Liberal	Constitutional amendment prohibiting same-sex marriage passed (2008)
Colorado	Moderate	No	Conservative	Passed law prohibiting same-sex marriage (2000)	Moderate	Failed to approve voter referendum on establishing domestic partnerships (2006)

State					
Connecticut	Liberal	Yes (2008 decision)	Liberal	Amended law in accordance with court ruling	Liberal	None
Delaware	Liberal	No	Liberal	Passed law prohibiting same-sex marriage (1996); Failed to pass bill allowing constitutional amendment banning same-sex marriage (2009)	Liberal	None
Florida	Moderate	No (2002 decision)	Conservative	None; Passed law prohibiting same-sex marriage (1997)	Liberal	Constitutional amendment prohibiting same-sex marriage passed (2008)
Georgia	Moderate	No (2002 decision)	Conservative	None; Passed law prohibiting same-sex marriage (1996)	Moderate	Constitutional amendment prohibiting same-sex marriage passed (2004)
Hawaii	Liberal	Yes (1993/1996 decision)	Liberal	Law passed in response to new constitutional amendment prohibiting same-sex marriage (1999); Failed attempt establish civil unions (2010)	Liberal	Constitutional amendment prohibiting same-sex marriage passed (1999)
Idaho	Conservative	No	Conservative	Passed law prohibiting same-sex marriage (1996)	Conservative	None
Illinois	Liberal	No	Conservative	Passed law prohibiting same-sex marriage (1996)	Liberal	None

(continued)

Table 8.5 Continued

State	State High Court Ideology	Court Decision Supporting Gay Marriage?	State Government Ideology	State Legislative Response	State Citizen Ideology	Voter-Initiated Response (generally by constitutional amendment)
Indiana	Moderate	No (2003 decision)	Conservative	Failed attempt every year since 2004 to place on ballot a constitutional amendment outlawing gay marriage; Passed law prohibiting same-sex marriage (1997)	Moderate	None
Iowa	Moderate	Yes (2009 decision)	Liberal	Amended law in accordance with court ruling	Moderate	3 judges defeated in retention elections (2010)
Kansas	Conservative	No	Conservative	Passed law prohibiting same-sex marriage (1996)	Moderate	Constitutional amendment prohibiting same-sex marriage passed (2005)
Kentucky	Moderate	No (1973 decision)	Liberal	None; Passed law prohibiting same-sex marriage (1998)	Moderate	Constitutional amendment prohibiting same-sex marriage passed (2004)
Louisiana	Moderate	No	Moderate	Passed law prohibiting same-sex marriage (1999)	Moderate	Constitutional amendment prohibiting same-sex marriage passed (2004)
Maine	Liberal	No	Liberal	Passed law allowing same-sex marriage (2009); originally passed law prohibiting same-sex marriage (1997)	Liberal	Ballot measure reversed state law allowing same-sex marriages (2009)

State						
Maryland	Liberal	No (2007 decision)	Liberal	Domestic partnership law enacted (2008); Passed law prohibiting same-sex marriage (1984)	Liberal	None
Massachusetts	Liberal	Yes (2004 decision)	Liberal	Amended law in accordance with court ruling	Liberal	None
Michigan	Liberal	No	Conservative	Passed law prohibiting same-sex marriage (1996)	Moderate	Constitutional amendment prohibiting same-sex marriage passed (2004)
Minnesota	Liberal	No (1971 decision)	Conservative; Moderate; Liberal	None; Passed law prohibiting same-sex marriage (1997); Failed attempt to create domestic partnerships (2010)	Moderate	None
Mississippi	Moderate	No	Conservative	Passed law prohibiting same-sex marriage (1997)	Moderate	Constitutional amendment prohibiting same-sex marriage passed (2004)
Missouri	Moderate	No	Liberal	Passed law prohibiting same-sex marriage (1996)	Moderate	Constitutional amendment prohibiting same-sex marriage passed (2004)
Montana	Moderate	No	Conservative	Passed law prohibiting same-sex marriage (1997)	Moderate	Constitutional amendment prohibiting same-sex marriage passed (2004)
New Hampshire	Moderate	No	Conservative; Liberal	Passed law prohibiting same-sex marriage (1987); Passed law allowing gay marriage (2010)	Moderate	None

(continued)

Table 8.5 Continued

State	State High Court Ideology	Court Decision Supporting Gay Marriage?	State Government Ideology	State Legislative Response	State Citizen Ideology	Voter-Initiated Response (generally by constitutional amendment)
Nebraska	Moderate	No	Conservative	None	Conservative	Constitutional amendment prohibiting same-sex marriage passed (2000)
Nevada	Moderate	No	Conservative	None	Moderate	Constitutional amendment prohibiting same-sex marriage passed (2002)
New Jersey	Moderate	Yes (2005 decision)	Liberal	Amended law in accordance with court ruling	Liberal	None
New Mexico	Moderate	No	Liberal	Failed attempt to establish domestic partnerships (2008, 2009)	Moderate	None
New York	Liberal	No (2006 decision)	Liberal	Established domestic partnerships (2010); Failed attempt to pass bill authorizing same-sex marriage (2007, 2009)	Liberal	None
North Carolina	Moderate	No	Liberal	Passed law prohibiting same-sex marriage (1996)	Moderate	None
North Dakota	Liberal	No	Conservative	Passed law prohibiting same-sex marriage (1997)	Liberal	Constitutional amendment prohibiting same-sex marriage passed (2004)

State						
Ohio	Moderate	No	Conservative	Passed law prohibiting same-sex marriage (2004)	Moderate	Constitutional amendment prohibiting same-sex marriage passed (2004)
Oklahoma	Moderate	No	Conservative	Passed law prohibiting same-sex marriage (1996)	Conservative	Constitutional amendment prohibiting same-sex marriage passed (2004)
Oregon	Liberal	No	Liberal	Established domestic partnerships (2007)	Liberal	Constitutional amendment prohibiting same-sex marriage passed (2004)
Pennsylvania	Liberal	No	Conservative	Pass law prohibiting gay marriage (1996)	Moderate	None
Rhode Island	Liberal	No	Liberal	Passed law creating domestic partnership benefits (2001)	Liberal	None
South Carolina	Moderate	No	Conservative	Passed law prohibiting same-sex marriage (1996)	Moderate	None
South Dakota	Moderate	No	Conservative	Passed law prohibiting same-sex marriage (1996, 2000)	Moderate	Constitutional amendment prohibiting same-sex marriage passed (2006)
Tennessee	Moderate	No	Conservative	Passed law prohibiting same-sex marriage (1996)	Moderate	None
Texas	Moderate	No (2010 decision)	Conservative	None; Passed law prohibiting same-sex marriage (1973)	Moderate	Constitutional amendment prohibiting same-sex marriage passed (2005)
Utah	Conservative	No	Conservative	Passed law prohibiting same-sex marriage (1995)	Conservative	Constitutional amendment prohibiting same-sex marriage passed (2004)

(continued)

Table 8.5 Continued

State	State High Court Ideology	Court Decision Supporting Gay Marriage?	State Government Ideology	State Legislative Response	State Citizen Ideology	Voter-Initiated Response (generally by constitutional amendment)
Vermont	Liberal	Yes (1998 decision)	Liberal	Amended law in accordance with court ruling (1999); Passed law allowing same-sex marriage (2009)	Liberal	None
Virginia	Moderate	No	Conservative	Passed law prohibiting same-sex marriage (1997)	Moderate	None
Washington	Moderate	No (2006 decision)	Liberal	None; Passed law creating domestic partnerships (2008); law prohibiting gay marriage originally enacted in 1998	Liberal	Passed voter referendum supporting legislative expansion of domestic partnerships (2009)
West Virginia	Liberal	No	Moderate	Passed law prohibiting same-sex marriage (2000)	Liberal	None
Wisconsin	Liberal	No	Moderate	Passed law placing constitutional amendment on ballot for voter approval (2006); law already in place as of 2000 defining marriage as between "husband and wife"	Moderate	Constitutional amendment prohibiting same-sex marriage passed (2006)
Wyoming	Conservative	No	Moderate	Passed law prohibiting same-sex marriage (2003)	Conservative	None

struck down (or indicated their attempt to strike down) a law prohibiting same-sex marriage, we see that any negative backlash was primarily voter-driven. In three states, Hawaii, Alaska and California, voters reversed the state high court's decision by approving ballot propositions to amend the state constitution to prohibit same-sex marriage. While Alaska is a case of a conservative electorate reversing a more moderate high court, Hawaii and California are both instances where a liberal citizenry still reacted negatively to a high court ruling. In the other five states, the state legislatures all promptly amended the relevant state laws in accordance with the high court's ruling and the citizenry accepted these changes. The only potential caveat to that conclusion is Iowa, where voters did not attempt to reverse the high court's decision per se, but voters did successfully defeat three of the high court justices in their retention elections. And, in Iowa, we see a moderate citizenry reacting to a decision by a moderate high court which was fairly easily accepted by a liberal legislature. In comparison, in the other four states where the legislature and public have seemingly accepted the high court's decision with equanimity, the legislature and citizenry are all quite liberal.

The results are much more mixed in terms of those states where legal challenges to laws prohibiting same-sex marriage failed. No actions were taken after the two decisions handed down in the early 1970s, and it is still too early tell if there will be any type of reaction to the 2010 decision by the Texas high court. In three of the states where existing laws prohibiting same-sex marriage were challenged and upheld (Florida, Georgia and Arizona), the voters all responded by further ensuring the continuation of these policies by approving constitutional amendments to the state constitution. As an interesting side note, Arizona actually represents the only state to date where such a ballot proposition failed: voters failed to approve a constitutional amendment in 2006, but a similar measure was then successful passed in 2008. Attempts have been made by the legislature in Indiana to place a similar measure on the ballot every year since 2004, but none has yet been successful. In the final three states, the legislatures all responded to the court rulings upholding gay marriage bans either by attempting to allow gay marriage or by successfully extending domestic partnerships to same-sex couples. Perhaps not surprisingly, in all three of these states, the legislatures and citizenry are all quite liberal. And, in the state of Washington, a voter referendum in 2009 concerning the legislature's expansion of domestic partnership benefits received support from the majority of voters.

Finally, we have the majority of states in which no lawsuits have been filed. However, the lack of lawsuits does not necessarily mean the lack of backlash; instead, almost every one of these states has *preemptively* acted to try and forestall challenges within their states. The first major wave of responses came in the late 1990s in response to the decisions by the Hawaii and Alaska high courts. Between 1996 and 1999, twenty-eight states passed statutes limiting marriage to heterosexual couples. The majority of these states possessed conservative legislatures, but moderate and liberal legislatures also passed similar laws, though not as consistently. The second major wave of responses was a result of the Massachusetts's high court's decision in *Goodridge*. These responses were almost all voter-driven, as the Massachusetts decision suggested that mere laws were not enough; rather, the state constitution itself needed to explicitly prohibit same-sex marriage.

Thus, between 2004 and 2008, nineteen states saw their constitutions explicitly amended through ballot measures. The majority of these states actually possessed "moderate" voters, and a number possessed liberal voters. Lastly, there have been some states which have, as noted above, responded by increasing the rights and protections offered to same-sex couples. Seven states, other than those under court order, have successfully passed laws which either extended the definition of marriage to cover same-sex couples or created some type of civil union or domestic partnership status for gay and lesbian couples. All seven of these states possessed liberal state governments at the time. And, in every state but Maine (which notably also possessed a liberal citizenry), the state's citizens have either accepted the law or voted in favor of the law. Again, perhaps not surprisingly, the citizenry in all of these states was liberal.

Overall, these results suggest that opposition to gay marriage is not completely a function of a state's level of liberalism, but rather that such opposition does in many ways span the spectrum. On the one hand, those states where court decisions have been accepted by the state government and the public are all ones considered "liberal" under the ideology scores used here. Similarly, those states which have acted on their own to extend legal protections to same-sex couples are also all liberal. On the other hand, in a number of liberal and moderate states, as well as conservative states, the state government, the public or both have taken decisive steps to express their opposition to gay marriage. For example, while Maine is extremely liberal across the board, Maine voters successfully reversed a Maine law recognizing same-sex marriage. Thus, these results in tandem suggest that a state possessing a liberal state government and a liberal citizenry are necessary, but not sufficient conditions for same-sex couples to receive some type of legal recognition. Alternatively, the likelihood of a state government or citizenry accepting a high court ruling in favor of gay marriage—or even accepting legislation—is extremely small.

7. Conclusion: Impact of State-Level Pushes for Policy Changes Through the Courts: Prospects and Perils

It is difficult to determine whether state-level litigation strategies aimed at securing the right of marriage for same-sex couples have been successful. On the one hand, gay marriage advocates have won a number of court cases in the United States, including in the Northeast and in seemingly unlikely states such as Iowa. Since the court cases in each of these states struck down laws which prohibited same-sex marriage—and prospects of legislative repeal seemed unlikely—without these court cases, these rights would not have been secured. These wins have also prompted both other court cases as well as some state legislatures, such as New Hampshire, to amend their state marriage laws to include same-sex marriage. Thus, scholars such as McCann (1994) and Scheingold (2004) would argue that these cases show how courts can help to influence broad social change and that by securing court victories smart strategists have in turn exercised the "politics of rights." While the number of victories has been small, these scholars would argue that the rights gained to date by gays and lesbians—whether with respect to marriage or other issues, such as adoption—would not be possible without the courts leading the way (see Gash 2010).

On the other hand, these wins have not come without peril: in a number of these states, public and legislative backlash resulted in constitutional amendments reversing the high court decision and prohibiting gay marriage. Thus, the court decisions handed down in Alaska, Hawaii and California also resulted in constitutional prohibitions against same-sex marriage. And, many more states have taken steps to either enact legislative or constitutional prohibitions against gay marriage. Even in states where gay marriage has been legal the longest are not without ongoing controversy—in many of these states, organized groups are pushing to utilize state ballot initiatives or other methods to try and restore marriage to its traditional definition of one man and one woman. These stories of backlash thus give credence to the argument advanced by Rosenberg (2008) that courts are ill-suited for the job of creating broad-based social change. A central part of Rosenberg's thesis is that courts are most successful in influencing matters of social policy when they have the support of the other branches of government or the public, and this likely occurs when external conditions suggest social change is already occurring. While some gains have been realized, these scholars argue that the setbacks more than outweigh what few victories have been won. Rosenberg's second edition, published in 2008, includes an examination of same-sex marriage litigation. Rosenberg highlights how state courts may be even less suitable for achieving broad-scale social change: their decisions are only binding within their own state; these judges serve for set terms; and state court judges are many times elected, thus decreasing their level of independence from the political system (Rosenberg 2008, 340).

The views of those in favor of gay marriage concerning whether to continue pursuing litigation-based strategies reflect this complex state of affairs. Scholars such as Mucciaroni (2008) argue for the pursuit of a more diverse strategy:

> Proponents of gay marriage should reconsider their strategy of seeking to secure marriage rights and civil unions through the courts.... [G]oing through the courts is no guarantee of victory, and such efforts can backfire.... The backlashes that judicial victories ignited led to broad statutory and constitutional bans that jeopardize civil unions and domestic partnerships policies along with marriage—Legislative solutions are more likely to produce compromises, which may realistically be the best that gay rights advocates can accomplish on such a contentious subject at this time. (265)

More negatively, D'Emilio (2007) argues that "the attempt to achieve marriage through the courts has provoked a series of defeats that constitute the greatest calamity in the history of the gay and lesbian movement in the United States" (45). Specifically, building on Rosenberg's theory, D'Emilio argues that gay marriage litigation has faltered in part because of the magnitude of social change required and the lack of external clues suggesting that the courts are merely reflecting "the prevailing winds of history" (57).

However, Mucciaroni also acknowledges that "[e]ven if [courts] do not bring about thorough social reformation, courts can play a significant role in the advancement of minority rights.... Courts have been catalysts for getting issues on the agenda, producers of new policies, and enforcers of policies crafted by legislatures" (252). He argues that the issues on which litigation strategies have been most successful all share three characteristics: "a legacy of judicial involvement borne of legislative reluctance to address issues or difficulty in developing a legislative consensus; independence from other policy actors in order to authorize or implement court decisions; and policymaking at the state court level" (252). In other words, he suggests that courts are in fact *most* able to help when some of the conditions cited by Rosenberg (and D'Emilio) as impediments exist—namely, that the legislature and executive are unwilling to act and courts *can* operate independently. It is perhaps not unimportant that, unlike in *Brown v. Board of Education* where the Supreme Court needed the cooperation of all fifty states and the thousands of local school boards within them, state high courts have only one legislature that they must order to act, thereby increasing the likelihood of strict compliance, at least by the other branches of government. Rosenberg acknowledges this reality as well: "[I]f judicial decisions supporting same-sex marriage can survive political backlash then Constraint III, the judiciary's lack of the power of implementation, does not come into play. This is because little or no change is required to implement same-sex marriage" (2008, 350). And, perhaps most notably for the themes raised earlier in this chapter, gay rights advocates were able to utilize the state courts, which, as discussed above, can look to state constitutions which are many times more explicit and far-reaching in their guarantees of individual rights and equal protection.

More broadly, scholars such as Pinello point to some more practical and intangible changes resulting directly from these state high court decisions. Pinello (2006, 192) argues that the Massachusetts decision in particular led both to "a sizable population of legally married same-sex couples exist[ing] in the United States for the first time," as well as empowering the previously politically oppressed and spurring many gays and lesbians, as well as supporters of gay marriage, to political activism. Thus, these arguments suggest that, even with setbacks, significant court victories can activate and mobilize supporters and provide the political leverage necessary for these supporters to successfully engage in the "politics of rights" Scheingold first advocated for in 1974.

Part 3

CONCLUSION

9

CONCLUSION

Unnecessary Judicial Activism or a Necessary Part of the Policy Process?

1. Introduction

In this concluding chapter, we first summarize the findings presented in the earlier chapters and then we offer an assessment of the role of courts in creating and influencing public policy. We analyze how the structural and institutional features which define courts also aid as well as impede their ability to effectively make policy. Finally, we end by arguing that the courts' primary, constitutionally prescribed job of interpretation necessarily means that judges must enter policy disputes, and that so long as statutory and constitutional questions exist, they will continue to do so.

We began this book by examining certain American myths and, in particular, we explored the persistent myth of judicial neutrality. We argued that it has been a core idea in American political life to ignore the political nature of judges and judging and instead espouse the idea that all judges merely apply the law to the case at hand and have neither the ability nor the will to impose their personal policy preferences when deciding cases. As a result, any impact on social and public policy becomes a dictate of the law and not the consequence of the deliberate choice of the judge or of the court. Chief Justice Roberts in his statements to the Senate Judiciary Committee during his confirmation hearings epitomized this ideal of judicial neutrality and self-restraint. He maintained that judges are merely umpires who apply the rules and are constrained by precedent. Judicial decisions or outcomes are therefore almost preordained by the law and the facts.

However, this myth creates a conundrum: If facts, law and precedent mandate one certain outcome, then a decision that one disagrees with must be the result of an incorrect interpretation of the law. The judge or court writing the opinion or making the ruling obviously refused to apply the proper legal interpretation, and this failure to follow the law led to the wrong decision. This in turn leads to the inescapable conclusion that the judge substituted his or her own personal policy preferences for the proper legal standard. Failing to follow the law—using the plain meaning of the words, the intent of the Framers and most of all precedent—and instead inserting judicial policy preferences lies at the heart of the charge of judicial activism. This accusation carries particular weight when a court strikes down majoritarian legislation. In other words, critics charge that courts should not be able to substitute their judgment for the will of the majority. Judicial activism is treated with scorn and derision and it rarely has any defenders. All nominees to the U.S. Supreme Court, for example, assert that they are faithful to the law. Certainly no nominee appearing before the Senate Judiciary Committee can admit to possessing fixed principles such as ideological preferences or a belief structure that the nominee would use to decide cases, as opposed to following the dictates of the law.

Thus, when judges and courts decide controversial cases and those cases result in the overturning of state or federal law or mandating action and behavior that displeases majority preferences, the court is accused of engaging in judicial activism. This charge arises whether a court creates a right to privacy and then finds that a woman's right to abortion is covered by this right to privacy, or if the court declares a state's system of financing education is unconstitutional, or if it mandates changes in prior interpretations of legislation by a regulatory agency in environmental matters. If one believes that abortion is wrong, any constitutional interpretation that mandates a right to an abortion must be incorrect and becomes an example of judicial activism. The same is true if one disagrees with a court ordering a change in taxation to fund public education or an increase in the enforcement of air quality regulations. All become examples of activism whereby the courts failed to adhere to precedent, plain meaning or legislative or Framers' intent. For example, in April of 2005, Senator John Cornyn (R-TX) argued that there may even be a connection between violence against judges and public distaste of their rulings: "I don't know if there is a cause-and-effect connection, but we have seen some recent episodes of courthouse violence in this country.... I wonder whether there may be some connection between the perceptions in some quarters on some occasions where [federal] judges are making political decisions yet are unaccountable to the public that it builds and builds to the point where some people engage in violence."[1]

Justices and judges are very aware of such criticisms and their potential effects on both judicial legitimacy and even the safety of members of the judiciary. In March of 2006, former Supreme Court Justice Sandra Day O'Connor made headlines when she gave a speech warning against attacks on the judiciary by elected officials. In particular, she argued that if courts "don't make [elected officials] mad some of the time we probably aren't doing our jobs as judges, and our effectiveness is premised on the notion that we won't be subject to retaliation for our judicial acts.... We must be ever-vigilant against those who would strong arm the judiciary into adopting their preferred policies" (Totenberg 2006). Such strong statements from a Supreme Court justice suggest that the Court itself is concerned about the potential damage to the judiciary and its legitimacy if claims of judicial activism are routinely aired.

However, our results overall suggest that the label of "activism" is many times a function of whether or not one agrees with the policy changes implemented by these courts. In other words, judicial decisions are declared "activist" when people dislike the ruling. Critics of the Warren Court decry the vast advances in rights for criminal defendants, instead arguing that decisions such as *Miranda v. Arizona* (1966), which established that criminal suspects must be informed of their rights before being questioned, or *Mapp v. Ohio* (1961), which incorporated Fourth Amendment search-and-seizure protections and applied them to the states, weaken the ability of law enforcement to prevent crime and result in criminals going free merely because the constable has blundered. Not surprisingly, Warren Court supporters argue the opposite: that the Court's decisions ensured the protection of innocent persons from police abuses and granted important civil rights to all persons in the United States.

On the other hand, critics of the Rehnquist and Roberts Courts claim that these justices systematically undercut needed protections for the most powerless in society, while granting more and more protections for the government and large corporations. And, once again, advocates of these decisions conversely maintain that they were necessary to ensure fairness for all, rather than just for some favored groups, and to stop the federal government from encroaching on the states' constitutionally protected powers. Of course, advocates of both claim that each Court merely followed the law while the other engaged in judicial activism.

In the end, all courts run the risk of being labeled "activist" by their detractors and by those unwilling to recognize the crucial and unavoidable role that courts play in interpreting and making policy. The courts in the American system of government are constitutionally charged with interpreting the laws of the land. Interpreting the law, and thus fulfilling their constitutional duty, leads courts to make choices about the meaning and intent of legislation and the Constitution. This interpretative responsibility also necessarily means that courts frequently make and change public and social policy. Thus, criticisms of courts for making policy are really criticisms of the courts' prescribed constitutional role in our political system.

One of the major premises of our book is to rebut the myth of neutrality and demonstrate both how and why courts can—and, in fact, should—structure and change social and public policy. Without delving into whether these judicial decisions are legally correct, we have attempted to show that judicial decision making is not a neutral process. Rather, we have shown that judges and courts are part of the American political system. Presidents nominate judges to the federal bench and the Senate confirms (or rejects) these nominations. Almost exclusively, Democratic presidents nominate Democrats and Republican presidents nominate Republicans. In many states, judicial candidates run for office, sometimes in nonpartisan elections, but often with partisan affiliations noted on the ballot, while in other states appointments follow partisan lines. Once on the bench, judges are often asked to decide questions with important and far-reaching political and policy implications, but when they rule—appropriately—on such matters, they are accused of activism.

Scholars in law and the social sciences started to erode the myth of neutrality many decades ago with advent of the Legal Realism movement. This scholarly movement recognized the inherent and nonremovable biases that are always present in judicial decision making. Social scientists then advanced this scholarship by investigating, measuring and testing for attitudinal or ideological influences on judicial decision making at the Supreme Court level and other state and federal courts. Scholars have repeatedly found, using a variety of methods, that judges' personal preferences, in part due to the political nature of judicial selection, influence their ultimate decisions (see e.g., Dahl 1957; Segal and Spaeth 1993, 2002). And, even when judges rely solely (or even mostly) on the law when deciding cases, they cannot escape the political and policy ramifications of their decisions. Thus, the most problematic implication of the continued reliance on the myth of judicial neutrality is that judges are criticized for performing their constitutionally mandated duties.

After we introduced the idea of the myth of judicial neutrality and the difficulty of using the term "judicial activism," we examined another line of research which, while acknowledging that judges' decisions necessarily influence policy, argues that judges have limited ability to actually change policy. Because of constraints inherent within the political system that courts must overcome, courts are generally incapable of actually bringing about significant social and public policy change. Gerald Rosenberg (1991, 2008), the foremost proponent of this idea, argues that American courts are ineffective and weak in comparison to the president and Congress. Rosenberg argues that courts lack the ability to influence public and social policy to the degree feared by Meese and others. Rather, Rosenberg maintains that changes in policy occur only through the active involvement of the executive and legislature.

We critiqued this position as well. It is our contention that all judges, conservative or liberal, Republican or Democrat, originalist or adherents to a "living constitution," promote and make policy and create policy changes. Judges throughout the judicial hierarchy make policy, including the trial judges of the federal system, the federal district courts and the federal appellate courts, which consist of the U.S. circuit courts of appeals and the U.S. Supreme Court. As many scholars have repeatedly shown, courts can influence policy changes in numerous ways, both large and small (see e.g., Feeley and Rubin 2000; Mather 1995; McCann 1994). However, while we argue that judges play an important role in the policymaking process, we also acknowledge that, like every other political actor, they confront political and institutional constraints that may mitigate their policy making capabilities. The myth of neutrality and the myth of activism also contain a myth that exaggerates the policymaking power and influence of the courts (see also Scheingold 2004).

In order to explain this view, we then introduced the concept of a "legal set." We argue that the legal set is a policy domain for courts that essentially falls within the domain of policy choices left to courts through choices by other political actors in the American political system. Within an acceptable range of alternative policy choices, courts can have a huge impact and the other political actors have little choice but to accept the courts' rulings. Simply put, if the political system lacks the ability or will to overturn the decision—whether due to ideological discordance or widespread agreement with the court's decision—then courts can have a significant impact on policy. However, if a court's policy choice falls too far outside the acceptable range of alternatives, then other political actors will override the decision through new legislation, constitutional change or even a public assault on judicial independence.

National courts, like the Supreme Court, can induce national variation in policy, while regional courts and state courts can create regional and state-level policy change. We also noted, however, that the number of laws that the Supreme Court overturns or declares unconstitutional is a very small percentage of all laws that the Court is asked to review. Overall, within this domain and within these external and internal constraints, courts can exert significant influence over public and social policy.

After introducing the concepts and theme of our book, we examined several important social and public policy domains. Our first examination concerned courts and tax law. We showed that courts have significant influence over economic policy. We analyzed the influence of the Supreme Court and lower federal courts on U.S. tax policy and on the actions and behavior of the Internal Revenue Service, the federal tax enforcement agency. We showed how the Supreme Court, through a series of decisions, greatly influenced the development of tax law and how most of those decisions supported efforts to expand tax collection.

We also showed how lower federal courts can shift the focus of audits between high income and low income taxpayers and between individuals and businesses depending upon the ideology of the respective courts. This judicial influence was strong; however, the influence of the elected officials was more dramatic due to the more rapid shifts in ideology of the president and the Congress. However, while the influence of courts was not as dramatic as that of elected officials, their influence can last much longer.

We next reviewed environmental law, with a specific focus on air and water policy. We began by noting how much of the scholarly literature was split on the extent of court influence on environmental policy, with some asserting an inordinate and harmful impact on policy, while others argued that the federal courts had abandoned any attempt to influence environmental policy, leading to charges that this dereliction of duty was harmful to environmental law and policy. Indeed, we discerned that the Supreme Court and lower federal courts had a mixed record in their rulings, which led perhaps to this scholarly debate. However, we also found that a court's position on the environment depended in large part upon the ideological makeup of the court at the time of the particular ruling. Similar to our examination of tax policy, we found that lower courts matter a lot to the regional enforcement of water and air policy and much depended upon the core preferences of the lower courts. More liberal courts drive the EPA to greater enforcement, while more conservative courts lead to less enforcement.

Over the next several chapters, we switched our focus to the influence of courts on social policy. We began by documenting the importance of the

Supreme Court and lower federal courts in the movement toward gender equality. We argued that the gender equality domain provides a timely examination of the role of the legal set and the importance of courts in moving policy forward, provided, however, that court-motivated policy is supported within the political domain.

We showed how the Court, even in the absence of an Equal Rights Amendment, was able to push gender discrimination to a category almost on the same level as race. We showed that the level of scrutiny applied by the Supreme Court in reviewing allegations of gender discrimination moved from a rational basis test for laws that discriminate based on gender to a standard of "heightened scrutiny." We also found, however, that the Court was moving in tandem with the preferences of the elected branches of government and that the gender equality rulings came within a policy space that denied the political system any opportunity to override or void these rulings.

We continued examining social policy and gender with our chapter that analyzed the influence of the courts on reproductive rights. With its decision in *Roe v. Wade* (1973), the Supreme Court determined that the right to privacy, established in *Griswold v. Connecticut* (1968), encompassed a woman's right to choose whether to terminate a pregnancy. This decision sparked an ongoing legal and political battle which shows no signs of being resolved in the near future. The policy space within which the Court operated has been limited over time by successive electoral battles which have also led to changes in Court membership, restricting and narrowing the right to an abortion advanced in *Roe v. Wade*. Furthermore, given these more recent Supreme Court rulings, states have responded by passing laws which test the limits and reaches of these rights, including enacting legislation which limits access to prescription contraceptives or imposes potential criminal penalties based on the actions of pregnant women. As a result, due to the courts' central role in establishing the right to privacy, the federal courts will continue to play a key role in shaping its limits and boundaries, and determining whether federal and state laws are permissible.

We moved from social policy back to public policy in Chapter 6 with our examination of discrimination and educational affirmative action. We noted that the Court during the post-World War II period, when the country was moving to end racial discrimination, was not out of alignment with the political actors. The Court operated within the parameters of the dominant policy space, breaking down segregation and providing political actors with the justification to enact much more sweeping civil rights and voting rights legislation. We also noted that in the controversial area of affirmative action, the Court carved out a very narrow but constitutionally permissible niche allowing educational affirmative action programs to proceed on as long as such programs were targeted at promoting diversity.

We then moved to an examination of two examples of state court policymaking. We continued our analysis of courts and education with an assessment of public school financing, an area almost exclusively within the domain of state courts and state constitutions. With the U.S. Supreme Court rejecting the use of the equal protection clause in *San Antonio Independent School District v. Rodriguez* (1973) to alleviate imbalances in public school financing, those seeking to make changes turned to state constitutions. Most importantly, every state's constitution contains an education clause that mandates, to some extent, a free public education. Legal challenges to educational financing schemes based on these state constitutional provisions ultimately led to significant changes in the pattern of education expenditures in many states. As our assessment shows, state court patterns mimic federal court patterns in that ideological preferences highly influence court decisions but ultimately the courts must rely on the elected branches of government to enact legislative or constitutional change in order to amend the education financing system throughout the state. The courts' ability to influence state education reform policy works best when their decisions lie within the legal set and policy preferences of the other branches of government. In this particular policy arena, state legislatures were not acting, nor was the federal court system offering any relief. The state courts, by utilizing their state constitutions, became the prime motivators of policy change and were able to move state educational finance policy and help minimize the level of inequality in educational opportunity for children.

Our final chapter continued our look at the state courts by examining a highly controversial social policy—that of same-sex marriage. Same-sex marriage litigation attempts present a particularly stark example of how courts may face significant backlash when their rulings fall outside the policy preferences held by the other branches of government and the public. In many instances, state legislatures and the public reacted to court decisions by amending state law and state constitutions, and, in a number of states, taking such actions preemptively in order to forestall progay marriage court rulings. However, we also noted the important role of courts in moving the same-sex marriage debate onto the national agenda. For example, several scholars argue that, even with subsequent legislative defeats, significant court victories can activate and mobilize supporters and provide the political leverage necessary for these supporters to successfully engage in the "politics of rights."

2. Courts and the Political System

Clearly courts contribute to, change, alter and help define public and social policy in the United States at both the federal and state levels. Several factors contribute to the courts' ability to influence and change policy, even though, at the federal level, they lack electoral support or accountability. For one thing, courts are held in high esteem, particularly when compared to the other branches of government. The Supreme Court, the most extensively studied of all courts, is unusual among the branches of government in that it enjoys consistently high levels of public support (Adamany and Grossman 1983; Caldeira and Gibson 1992; Jaros and Roper 1980; Mondak and Smithey 1997; Murphy and Tanenhaus 1968). What distinguishes the Supreme Court from the executive and legislative branches is the "cult of the robe" (Frank 1963, 254–61), or the widely held perception that the Court operates "above politics" (Jaros and Roper 1980).

Scholars have broken down the support for the Court into two different categories, diffuse support and specific support (Easton 1965). Specific support involves citizens' attitudes toward particular officials and policies while diffuse support implies support for an institution. Thus, specific support measures public attitudes toward the Supreme Court justices and the Court's rulings, while diffuse support measures the public's support for the legitimacy of the Court apart from its membership and decisions. In many instances, the Court's controversial decisions affect specific support (e.g., confidence in the justices) but not diffuse support (e.g., legitimacy of the institution). As a result, courts possess long-term legitimacy in the public's eyes. Even a controversial "activist" decision, while impeding a court's short-term specific support, does little to diminish its long-term diffuse support.

This distinction means that the Court has the ability to render controversial decisions, which while potentially affecting support in the short-term, do not diminish the institution of the judiciary. Consequently, the Court possesses the freedom to issue controversial rulings and forestall backlash while still retaining the respect and support of the public and the political system. The cult of the robe also allows the political system to adopt and eventually enforce Court rulings. We rarely see effective, sustained opposition to federal judicial rulings in the present day United States.

The disadvantage to the "cult of the robe" is that it leads to the myth of neutrality. If courts are above politics, they should not and cannot engage in policy debates and make political decisions. However, as we note throughout this book, judges are political actors and make political decisions all the time. Law is dynamic rather than static, and sometimes there are conflicting or open-ended precedents supporting both sides of the debate. Other times, courts are called upon to issue rulings or render opinions on novel areas or questions of the law.

The Supreme Court in particular, aided by its discretionary docket and seat at the top of the judicial hierarchy, often takes controversial cases and renders decisions that fail to generate support by many political leaders and large segments of the voting public. Many times these decisions are derided as judicial activism and biased judging. The failure to acknowledge the ideological nature of judges and judging and the unavoidability of preferences in judicial decision making, however, does a disservice to the nature and the difficulty of judicial decision making.

We also have tried to demonstrate that supporters and defenders of courts and policymaking both over- and underestimate the extent of the ability of courts to move and change policy. Courts do play an important and substantive role in policy change. We have illustrated this role with seven chapters showing the influence of both state and federal courts on areas ranging from gender equality to environmental policy to same-sex marriage.

However, the political system is not bound to take a court's decision as the final word. Even a federal constitutional ruling can be, and has been, altered through the amendment process, albeit rarely in American political history. Rulings can also be changed or undercut through subsequent legislation, executive action, defiance or the selection of new judges (see e.g., Steigerwalt 2010).

Most notably, changes in judicial preferences and rulings naturally occur as a result of changes in the dominant political coalition. Over time, unpopular decisions out of sync with the dominant political and societal preferences will likely be overturned simply through the replacement of court personnel. Political actors will be elected who reflect the majority's preferences and, in turn, these actors will nominate and confirm judges who reflect their preferences and ideological beliefs, leading eventually to changes in court rulings. One of the most prominent examples involves the rulings of the Supreme Court during the first several years of the administration of Franklin D. Roosevelt. This conservative court, a relic of twelve years of Republican appointments, was known as the Court of the "Four Horsemen of the Apocalypse" (see Jenson 1992). This name reflected a concerted bloc of four conservative justices, Pierce Butler, James McReynolds, George Sutherland and Willis Van Devanter, who opposed and consistently voted against Roosevelt's New Deal agenda. This solid voting bloc often meant judicial defeat of New Deal legislation. Roosevelt's response, following his landslide reelection victory in the 1936 presidential election, was to suggest a "court packing" plan which would enable him to expand the size of the Court and appoint new justices for each current justice over the age of seventy. While Roosevelt's plan was defeated, the pressure asserted by Roosevelt and other New Deal supporters allegedly led Justice Owen Roberts to switch his vote to support the New Deal legislation. This change by Roberts is often called the "switch in time that saved nine."

Eventually Roosevelt was able to replace all of these justices, and the Court moved in the ideological and philosophical direction of Roosevelt and the New Deal majority in Congress. The prior Court was outside of the legal set established by the politically elected actors and they ultimately lost control of the policy process. The implication of this story is that the Supreme Court, as well as other courts, can influence and even challenge public and social policy, but also that the Court must be aware of how its rulings correlate with the preferences of elected officials and the broader public.

3. Conclusion: Judges, Judicial Decisions and Politics

We do not mean to suggest that courts willfully ignore the law in their decisional process, nor do we mean to suggest that judges and courts strictly pay attention to executive and legislative preferences and rigidly calculate their potential response when rendering their decisions. In fact, the extent of the influence of the law is an ongoing topic of research for legal and social science scholars, with a number of recent studies suggesting that the law plays a far more important and dynamic role in judicial policymaking than previously acknowledged (see e.g., Bartels 2009; Corley, Steigerwalt and Ward n.d.; Lax 2007; Richards and Kritzer 2002).

The tension, however, is that we call upon courts to resolve issues and render opinions in a multitude of areas that have been left to them by the elected actors in the American political system. In fact, there are numerous instances where legislatures have consciously written vague laws or left important questions unanswered, knowing that the courts will be asked to resolve these issues (see e.g., Melnick 1994). And, once a proper legal challenge is raised, courts have no choice but to resolve these issues. For example, Melnick (1985) details how Congress passed the Education for All Handicapped Children Act in 1975, requiring that all children must be given an "appropriate" education by public schools. The problem, however, is that the legislation failed to define what comprised an "appropriate" education. Moreover, the law explicitly gave parents the standing to challenge the educational plans devised by schools for their children and required judges to make an "independent" decision based on the evidence. The end result was to deliberately transfer power for such decisions from state and local officials to federal judges. Not surprisingly, many local officials decried the decisions judges reached, but the reality is that these judges were simply acting as Congress had prescribed.

Furthermore, legislatures may even pass laws in order to strategically utilize judicial decisions for political reasons. The debate over flag burning in 1989 illuminates how Congress may knowingly pass unconstitutional laws in order to force a Supreme Court decision to aid Congress's ultimate goal. After the U.S. Supreme Court struck down a Texas law banning flag burning in *Texas v. Johnson* in 1989, Congress passed the Flag Protection Act later that year. What made the debate over the law notable was the rather large contingent of lawmakers who voted for the law while also acknowledging that the law would likely not survive constitutional challenge. Why would members vote for a law they knew to be constitutional? Simply put, because these members *wanted* the Supreme Court to strike down this federal law in the hopes that the Court's decision would mobilize enough support for successfully enacting a constitutional amendment. As Senator Robert Kasten remarked, "The matter before us tonight is an attempt to provide, by statute, the protection our flag deserves. Given the decision of five Supreme Court Justices that the statute in *Texas versus Johnson* violated the Constitution, I don't believe this vehicle will work. But I will support this effort until the Senate considers the constitutional amendment which will provide the protection the flag deserves."[2] Members of Congress thus tried to strategically conjure a Supreme Court decision—having also written into the law a provision for a direct appeal to the Court, and knowing full well the likely outcome—in order to achieve their real political goal.[3]

The consequence of such legislative actions—and, indeed, the constitutional duties imposed on courts—is that courts will always have an influential role in policy formation and change. Courts will continue to be asked to fulfill their duty of interpreting state and federal laws as well as state and federal constitutions. And, they will may many times do so in the face of vague and ambiguous phrases which make their job all the more difficult, and in the midst of contentious political debates which heighten the implications of their decisions. However, if courts were to decline to answer these legal questions—if they were to decline to fulfill their constitutionally imposed duties—we the people would only suffer. We would thus be well served by acknowledging the courts' important—and many times misunderstood and much-maligned—role in interpreting laws and constitutions and ultimately affecting the development and direction of policy in the United States.

TABLE OF CASES

NOTES

1 Introduction

1. For a review of the contributions of the scholars who developed the concept of judicial attitudes, see *Pioneers of Judicial Behavior* (Maveety 2003).
2. Segal, Timpone and Howard (2000) also constructed a social liberalism score.
3. Songer constructed a civil liberties ideology score, as well (see Songer, Davis and Haire. 1994).
4. Because of the heavy and growing workload of the courts of appeals in the post-World War II era, en banc hearings constitute only a negligible number of appeals. For example, excluding the Federal Circuit, the courts of appeals employ three-judge panels in over 99% of all administrative hearings (Schuck and Elliott 1990).
5. 135 *Congressional Record* S12650-02, *S12650 (101st Congress, 1st session, October 5, 1989. Remarks concerning the Flag Protection Act of 1989).
6. Subsequent to *Marbury v. Madison* (1803), the Court did not strike another federal law for more than fifty years. But the pace of judicial invalidation of both state and federal legislation picked up considerably after the Civil War. With the end of the war, the Court began using its power of judicial review on a more regular basis, with peaks occurring during the 1860s, the administration of Theodore Roosevelt, after World War I, during the 1920s and 1930s and since the 1960s (Caldeira and McCrone 1982).

2 Courts and Taxes

1. The first act was passed July 6, 1861, although no income tax revenue was collected under this act. The second and more important act was passed July 1, 1862. By this time, Congress knew the Civil War was going to last more than 90 days, creating a need for increased government revenue.
2. The office of the Commissioner of Internal Revenue as part of the Bureau of Internal Revenue (Chommie 1970), was created to collect income tax. Although successful in financing the Civil War, the income tax act expired in 1872. The Bureau of Internal Revenue still existed, however, to administer and collect other taxes that had been established, and had almost 4,000 employees. That figure remained constant for the next fifty years.

3. The Amendment states that: "Congress shall have power to lay and collect taxes on incomes, from whatever source derived, without apportionment among the several states, and without regard to any census or enumeration."

4. Constitutional amendments have been used to overturn four Supreme Court rulings. The last was the Twenty-Sixth Amendment, ratified in 1971, that allowed 18-year-olds the right to vote; this amendment overturned the Supreme Court's decision in *Oregon v. Mitchell* (1970).

5. Sears wrote: "It is intended that Part I shall be frank and devoid of that mock patriotism which preaches from the taxing power's vantage point and secretly takes advantage of any loophole in the law. No tricks are advocated or alluded to in this book, except to illustrate the fundamental differences between avoidance and evasion" (1922, iii).

6. Quoted by Judy Mann, "We All End Up Paying For Deadbeats," *Washington Post*, January 6, 1995, p. E3. As evidence of the lack of compliance, Brand noted that when the law was changed to require the listing of social security numbers for dependents, "Seven million dependents disappeared in the United States."

7. I.R.C. § 7482.

8. Congress has the power to create courts under the Constitution. The Tax Court is a constitutional court established by Congress under Article I as opposed to Article III. Article III, Section 1 of the.U.S. Constitution states: "The judicial power of the United States shall be vested in one Supreme Court, and in such inferior courts as the Congress may from time to time ordain and establish." These judges have lifetime tenure and salary protection. By contrast, Article I legislative court judges have fixed terms and lack the salary guarantee.

9. Criminal tax cases are prosecuted in a much shorter time frame, in part because a criminal defendant has a constitutional right to a speedy trial before a jury.

4 The Status of Women

1. It should be noted that the facts of the case suggest that the sexual encounter was not, in fact, consensual: The minor female described how she initially told Michael "no" when he began pushing her to have sex. It was only after he physically assaulted her that she "consented." It is not clear from the Supreme Court's opinion why the decision was made to bring statutory, as opposed to general rape charges. However, that decision is what led to this case, since the statute governing statutory rape distinguished explicitly between minor females and minor males.

2. The Supreme Court's decision in *Geduldig* did *not* prohibit the states or federal government from enacting statutes which protect pregnant women against discrimination. Rather, the ruling stipulated that laws which treated pregnant women differently from other persons would not be viewed as sex-based laws for the purposes of equal protection analysis. However, that does not make laws which protect pregnant women unconstitutional.

3. Information on EEOC enforcement statistics. Retrieved from http://www.eeoc.gov/eeoc/statistics/enforcement/sex.cfm. The EEOC is what many refer to as a quasi-judicial executive agency, since it can investigate charges, file lawsuits on behalf of individuals and oversee mediation between employers and employees, a type of alternative dispute resolution which produces a legally binding settlement.

6 Discrimination and Educational Affirmative Action

1. While the Fifteenth Amendment guaranteed the right of all citizens to vote, it was subsequently interpreted to mean that all male citizens possessed the right to vote. It was not until the ratification of the Nineteenth Amendment in 1920 that women were also constitutionally guaranteed the right to vote.
2. Courts in the American system can only hear and rule on cases involving actual, and not hypothetical, disputes for which a court decision can remedy the legal wrong alleged. However, a case is considered "moot" when the facts of the case have changed such that a court-ordered remedy is no longer necessary or applicable. In *DeFunis*, since the petitioner was already enrolled in law school, an order forcing the school to admit him would be necessarily useless, and thus the case was rendered moot.

7 School Finance Reform

1. The six states where the courts have not ruled on education finance litigation are Delaware, Hawaii, Mississippi, Nevada, Utah and Iowa. No litigation has been filed in the first five states, while in Iowa there has not been a court decision (National Access Network http://www.schoolfunding.info/index.php3). Hawaii has a statewide unified school district and therefore no variation across districts.
2. Scholarly literature shows courts can send signals to the legislature (see Hausegger and Baum 1999), and this happened with the Nebraska Supreme Court and the Nebraska legislature (Bosworth 2001).

8 Same-Sex Marriage

1. It should be noted that we are interested here in the state regulation of civil marriage, which is wholly distinct from religious marriage. The recognition of marriage by religious denominations and their affiliates is determined by the individual religions, and the decision of a state to recognize (or not) same-sex marriages is separate from the question of whether a particular religious denomination decides to recognize the marriage.

9 Conclusion

1. Speech given on the Senate floor on April 4, 2005. *Congressional Record* at S3126.
2. Senator Robert Kasten, October 5, 1989. Remarks on the Senate floor concerning the Flag Protection Act of 1989.135 *Congressional Record* S12650-02, *S12650.
3. These members were indeed prescient: the Supreme Court struck down the law in the 1990 case of *United States v. Eichman* (496 U.S. 310). However, the resultant efforts to pass a constitutional amendment prohibiting flag burning failed.

REFERENCES

Aamot, Gregg. 1998. "New Laws Target Pregnant Drinkers." *Associated Press*, May 31.

Adamany, David, and Joel B. Grossman. 1983. "Support for the Supreme Court as a National Policymaker." *Law and Politics Quarterly* 5: 405–37.

Allen, James. 1996. "Bills of Rights and Judicial Power—A Liberal's Quandary." *Oxford Journal of Legal Studies* 16: 337.

American Civil Liberties Union (ACLU). 2009. Letter Re: House Bill 12, "Criminal Homicide and Abortion Amendments." American Civil Liberties Union of Utah, February 19.

Balkin, Jack M. 2001. "*Bush v. Gore* and the Boundary between Law and Politics." *Yale Law Journal* 110: 1450–58.

Bartels, Brandon L. 2009. "The Constraining Capacity of Legal Doctrine on the U.S. Supreme Court." *American Political Science Review* 103: 474–95.

Baum, Lawrence. 1990. *American Courts: Process and Policy.* Boston: Houghton Mifflin.

Baum, Lawrence. 1994. "Specialization and Authority Acceptance: The Supreme Court and Lower Federal Courts." *Political Research Quarterly* 47: 693–703.

Baum, Lawrence. 2001. *The Supreme Court* (7th ed.). Washington, DC: Congressional Quarterly Press.

Baumgartner, Frank R. 2001. Political Agendas. In *International Encyclopedia of Social and Behavioral Sciences: Political Science,* Niel J. Smelser and Paul B. Baltes, eds., pp. 288–90. New York: Elsevier Science and Oxford: Pergamon.

Beck, Nathaniel L., and Jonathan N. Katz. 1995. "What to Do (and Not to Do) with Time-Series—Cross-Section Data." *American Political Science Review* 89: 634–47.

Berry, Francis Stokes, and William D. Berry. 1990. "State Lottery Adoptions as Policy Innovations: An Event History Analysis." *American Political Science Review* 84: 395–415.

Berry, Frances Stokes, and William D. Berry. 1994. "The Politics of Tax Increases in the States." *American Journal of Political Science* 38: 855–59.

Berry, William D., Evan J. Ringquist, Richard C. Fording, and Russell L. Hanson. 1998. "Measuring Citizen and Government Ideology in the American States." *American Journal of Political Science* 42: 337–46.

Beth, Loren. 1999. Pollock vs. Farmers' Loan and Trust Company. In *The Oxford Guide to United States Supreme Court Decisions,* Kermit Hall, ed., pp. 241–42. New York: Oxford University Press.

Bookman, John T. 2008. *The Mythology of American Politics: A Critical Response to Fundamental Questions.* Dulles, VA: Potomac Books.

Bork, Robert H. 1971. "Neutral Principles and Some First Amendment Problems." *Indiana Law Journal* 47: 1–35.

Bork, Robert H. 2003. *Slouching towards Gomorrah: Modern Liberalism and American Decline.* New York: HarperCollins.

Bosworth, Matthew H. 2001. *Courts as Catalysts: State Supreme Courts and Public School Finance Equity.* Albany, NY: State University of New York Press.

Bowen, William G., and Derek Bok. 1998. *The Shape of the River.* Princeton, NJ: Princeton University Press.

Boyd, William Lowe, David N. Plank, and Gary Sykes. 1998. "Teachers' Unions in Hard Times." Paper presented at Conference on Teachers' Unions and Educational Reform, Kennedy School of Government, Harvard University, Cambridge, MA.

Brace, Paul, and Melinda Gann Hall.1990. "Neo-Institutionalism and Dissent in State Supreme." *Journal of Politics* 52: 54.

Brace, Paul, Laura Langer, and Melinda Gann Hall. 2000. "Measuring the Preferences of State Supreme Court Judges." *Journal of Politics* 62: 387–413.

Brennan, William J., Jr. 1977. "State Constitutions and the Protection of Individual Rights." *Harvard Law Review* 90: 489–504.

Brennan, William J., Jr. 1985. "The Great Debate: Speech to the Text and Teaching Symposium." Georgetown University, Washington, DC, October 12. http://www.fed-soc.org/resources/id.50/default.asp

Cahill, Sean Robert. 2004. *Same-Sex Marriage in the United States: Focus on the Facts.* Lanham, MD: Lexington Books.

Caldeira, Gregory A., and James L. Gibson. 1992. "The Etiology of Public Support for the Supreme Court." *American Journal of Political Science* 36: 635–64.

Caldeira, Gregory A., and Donald J. McCrone. 1982. "Of Time and Judicial Activism: A Study of the U.S. Supreme Court, 1800–1973." In *Supreme Court Activism and Restraint*, Stephen C. Halpern and Charles M. Lamb, eds., pp. 103–27. Lexington, MA: Lexington Books.

Canes-Wrone, Brandice. 2003. "Bureaucratic Decisions and the Composition of the Lower Courts." *American Journal of Political Science* 47: 302–14.

Cann, Damon, and Teena Wilhelm. 2011. "Policy Reform via Courts, Legislatures and Citizens: The Case of Education Finance." *Social Science Quarterly* (forthcoming).

Caron, Paul L., ed. 2003. *Tax Stories: An In-Depth Look at Ten Leading Federal Income Tax Cases.* New York: Foundation Press.

Carson, Rachel. 1962. *Silent Spring.* New York: Houghton Mifflin.

Chavez, Linda. 2003. "Women in Combat Will Take a Toll on Our Culture," April 30. http://www.Townhall.com.

Chommie, John C. 1970. *The Internal Revenue Service.* New York: Praeger.

Clune, William H. 1994. "The Shift from Equity to Adequacy in School Finance." *Educational Policy* 8: 376–94.

Collins, Ronald K. L., and Peter J. Galie. 1986. "Models of Post-Incorporation Judicial Review: 1985 Survey of State Constitutional Individual Rights Decisions." *Publius: The Journal of Federalism* 16: 111–39.

Collins, Ronald K. L., Peter J. Galie, and John Kincaid. 1986. "State High Courts, State Constitutions, and Individual Rights Litigation since 1980: A Judicial Survey." *Publius: The Journal of Federalism* 16: 141–62.

Commager, Henry Steele. 1943. *Majority Rule and Minority Rights.* New York: Oxford University Press.

Cooley, Thomas. 1868. *A Treatise on the Constitutional Limitations Which Rest upon the Legislative Power of the States of the American Union.* Boston: Little, Brown.

Coons, John E., William H. Clune, and Stephen D. Sugarman. 1971. *Private Wealth and Public Education.* Cambridge, MA: Belknap Press of Harvard University Press.

Corley, Pamela C., Amy Steigerwalt, and Artemus Ward. (n.d.). *Deciding to Agree: Explaining Consensus on the United States Supreme Court.* Unpublished book manuscript.

Culver, John H., and John T. Wold. 1986. "Rose Bird and the Politics of Judicial Accountability in California." *Judicature* 70: 81.

Dahl, Robert A. 1957. "Decision-Making in a Democracy: The Supreme Court as a National Policy Maker." *Journal of Public Law* 6: 279–95.

Daily, Frederick W. 1992. *Stand Up to the IRS.* Berkeley, CA: Nolo Press.

Davis, Devra L. 2002. *When Smoke Ran Like Water: Tales of environmental deception and the Battle Against Pollution.* New York: Basic Books.

D'Emilio, John. "Will the Courts Set Us Free? Reflections on the Campaign for Same-Sex Marriage." In *The Politics of Same-Sex Marriage*, Craig A. Rimmerman and Clyde Wilcox, eds., pp. 39–64. Chicago: University of Chicago Press.

Dixon, Ken. 2009. "Rell Signs Gay Marriage Bill." *Connecticut Post*, April 23, News section.

Dolan, Maura. 2008. "Gay Pairs are Urged Not to Sue." *Los Angeles Times*, June 11, http://articles.latimes.com/2008/jun/11/local/me-gaymarriage11

Donovan, Todd, Christopher Z. Mooney, and Daniel A. Smith. 2008. *State and Local Politics: Institutions and Reform.* Independence, KY: Cengage Learning.

Dornbusch, Sanford M., Philip L. Ritter, and Laurence Steinberg. 1991. "Community Influences on the Relation of Family Statuses to Adolescent School Performance: Differences between African-Americans and Non-Hispanic Whites." *American Journal of Education* 99: 543–67.

Dubroff, Harold. 1979. *The United States Tax Court: An Historical Analysis.* Chicago: Commerce Clearing House.

Easterbrook, Frank H. 1990. "Success and the Judicial Power." *Indiana Law Journal* 65: 277–82.

Easton, David. 1965. *A Systems Analysis of Political Life.* New York: Wiley.

Elazar, Daniel J. 1966. *American Federalism: A View from the States.* New York: Crowell.

Epstein, Lee, Valerie Hoekstra, Jeffrey A. Segal, and Harold J. Spaeth. 1998. "Do Political Preferences Change? A Longitudinal Study of U.S. Supreme Court Justices." *Journal of Politics* 60: 801–18.

Epstein, Lee, and Jack Knight. 1998. *Choices Justices Make.* Washington, DC: Congressional Quarterly Press.

Epstein, Lee, Andrew D. Martin, Jeffrey A. Segal, and Chad Westerland. 2007. "The Judicial Common Space." *Journal of Law, Economics and Organization* 23: 303–25.

Epstein, Lee, Jeffrey A. Segal, Harold J. Spaeth, and Thomas G. Walker. 2003. *Supreme Court Compendium.* Washington, DC: Congressional Quarterly Press.

Erikson, Robert S., Gerald C. Wright, and John P. McIver. 1989. "Political Parties, Public Opinion, and State Policy in the United States." *American Political Science Review* 83: 729–50.

Evans, William N., Sheila E. Murray, and Robert M. Schwab. 1997. "Schoolhouses, Courthouses, and Statehouses after *Serrano*." *Journal of Policy Analysis and Management* 16: 10–31.

Feder, Jody. 2005. *Federal and State Laws Regarding Pharmacists Who Refuse to Dispense Contraceptives* (CRS Report RS2293). Washington, DC: Congressional Research Service.

Feeley, Malcolm, and Edward Rubin. 2000. *Judicial Policy Making and the Modern State: How the Courts Reformed America's Prisons*. New York: Cambridge University Press

Fentiman, Linda C. 2009. "In the Name of Fetal Protection: Why American Prosecutors Pursue Pregnant Drug Users (And Other Countries Don't)." *Columbia Journal of Gender and Law* 18: 647–69.

Ferejohn, John, and Charles Shipan. 1990. "Congressional Influence on Bureaucracy." *Journal of Law, Economics, & Organization* 6: 1–20.

Fisher, Patrick, and Travis Pratt. 2006. "Political Culture and the Death Penalty." *Criminal Justice Policy Review* 17: 48–60.

Flemming, Roy B., John Bohte, and B. Dan Wood. 1997. "One Voice among Many: The Supreme Court's Influence on Attentiveness to Issues in the United States, 1947–92." *American Journal of Political Science* 41: 1224–50.

Franck, Matthew J. 1996. *Against the Imperial Judiciary: The Supreme Court vs. the Sovereignty of the People*. Lawrence, KY: University Press of Kansas.

Frank, Jerome. 1930. *Law and the Modern Mind*. New York: Brentano.

Frank, Jerome. 1949. *Courts on Trial: Myth and Reality in American Justice*. Princeton, NJ: Princeton University Press.

Frank, Jerome. 1963. *Courts on Trial: Myth and Reality in American Justice* (paperback edition). New York: Atheneum.

Fuller, Lon L. 1960. "Adjudication and the Rule of Law." *Proceedings of the American Society of International Law* 54: 1–8.

Gambitta, Richard A. L. 1981. "Litigation, Judicial Deference, and Policy Change." In *Governing Through Courts*, Richard A. L. Gambitta, Marlynn L. May, and James C. Foster, eds., pp. 259–84. Beverly Hills, CA: Sage.

Gash, Alison. 2010. *Below the Radar: How Silence Saved Civil Rights*. Ph.D. Dissertation, University of California, Berkeley, May.

Geier, Deborah A. 1991. "The Tax Court, Article Three, and the Proposal Advanced by the Federal Courts Study Committee: A Study in Applied Constitutional Theory." *Cornell Law Review* 76: 985–1035.

Giles, Micheal W., Virginia A. Hettinger, and Todd Peppers. 2001. "Picking Federal Judges: A Note on Policy and Partisan Selection Agendas." *Political Research Quarterly* 54: 623–41.

Golden, Tim. 1997. "California's Ban on Preferences Goes into Effect." *New York Times*, August 29, A1.

Gonzales, Nancy A., Ana Mari Cauce, Ruth J. Friedman, and Craig A. Mason. 1996. "Family, Peer, and Neighborhood Influences on Academic Achievement among African-American Adolescents: One-Year Prospective Effects." *American Journal of Community Psychology* 24: 365–87.

Graber, Mark A. 1993. "The Non-Majoritarian Problem: Legislative Deference to the Judiciary." *Studies in American Political Development* 7: 35.

Graglia, Lino A. 2005. "Constitutional Law without the Constitution: The Supreme Court's Remaking of America." In *"A Country I Do Not Recognize": The Legal Assault on American Values*, Robert H. Bork, ed., pp. 1–55. Stanford, CA: Hoover Institution Press.

Graham, Troy. 2006. "Legislature OKs Civil-Union Bill." *Philadelphia Inquirer*, December 15, B1.

Gray, Virginia. 1973. "Innovations in the States: A Diffusion Study." *American Political Science Review* 67: 1174–85.

Greene, William H. 1997. *Econometric Analysis*. New York: Prentice Hall.

Greenhouse, Linda. 2005. *Becoming Justice Blackmun: Harry Blackmun's Supreme Court Journey*. New York: Times Books/Henry Holt.

Gregg, Katherine. 2011. "Same-Sex Marriage Bill to Be Introduced Thursday." *The Providence Journal*, January 6, Local section, p.8.

Gunther, Gerald. 1986. *Individual Rights in Constitutional Law*. New York: Foundation Press.

Guttmacher Institute. 2010. "State Policies in Brief: Refusing to Provide Health Services." Policy brief by the Guttmacher Institute, updated December 1. http://www.guttmacher.org/statecenter/spibs/spib_RPHS.pdf

Haider-Markel, Donald P., and Ronald La Due Lake. 1998. "The Importance of Institutional Structures on Legislative Outcomes: Lessons from the American States." Paper presented at the Annual American Political Science Association Conference, Boston, MA, September.

Haigh, Susan. 2005. "Conn. House OKs Civil Unions." *Boston Globe* (reprinted from *The Associated Press*), April 14.

Hall, Kermit L., Paul Finkelman, and James W. Ely Jr. 2005. *American Legal History: Cases and Materials* (3rd ed.). New York: Oxford University Press.

Hall, Melinda Gann. 1992. "Electoral Politics and Strategic Voting in State Supreme Courts." *Journal of Politics* 54: 427.

Hall, Melinda Gann. 2001. "State Supreme Courts in American Democracy: Probing the Myths of Judicial Reform." *American Political Science Review* 95: 315–30.

Hammond, Thomas H., and Jack H. Knott. 1996. "Who Controls the Bureaucracy? Presidential Power, Congressional Dominance, Legal Constraints, and Bureaucratic Autonomy in a Model of Multi-Institutional Policymaking." *Journal of Law, Economics and Organization* 12: 121–68.

Hand, Learned. 1952. *The Spirit of Liberty: Papers and Addresses of Learned Hand Collected, and with an Introduction and Notes by Irving Dilliard*. New York: Knopf.

Hand, Learned. 1959. *Spirit of Liberty: Papers and Addresses*. New York: Vintage Books.

Hansen, Wendy L., Renee J. Johnson, and Isaac Unah. 1995. "Specialized Courts, Bureaucratic Agencies, and the Politics of U.S. Trade Policy." *American Journal of Political Science* 39: 529–57.

Harriman, Ann. 1996. *Women/Men/Management* (2nd ed.). Westport, CT: Greenwood.

Harris, Lisa H., and Lynn Paltrow. 2003. "The Status of Pregnant Women and Fetuses in U.S. Criminal Law." *Journal of the American Medical Association* 13: 1697–1999.

Hausegger, Lori, and Lawrence Baum. 1999. "Inviting Congressional Action: A Study of Supreme Court Motivations in Statutory Interpretation." *American Journal of Political Science* 43: 162–85.

Headlam, Bruce. 2002 "Nothing Personal." *New York Times Magazine*, February 17. http://www.nytimes.com/2002/02/17/magazine/17WWLN.html

Hill, Kim Quaile, and Jan E. Leighly. 1992. "The Policy Consequences of Class Bias in American State Electorates." *American Journal of Political Science* 36: 351–65.

Hoekstra, Valerie. 2000. "The Supreme Court and Local Public Opinion." *American Political Science Review* 94: 89–100.

Hogan, Cara. 2011. "Gay Marriage Law Could Be Repealed." *Eagle Tribune*, January 9, State and Regional News section.

Howard, Robert M. 2001. "Wealth, Audits and Lawsuits: Responsiveness of the IRS to Wealth and Power." *Social Science Quarterly* 82: 268–80.

Howard, Robert M. 2005. "Comparing the Decision Making of Specialized Courts and General Courts: An Exploration of Tax Decisions." *The Justice System Journal* 26: 135–48.

Howard, Robert M. 2009. *Getting a Poor Return: Courts, Justice and Taxes*. Albany, NY: State University of New York Press.

Howard, Robert M., and David C. Nixon. 2002. "Regional Influences within a Separation of Powers Framework: Courts, Ideological Preferences and IRS Local Policymaking." *Political Research Quarterly* 55: 907–22.

Howard, Robert M., and David C. Nixon. 2003. "Local Control of the Bureaucracy: Federal Appeals Courts, Ideology, and the Internal Revenue Service." *Washington University Journal of Law & Policy* 13: 233–356.

Howard, Robert M., and Jeffrey A. Segal. 2004. "A Preference for Deference? The Supreme Court and Judicial Review." *Political Research Quarterly* 57: 131–43.

Huber, Gregory A., and Sanford C. Gordon. 2004. "Accountability and Coercion: Is Justice Blind when It Runs for Office?" *American Journal of Political Science* 48: 247–63.

Humphries, Martha Anne, and Donald R. Songer. 1999. "Law and Politics in Judicial Oversight of Administrative Agencies." *Journal of Politics* 61: 207–20.

Hunter, Susan, and Richard W. Waterman. 1992 "Determining an Agency's Regulatory Style: How Does the EPA Water Office Enforce the Law?" *Western Political Quarterly* 45: 403–17.

James, Susan Donaldson. 2010. "Pregnant Woman Fights Court-Ordered Bed Rest." *ABC News.com*, January 14. http://abcnews.go.com/Health/florida-court-orders-pregnant-woman-bed-rest-medical/story?id=9561460&page=1.

Jaros, Dean, and Robert Roper. 1980. "The U.S. Supreme Court: Myth, Diffuse Support, Specific Support and Legitimacy." *American Politics Quarterly* 8: 85–105.

Jenson, Carol E. 1992. "New Deal". In *Oxford Companion to the United States Supreme Court*, Kermit L. Hall, ed., pp. 1067–68. Oxford: Oxford University Press.

Johnson, Timothy, and Andrew Martin. 1998. "The Public's Conditional Response to Supreme Court Decisions." *American Political Science Review* 92: 299–309.

Kairys, David. 2001. "Bush v. Gore Blues." *Jurist: The Legal Education Network*. http://jurist.law.pitt.edu/forumnew23.htm.

Kane, Thomas J., Stephanie K. Riegg, and Douglas O. Staiger. 2006. "School Quality, Neighborhoods and Housing Prices." http://home.gwu.edu/-scellini/KaneRiegg Staiger_web.pdf

Karch, Andrew. 2007. *Democratic Laboratories: Policy Diffusion among the American States*. Ann Arbor, MI: University of Michigan Press.

Katzmann, Robert A. 1997. *The Courts and Congress*. Washington, DC: Brookings Institution.

Keck, Thomas M. 2004. *The Most Activist Supreme Court in History: The Road to Modern Judicial Conservatism*. Chicago: University of Chicago Press.

Kingdon, John. 1989. *Congressmen's Voting Decisions*. Ann Arbor: University of Michigan Press.

Klarner, Carl. 2003. "The Measurement of the Partisan Balance of State Government." *State Politics & Policy Quarterly* 3: 309–19.

Koven, Steven G., and Christopher Mausolff. 2002. "The Influence of Political Culture on State Budgets: Another Look at Elazar's Forumulation." *American Review of Public Administration* 32: 66–77.

Krehbiel, Keith. 1991. *Information and Legislative Organization.* Ann Arbor: University of Michigan Press.

Krehbiel, Keith. 1996. "Institutional and Partisan Sources of Gridlock." *Journal of Theoretical Politics* 8: 7–40.

Krehbiel, Keith. 1998. *Pivotal Politics: A Theory of U.S. Lawmaking.* Chicago: University of Chicago Press.

Kroll, Glenn. 1996. "Are Tax Court Judges Partial to the Public?" *Oil & Gas Tax Quarterly* 45: 135.

Kuklinski, James H., and John E. Stanga. 1979. "Political Participation and Government Responsiveness: The Behavior of California Superior Courts." *American Political Science Review* 73: 1090–99.

Langer, Laura. 2002. *Judicial Review in State Supreme Courts: A Comparative Study.* Albany, NY: State University of New York Press.

Lax, Jeffrey R. 2007. "Constructing Legal Rules on Appellate Courts." *American Political Science Review* 101: 591–604.

Lazarus, Richard James. 2000. "Restoring What's Environmental about Environmental Law in the Supreme Court." SSRN eLibrary. http://papers.ssrn.com/sol3/papers.cfm?abstract_id=216433

Legomsky, Stephen. 1990. *Specialized Justice: Courts, Administrative Tribunals, and a Cross-National Theory of Specialization.* Oxford: Oxford University Press.

Leland, John. 2010. "Abortion Foes Advance Cause at State Level." *New York Times,* June 3, A18.

Leonard, Arthur S. 1997. *Homosexuality and the Constitution: Volume 4, Homosexuality and the Family.* Florence, KY: Taylor and Francis.

Leventhal, Harold. 1974. "Environmental Decision Making and the Role of the Courts." *University of Pennsylvania Law Review* 122: 509–55.

Levy, Richard E., and Robert L. Glicksman. 1989. "Judicial Activism and Restraint in the Supreme Court's Environmental Law Decisions." *Vanderbilt Law Review* 42: 343–431.

Lieb, David A. 2010. "Missouri Governor Lets Abortion Law Take Effect." *Associated Press,* July 14.

Llewelyn, Karl N. 1930. "A Realistic Jurisprudence: The Next Step." *Columbia Law Review* 30: 431–65.

Llewelyn, Karl N. 1962. *Jurisprudence: Realism in Theory and Practice.* Chicago: University of Chicago Press.

Lovell, George I. 2003. *Legislative Deferrals: Statutory Ambiguity, Judicial Power and American Democracy.* New York: Cambridge University Press.

Luker, Kristen. 1985. *Abortion and the Politics of Motherhood.* Berkeley: University of California Press.

Mann, Judy. 1995. "We All End Up Paying For Deadbeats." *Washington Post,* January 6, E3.

Martin, Andrew D., and Kevin Quinn. 2002. "Dynamic Ideal Point Estimation via Markov Chain Monte Carlo for the U.S. Supreme Court, 1953–1999." *Political Analysis* 10: 134–53.

Martin, Andrew D., and Kevin Quinn. 2007. "Assessing Preference Change on the U.S. Supreme Court." *Journal of Law Economics and Organization* 23: 365–85

Martinek, Wendy L., Mark Kemper, and Steven R. Van Winkle. 2002. "To Advise and Consent: The Senate and Lower Federal Court Nominations, 1977–1998." *Journal of Politics* 64: 337–61.

Massey, Calvin. 2011. "The Originalist: Interview with Justice Antonin Scalia." *California Lawyer*. http://www.callawyer.com/story.cfm?eid=913358&evid=1, January.

Mather, Lynn. 1995. "The Fired Football Coach (Or, How Trial Courts Make Policy)." In *Contemplating Courts*, Lee Epstein, ed., 170–202. Washington, DC: Congressional Quarterly Press.

Maule, James Edward. 1999. "Instant Replay, Weak Teams, and Disputed Calls: An Empirical Study of Alleged Tax Court Bias." *Tennessee Law Review* 66: 351–426.

Maveety, Nancy, ed. 2003. *Pioneers of Judicial Behavior*. Ann Arbor: University of Michigan Press.

Mayhew, David. 1974. *The Electoral Connection*. New Haven, CT: Yale University Press.

McCann, Michael. 1994. *Rights at Work: Pay Equity Reform and the Politics of Legal Mobilization*. Chicago: University of Chicago Press.

McClosky, Herbert, and John Zaller. 1984. *The American Ethos: Public Attitudes toward Capitalism and Democracy*. Cambridge, MA: Harvard University Press.

McFadden, Robert D. 2008. "Gay Marriage is Ruled Legal in Connecticut." *New York Times*, October 11, A1.

McIver, John P., Robert S. Erikson, and Gerald C. Wright. 1993. "Public Opinion and Public Policy: A View from the States." In *New Perspectives in American Politics*, Lawrence C. Dodd and Calvin Jillson, eds., pp. 249–66. Washington, DC: Congressional Quarterly Press.

Mead, Lawrence M . 2004. "State Political Culture and Welfare Reform." *Policy Studies Journal* 32(2): 271–96

Meese, Edwin. 1985. "Great Debate: Speech Before the American Bar Association," Washington, DC, July 9. http://www.fed-soc.org/resources/id.49/default.asp

Melnick, R. Shep. 1983. *Regulation and the Courts: The Case of the Clean Air Act*. Washington, DC: The Brookings Institution

Melnick, R. Shep. 1985. "The Politics of Partnership." *Public Administration Review* 45: 653–60.

Melnick, R. Shep. 1994. *Between the Lines: Interpreting Welfare Rights*. Washington, DC: Brookings Institution Press.

Melnick, R. Shep. 2004. "Courts and Agencies." In *Making Policy, Making Law: An Interbranch Perspective*, Mark C. Miller and Jeb Barnes, eds., pp. 89–106. Washington, DC: Georgetown University Press.

Mondak, Jeffery J., and Shannon Ishiyama Smithey. 1997. "The Dynamics of Public Support for the Supreme Court." *Journal of Politics* 59: 1114–42.

Mooney, Christopher Z. 2001. "Modeling Regional Effects on State Policy Diffusion. *Political Research Quarterly* 54(1): 103–24.

Mucciaroni, Gary. 2008. *Same Sex, Different Politics: Success and Failure in the Struggles over Gay Rights*. Chicago: University of Chicago Press.

Murphy, Walter F., and Joseph Tanenhaus. 1968. "Public Opinion and the Supreme Court: The Goldwater Campaign." *Public Opinion Quarterly* 32: 31–50.

National Access Network. 2001–2010. "State by State Litigation" http://www.schoolfunding.info/index.php3

Nechyba, Thomas, and Michael Heise. 2000. "School Finance Reform: Introducing the Choice Factor." In *City Schools: Lessons from New York*, D. Ravitch and J. Vitteritti, eds., pp. 367–92 Baltimore, MD: Johns Hopkins University Press.

Neubauer, David W., and Stephen S. Meinhold. 2009. *Judicial Process: Law, Courts and Politics in the United States*. New York: Cengage Learning.

Nixon, David C. 2004 "Political Ideology Measurement Project." http://www2.hawaii.edu/~dnixon/PIMP/

Noonan, John T. 2002. *Narrowing the Nation's Power: The Supreme Court Sides with the States*. Berkeley: University of California Press.

Oakes, James L. 1977. "The Judicial Role in Environmental Law." *New York University Law Review* 52: 498–517.

Omaha World-Herald. 2010. "Chief Justice: Don't Politicize Court." *Omaha World-Herald*, October 21. http://www.omaha.com/article/20101021/NEWS97/710229906.

Pasternak, Judy. 1998. "Wisconsin OKs Civil Detention for Fetal Abuse." *Los Angeles Times*, May 2, A1.

Perry, H.W., Jr. 1991. *Deciding to Decide: Agenda Setting in the United States Supreme Court*. Cambridge, MA: Harvard University Press.

Pierceson, Jason. 2005. *Courts, Liberalism, and Rights: Gay Law and Politics in the United States and Canada*. Philadelphia: Temple University Press.

Pinello, Daniel R. 2006. *America's Struggle for Same-Sex Marriage*. New York: Cambridge University Press.

Posner, Richard A. 1973. An Economic Approach to Legal Procedure and Judicial Administration. *Journal of Legal Studies* 2: 399–458.

Posner, Richard A. 1996. *The Federal Courts: Challenge and Reform* (2nd ed.). Cambridge, MA: Harvard University Press.

Pritchett, C. Herman. 1948. *The Roosevelt Court: A Study of Judicial Values and Votes, 1937–48*. New York: Macmillan.

Ratner, Gary M. 1985. "A New Legal Duty for Urban Public Schools: Effective Education in Basic Skills." *Texas Law Review* 63: 777–864.

Reid, Eric. 1995. "Assessing and Responding to Same-Sex "Marriage" in Light of Natural Law." *Georgetown Journal of Law & Public Policy* 3: 523–39

Reuters. 2004. "Utah Woman Pleads Guilty in Stillborn Case." *Reuters*, April 7.

Richards, Mark J., and Herbert M. Kritzer. 2002. "Jurisprudential Regimes in Supreme Court Decision Making." *American Political Science Review* 96: 305–20.

Ringquist, Evan J. 1993a. *Environmental Protection at the State Level*. Armonk, NY: M. E. Sharpe.

Ringquist, Evan J. 1993b. "Testing Theories of State Policy-Making." *American Politics Quarterly* 21: 320–42.

Ringquist, Evan J. 1995. "Political Control and Policy Impact in EPA's Office of Water Quality." *American Journal of Political Science* 39: 336–63.

Ringquist, Evan J., and Craig E. Emmert. 1999. "Judicial Policymaking in Published and Unpublished Decisions: The Case of the Clean Air Act." *Political Research Quarterly* 52: 7–37.

Roberts. John. 2005. "Transcript: Day One of the Roberts Hearings." Tuesday, September 13. http://www.washingtonpost.com/wpdyn/content/article/2005/09/13/AR2005091300693.html,

Roch, Christine, and Robert M. Howard. 2008. "State Policy Innovation in Perspective: Courts, Legislatures, and Educational Finance Reform." *Political Research Quarterly* 61: 333–44.

Rogers, James. 2001. "Information and Judicial Review: A Signaling Game of Judicial-Legislative Interaction." *American Journal of Political Science* 45: 84–99.

Rohde, David W., and Harold J. Spaeth. 1976. *Supreme Court Decision Making*. San Francisco: W.H. Freeman.

Rosenberg, Gerald N. 1991. *The Hollow Hope: Can Courts Bring About Social Change?* Chicago: University of Chicago Press.

Rosenberg, Gerald N. 2008. *The Hollow Hope: Can Courts Bring About Social Change?* (2nd ed.). Chicago: University of Chicago Press.

Rossiter, Clinton L., ed. 1961. *The Federalist Papers: Alexander Hamilton, James Madison, John Jay*. New York: Mentor

Roth, Jeffrey A., John T. Scholz, and Ann Dryden Witte. 1989. *Taxpayer Compliance: An Agenda for Research—A National Academy of Sciences Report*. Philadelphia: University of Pennsylvania Press.

Russell, Joyce. 2010. "Gay-Marriage Critics Try to Oust Iowa Justices." *NPR*, October 19. http://www.npr.org/templates/story/story.php?storyId=130670582.

Sacchetti, Maria. 2009. "Maine Voters Overturn State's New Same-Sex Marriage Law." *Boston Globe, Local Maine Section* November 4. Scheingold, Stuart. 2004. *The Politics of Rights: Lawyers, Public Policy and Political Change* (2nd ed.). Ann Arbor: University of Michigan Press.

Scherer, Nancy, Brandon L. Bartels, and Amy Steigerwalt. 2008. "Sounding the Fire Alarm: The Role of Interest Groups in the Lower Federal Court Confirmation Process." *Journal of Politics* 70: 1026–39.

Schlafly, Phyllis. 1986. "A Short History of the E.R.A." *The Phyllis Schlafly Report*, September.

Scholz, John T., and B. Dan Wood. 1998. "Controlling the IRS: Principals, Principles and Public Administration." *American Journal of Political Science* 42: 141–62.

Scholz, John T., and B. Dan Wood. 1999. "Efficiency, Equity and Politics: Democratic Controls over the Tax Collector." *American Journal of Political Science* 43: 1166–88.

Schubert, Glendon. 1959. *Quantitative Analysis of Judicial Behavior*. New York: Free Press of Glencoe.

Schuck, Peter H., and E. Donald Elliott. 1990. "To the Chevron Station: An Empirical Study of Federal Administrative Law." *Duke Law Journal* 5: 984–1077.

Schulte, Grant. 2010. "Democrats Seek Support to Keep Justices on Court." *Des Moines Register*, December 31.

Sclamberg, Alexis. 2010. "Utah's Feticide Law Puts Miscarriage on Trial." *WeNews*, April 20. http://womensenews.org/story/law/100419/utahs-feticide-law-puts-miscarriage-trial.

Sears, John Harold. 1922. *Minimizing Taxes*. Kansas City, MO: Vernon Law.

Segal, Jeffrey A., and Albert D. Cover. 1989. "Ideological Values and the Votes of U.S. Supreme Court Justices." *American Political Science Review* 83: 557–65.

Segal, Jeffrey A., Lee Epstein, Charles M. Cameron, and Harold J. Spaeth. 1995. "Ideological Values and the Votes of U.S. Supreme Court Justices Revisited." *Journal of Politics* 57: 812–23.

Segal, Jeffrey A., and Harold J. Spaeth. 1993. *The Supreme Court and the Attitudinal Model*. New York: Cambridge University Press.

Segal, Jeffrey A., and Harold J. Spaeth. 2002. *The Supreme Court and the Attitudinal Model Revisited.* New York: Cambridge University Press.

Segal, Jeffrey A., Richard Timpone, and Robert M. Howard. 2000. "Buyer Beware? Presidential Influence Through Supreme Court Appointments." *Political Research Quarterly* 53(3): 557–73.

Shain, Barry Alan. 1996. *The Myth of American Individualism: The Protestant Origins of American Political Thought.* Princeton, NJ: Princeton University Press

Shilton, David C. 1990. "Is the Supreme Court Hostile to NEPA—Some Possible Explanations for a 12-0 Record." *Environmental Law* 20: 551.

Shipan, Charles R. 1998. "Political Influence, Regulatory Regimes, and the FDA." Paper presented at the Annual Meeting of the Public Choice Society, New Orleans, LA.

Shook, Susan M. 1996. "The Title IX Tug-of-War and Intercollegiate Athletics in the 1990s: Nonrevenue Men's Teams Join Women Athletes in the Scramble for Survival." *Indiana Law Journal* 71: 773–814.

Shprentz, Deborah Sheiman. 1996. Natural Resources Defense Council. Breath-taking Premature Mortality Due to Particulate Air Pollution in 239 American Cities http://www.nrdc.org/air/pollution/bt/btinx.asp

Sirin, Selcuk R. 2005. "Socioeconomic Status and Academic Achievement: A Meta-Analytic Review of Research." *Review of Educational Research* 75: 417–53.

Skrentny, John David. 2002. *The Minority Rights Revolution.* Cambridge, MA: Harvard University Press.

Sommers, Christina Hoff. 2010. "Fair Pay Isn't Always Equal Pay." *Wall Street Journal,* September 22, A25.

Songer, Donald R., Charles M. Cameron, and Jeffrey A. Segal. 1995. "An Empirical Test of the Rational Actor Theory of Litigation." *Journal of Politics* 57: 1119–29.

Songer, Donald R., Sue Davis, and Susan Haire. 1994. "A Reappraisal of Diversification in the Federal Courts: Gender Effects in the Courts of Appeals." *The Journal of Politics* 56(2) pp. 425-39.

Songer, Donald R., and Martha Humphries Ginn. 2002. "Assessing the Impact of Presidential and Home State Influences on Judicial Decision Making in the United States Courts of Appeals." *Political Research Quarterly* 55: 299–328.

Spaeth, Harold J. 1964. "The Judicial Restraint of Mr. Justice Frankfurter—Myth or Reality." *Midwest Journal of Political Science* 8: 22–38.

Spaeth, Harold J. 1972. *An Introduction to Supreme Court Decision Making* (Rev. ed.). New York: Chandler.

Steigerwalt, Amy. 2010. *Battle Over the Bench: Senators, Interest Groups and Lower Court Confirmations.* Charlottesville, VA: University of Virginia Press.

Steuerle, Eugene. 2008. *Contemporary U.S. Tax Policy* (2nd ed.). Washington, DC: Urban Institute Press.

Stevenson, Richard W. 1997. "Leading Republican Plans Bill to Shift Burden of Proof in Tax Disputes." *Infoseek Business,* October 20.p. 15.

Stewart, Richard B. 1976. "Development of Administrative and Quasi-Constitutional Law in Judicial Review of Environmental Decision Making: Lessons from the Clean Air Act." *Iowa Law Review* 62: 713–69.

Strauss, David A. 2010. *The Living Constitution.* New York: Oxford University Press.

Sulzberger, A. G. 2010. "Ouster of Iowa Judges Sends Signal to Bench." *New York Times,* November 4, A1.

Sutton, Jeffrey S. 2008. "*San Antonio Independent School District v. Rodriguez* and its Aftermath." *Virginia Law Review* 94: 1963–86.

Tarr, G. Alan. 1994."The Past and Future of the New Judicial Federalism." *Publius: The Journal of Federalism* 24: 63–79.

Tate, Neal C., and Roger Handberg. 1991. "Time Binding Theory Building in Personal Attribute Models of Supreme Court Voting Behavior, 1916–88." *American Journal of Political Science* 35: 460–80.

Taylor, Joan Kennedy. 1993. *Women's Issues: Feminism, Classical Liberalism and the Future.* Stanford, CA: Hoover Press.

Taylor, Marshall, W., Karen J. Simonson, Marc J. Winter, and Brian J. Seery. 1990. *Tax Court Practice.* Philadelphia: American Law Institute.

Thayer, James Bradley. 1893. "Origin and Scope of the American Doctrine of Constitutional Law." *Harvard Law Review* 7: 133.

Tiedeman, Christopher. 1886. A Treatise on the Limitations of Police Power in the United States: Considered From Both a Civil and Criminal Standpoint. Whitefish, MT: Kessinger, 2007.

Totenberg, Nina. 2006. "O'Connor Decries Republican Attacks on Courts." *National Public Radio*, March 10.

Tractenberg, Paul L. (n.d.) "Education Provisions in State Constitutions: A Summary of a Chapter for the State Constitutions for the Twenty-First Century Project." http://camlaw.rutgers.edu/statecon/subpapers/tractenberg.pdf

Traub, James. 1999. "The Class of Prop. 209." *New York Times Magazine*, May 2, 44.

Tyler, Tom R. 1984. "The Role of Perceived Injustice in Defendants' Evaluations of Their Courtroom Experience." *Law and Society Review* 18: 51–74.

Tyler, Tom R. 1988. "What is Procedural Justice? Criteria Used by Citizens to Assess the Fairness of Legal Procedures." *Law and Society Review* 22: 301–55.

Tyler, Tom R. 1990. *Why People Obey the Law: Procedural Justice, Legitimacy and Compliance.* New Haven, CT: Yale University Press.

Unah, Isaac. 1997. "Specialized Courts of Appeals' Review of Bureaucratic Actions and the Politics of Protectionism." *Political Research Quarterly* 50: 851–87.

U.S. Department of Education, National Center for Education Statistics. 2000. *The Condition of Education 2000* (NCES 2000–602). Washington, DC: Government Printing Office. http://nces.ed.gov/programs/coe/

U.S. Supreme Court Database. 2010. Release 02. http://scdb.wustl.edu/

Van Dyk. Robert. 1998. "The Pro-Choice Legal Mobilization and Decline of Clinic Blockades." In *Leveraging the Law: Using the Courts to Achieve Social Justice*, ed. David A. Schultz, pp. 135–67 New York: Peter Lang

Van Slyke, Dore, Alexandra Tan, and Martin Orland 1994. "School Finance Litigation: A Review of Key Cases: Prepared for the Finance Project." http://76.12.61.196/publications/litigation.html

Verba, Sydney, and Norman H. Nie. 1972. *Participation in America: Political Democracy and Social Equality.* New York: Harper and Row.

Volden, Craig. 2006. "States as Policy Laboratories: Emulating Success in the Children's Health Insurance Program." *American Journal of Political Science* 50: 294–312.

Wade, Jack Warren, Jr. 1986. *Audit-Proofing Your Tax Return.* New York: Macmillan.

Waldron, Jeremy. 1993. "A Rights-Based Critique of Constitutional Rights." *Oxford Journal of Legal Studies* 13: 18.

Waldron, Jeremy. 1998. "Judicial Review and the Conditions for Democracy." *Journal of Political Philosophy* 6: 335.

Walker, Jack. 1969. "The Diffusion of Innovations among the American States." *American Political Science Review* 63: 880–99.

Wechsler, Herbert. 1961. *Principles, Politics, and Fundamental Law.* Cambridge, MA: Harvard University Press.

Whittington, Keith E. 2005. "'Interpose Your Friendly Hand': Political Supports for the Exercise of Judicial Review by the United States Supreme Court." *American Political Science Review* 99: 583–96.

Wilhelm, Teena. 2007. "The Policymaking Role of State Supreme Courts in Education Policy." *Legislative Studies Quarterly* 23: 309–33.

Wiseman, Paul. 1997. "IRS May Not Be the Monster Critics Say It Is." *USA Today,* November 5, A17.

Witte, John. 1985. *The Politics and Development of the Federal Income Tax.* Madison: University of Wisconsin Press

Wolfe, Margaret Ripley. 1991. "The View from Atlanta: Southern Women and the Future." In *The Future South: A Historical Perspective for the Twenty-First Century,* Joe P. Dunn and Howard Lawrence Preston, eds., 123–57. Champagne, IL: University of Illinois Press.

Wood, B. Dan, and Nick A. Theobald. 2003. "Political Responsiveness and Equity in Education Finance." *Journal of Politics* 65: 718–38.

Wood, B. Dan, and Richard W. Waterman. 1993. "The Dynamics of Political-Bureaucratic Adaptation." *American Journal of Political Science* 37: 1–39.

Wood, B. Dan, and Richard W. Waterman. 1994. *Bureaucratic Dynamics: The Role of Bureaucracy in a Democracy.* Boulder, CO: Westview Press.

Wright, Gerald C., Robert S. Erikson, and John P. McIver. 1985. "Measuring State Partisanship and Ideology with Survey Data." *Journal of Politics* 47: 469–89.

Wrightsman, Lawrence S. 1999. *Judicial Decision Making: Is Psychology Relevant?* New York: Springer.

Yarbrough, Tinsley. 2008. *Blackmun: The Outsider Justice.* New York: Oxford University Press.

Young, Saundra. 2009. "White House Set to Reverse Health Care Conscience Clause." *CNN,* February 27. http://articles.cnn.com/2009-02-27/politics/conscience.rollback_1_health-care-providers-health-care-family-planning?_s=PM:POLITICS

INDEX

O'Connor, Sandra Day, 65, 67, 80, 107, 176
Ohio v. Akron Center for Reproductive Health, 82
Oklahoma Education Association v. State, 124
Olsen v. State, 124
Opinions of the Justices to the Senate, 147
Orland, Martin, 120
Orr v. Orr, 58

P
Palin, Sarah, 68, 74
Paltrow, Lynn, 90, 91
Panama Refining Co. v. Ryan, 14
Pasternak, Judy, 91
Pauley v. Bailey, 125
Pauley v. Kelly, 125
Pelosi, Nancy, 68, 74
Pemberton, Laura, 94
Pemberton v. Tallahassee Memorial Regional Medical Center, 94
Pendleton School District v. State of Oregon, 124
Pennsylvania Association of Rural and Small Schools v. Ridge, 124, 132
Peppers, Todd, 8
Perkins Frances, 67
Perry, H. W., Jr., 27
Peterson, Phyllis, 67
Philadelphia v. New Jersey, 43, 45
Pierceson, Jason, 142
Pinello, Daniel R., 172
Plank, David N., 126
Planned Parenthood of Southeastern Pennsylvania v. Casey, 16, 80, 81, 82, 93
Plessy v. Ferguson, 97, 98, 99, 117
Poelker v. Doe, 81
Pollock v. Farmer's Loan and Trust Co., 14, 25, 26, 27
Posner, Richard A., 35, 36
Powell, Lewis, 62, 78, 104, 107, 119, 120
Pratt, Travis, 133
Pritchett, Herman, 5

Q
Quinn, Kevin, 7

R
Railroad Retirement Board v. Alton Railway Co, 14

Rankin, Jeannette, 66
Rapanos v. U.S., 43, 45
Ratner, Gary M., 126
Ray, Charlotte E., 66
Reagan, Ronald, 7, 46, 79
Reed, Cecil, 56
Reed, Richard, 56
Reed, Sally, 56
Reed v. Reed, 57, 58, 67, 71, 72
Regents of the University of California v. Bakke, 15, 19, 102,103, 104, 106, 107, 108, 110, 111
Rehnquist, William, 17, 77, 78, 119
Reilly, William K., 46, 47
Rell, M. Jodi, 148
Reno, Janet, 68
Reserve Mining v. EPA, 43, 45
Revere, Paul, 1, 2
Reyes v. Superior Court, 91
Rice, Condoleezza, 68
Richards, Mark J., 184
Richland County v. Campbell, 124
Ride, Sally K., 68
Riegg, Stephanie K., 116
Ringquist, Evan J., 8, 50, 51, 52, 53
Ritter, Philip L., 109
Roberts, John, 2, 3, 17, 175
Roberts, Owen, 183
Robinson v. Cahill, 122, 124
Roch, Christine, 117, 126, 138
Roe v. Wade, 4, 10, 16, 19, 67, 76, 77, 78, 79, 80, 81, 85, 89, 93, 94, 180
Rogers, James, 126, 133
Rohde, David, 5, 6
Rokeach, Milton, 5
Romer v. Evans, 143
The Roosevelt Court, 5
Roosevelt Elementary School Dist. No. 66 v. Bishop, 123, 131
Roosevelt, Franklin 7, 14, 15, 99, 183
Roper, Robert, 181, 182
Ros-Lehtinen, Ileana, 68
Rose v. The Council for Better Education, 123, 131
Rosenberg, Gerald, 4, 71, 101, 144, 159, 171, 172, 175, 178
Ross, Betsy, 1
Ross, Nellie Taylor, 67
Rostker v. Goldberg, 59
Rowland, Melissa, 91
Rubin, Edward, 178
Ruckelshaus, William D., 46

CPSIA information can be obtained
at www.ICGtesting.com
Printed in the USA
LVOW13s0231040418
572203LV00005B/55/P